SAMUEL TAYLOR COLERIDGE

SHAKESPEAREAN CRITICISM

IN TWO VOLUMES: VOLUME TWO

EDITED BY

THOMAS MIDDLETON RAYSOR

Professor of English Literature, University of Nebraska

LONDON   J. M. DENT & SONS LTD
NEW YORK   E. P. DUTTON & CO INC

600591

CONTENTS

VOLUME TWO

REPORTS OF COLERIDGE'S LECTURES

VOLUME II

REPORTS OF COLERIDGE'S LECTURES

THE LECTURES OF 1808

DURING Coleridge's twenty-third year, in 1795, he delivered at Bristol two series of lectures on historical and theological subjects, of which Cottle[1] preserves the prospectuses. Some remains of these lectures were reprinted in *Essays on His Own Times*, but nearly all have been lost. These two courses, with miscellaneous individual lectures in the same period, gave Coleridge his only experience in public lecturing until he began his literary lectures in 1808.

These lectures of 1808 were definitely the first which he delivered on literary subjects, although Coleridge's own letters have been used to support a contrary opinion. The letter which has been the chief cause of this mistake is that written to Mudford in February 1818, in which Coleridge says that '16 or rather 17 years ago, I delivered 18 lectures on Shakspeare, at the Royal Institution.'[2] This of course would throw the first series of lectures back to 1801. But we know a good deal about Coleridge's whereabouts during this period: he was in the Lake District during most of the year, and apparently in London only from 15 November till 25 December[3]—much too short a time for the supposed lectures. Moreover, no lectures on non-technical subjects were given at the Royal Institution until 1804.[4]

In the notes[5] to her edition of the *Notes and Lectures upon Shakespeare* (1849), Sara Coleridge suggests an error in copying from the letter to Mudford, the manuscript of which is lost. 'It now seems clear to me, that my Father here alludes to a course of lectures delivered in 1808, and I think it most probable that, from some momentary confusion of mind, he wrote "sixteen or seventeen," instead of "ten or eleven";[6] unless his writing was wrongly copied.' Since the numerals '6' and '7' may easily be carelessly written so as to be read '0' or '1,' this last suggestion probably explains the difficulty. In the same letter, Coleridge complains that Schlegel's lectures 'were not given orally till two years after mine,' and this alone proves that the first figures are incorrect.

This remark may, however, be taken as proof that Coleridge delivered lectures at the Royal Institution in 1806, for Schlegel's lectures were delivered in 1808. Such lectures, indeed, are possible, for Coleridge's negotiations with the Royal Institution actually began in the autumn of 1806, after his return from Malta,[7] and the minutes of the Royal Institution record an arrangement with Coleridge for 'two

---

[1] *Reminiscences*, pp. 17–19.
[2] Cf. ii. 244.
[3] Campbell, Introduction to Coleridge's *Poetical Works*, p. lix.
[4] Bence Jones, *The Royal Institution* (London, 1871), pp. 260–1, etc.
[5] Coleridge's *Works*, iv. 457.
[6] Mudford prints the numerals, not the words.
[7] *Letters*, pp. 507–8.

3

courses of eight lectures on the Principles Common to the Fine Arts
for £120; to commence in November, every Thursday at two.'[1] But
in the list of lecturers at the Royal Institution in 1805–6, 1806–7,
Coleridge's name does not appear.[2]   Coleridge seems to have thought
that Schlegel's lectures on Shakespeare were delivered in 1810, the
year before their publication.[3] The conclusive proof of this is his
statement in the note introductory to his criticism of Hamlet,[4] that he
gave these lectures in 'the spring of the same year in which Sir
Humphry Davy . . . made his great revolutionary discoveries in
chemistry.' Sir Humphry Davy isolated potassium and sodium from
their hydroxides, potash and soda, in October 1807, and announced his
discoveries in the Bakerian lecture to the Royal Society, 19 November
1807. Davy fell ill four days afterwards; and Coleridge would
scarcely have heard anything of scientific lectures before the Royal
Society. A public announcement was made at the Royal Institution
by the Rev. Mr Dibden,[5] 13 January 1808. This announcement
was printed 18 January 1808,[6] and Coleridge was present when it was
made orally in the Rev. Mr Dibden's opening lecture.[7] When
Coleridge dates his lectures by Sir Humphry Davy's discoveries, he
means, evidently, 1808, not 1807.

Our knowledge of Coleridge's programme in 1808 depends chiefly
on a long letter to Davy,[8] written 11 September 1807. The proposed
lectures on the fine arts were given up in favour of literature, to the
great advantage of Coleridge's audience, which would scarcely have
appreciated the combination of Kantian aesthetics and oral descriptions of Italian art galleries.

. . . After having discussed the subject with Poole, he entirely
agrees with me, that the former plan suggested by me is invidious
in itself, unless I disguised my real opinions; as far as I should
deliver my sentiments respecting the *arts*, [it] would require
references and illustrations not suitable to a public lecture room;
and, finally, that I ought not to reckon upon spirits enough to
seek about for books of Italian prints, etc. And that, after all,

---

[1] Bence Jones, *The Royal Institution*, p. 277. If these two courses were
eight lectures each, not together, they could not have been delivered, for
Coleridge was at Coleorton for Christmas and remained there until the spring
of 1807. *Letters*, pp. 507, 511.
[2] Bence Jones, *The Royal Institution*, p. 276. The present editor has
consulted the secretary of the Royal Institution on this point, with the same
result.
[3] He gives a date in the letter of 1811 which deals with this subject. (Cf.
ii. 189.) The date is badly blotted but seems to be 1810. Schlegel's lectures
were published in 1809 and 1811, the lectures on Shakespeare at the latter
date.
[4] Cf. i. 17.
[5] Bence Jones, *The Royal Institution*, p. 283.
[6] Ibid., p. 351.
[7] Unpublished letter to the Morgans, 14 January 1808. A transcript by
E. H. Coleridge.
[8] *Letters*, pp. 515–16.

the general and most philosophical principles, I might naturally introduce into lectures on a more confined plan—namely, the principles of poetry, conveyed and illustrated in a series of lectures. 1. On the genius and writings of Shakespeare, relatively to his predecessors and contemporaries, so as to determine not only his merits and defects, and the proportion that each must bear to the whole, but what of his merits and defects belong to his age, as being found in contemporaries of genius, and what belonged to himself. 2. On Spenser, including the metrical romances, and Chaucer, though the character of the latter as a manner-painter I shall have so far anticipated in distinguishing it from, and comparing it with, Shakespeare. 3. Milton. 4. Dryden and Pope, including the origin and after history of poetry of witty logic. 5. On Modern Poetry and its characteristics, with no introduction of any particular names. In the course of these I shall have said all I know, the whole result of many years' continued reflection on the subjects of taste, imagination, fancy, passion, the source of our pleasures in the fine arts, in the *antithetical* balance-loving nature of man, and the connexion of such pleasures with moral excellence. The advantage of this plan to myself is, that I have all my materials ready, and can rapidly reduce them into form (for this is my solemn determination, not to give a single lecture till I have in fair writing at least one half of the whole course), for as to trusting anything to immediate effort, I shrink from it as from guilt, and guilt in me it would be. . . .

A brief summary of this same programme appears in the minutes of the Royal Institution at the end of 1807, with the additional information that Coleridge would give a total of twenty-five lectures, five on each of the announced subjects. He was to receive 'a compliment of £140, of which £60 was proposed to be paid in advance.'[1] And at about the same time,[2] Coleridge explains to Southey that Davy's illness has been the cause of postponing the lectures until the middle of January.[3]

In an unpublished letter to the Morgans,[4] dated 14 January, Coleridge writes: 'My own Lecture commences to-morrow.' Campbell[5] gives the date of this lecture as 12 January rather than 15 January, but he cites no authority, and it is rather improbable that Coleridge's first lecture would precede Dibden's on 13 January, when Davy's discovery was publicly announced. Coleridge writes again to

---

[1] Bence Jones, *The Royal Institution*, p. 284.
[2] 14 December.
[3] *Letters*, p. 522.
[4] Transcript by E. H. Coleridge.
[5] Campbell, Introduction to Coleridge's *Poetical Works*, p. lxxvi, note.

Mrs Morgan,[1] 'Friday morning, January 25,' speaking of his successful lecture 'on Friday evening,' presumably of the preceding week. If the week-days are correct this letter is misdated 25 January[2] for 22 January, and Coleridge refers to the first lecture already mentioned, on 15 January. In the same letter he says, 'I have been obliged, of course, to put off my lecture of to-day,' a remark which is scarcely compatible with an error in week-days.

The unpublished or published documents seem to give no hint of further lectures until Friday, 5 February. Coleridge writes to De Quincey on 3 February, speaking of his illness, and expressing the hope that he will be able to give next Friday's lecture, though he has had another relapse recently. On 9 February, he tells Southey that he could scarcely read his 'last lecture.' And on 10 February, he writes to Mrs Morgan as follows: 'I went from my bed to the R. Institution on Friday last, and having with great difficulty read thro' my lecture with my eyes never off the book, I returned from thence again to my bed.'[3]

These discouraging remarks all refer to the lecture of 5 February, which was reported briefly by H. C. Robinson, and which also survived in manuscript.[4] Robinson's report is here reprinted from Sadler's third edition of the *Diary*.[5]

I find among my papers two pages of notes of Coleridge's lecture, Feb. 5th, 1808:—

'Feb. 5th, 1808.   Lecture 2nd on Poetry (Shakespeare), &c.

'Detached Minutes.

'The Grecian Mythology exhibits the symbols of the powers of nature and Hero-worship blended together. Jupiter both a King of Crete and the personified Sky.

'Bacchus expressed the organic energies of the Universe which work by passion—a joy without consciousness; while Minerva, &c., imported the pre-ordaining intellect. Bacchus expressed the physical origin of heroic character, a felicity beyond prudence.

'In the devotional hymns to Bacchus the germ of the first Tragedy. Men like to imagine themselves to be the characters they treat of—hence dramatic representations. The exhibition of action separated from the devotional feeling. The Dialogue became distinct from the Chorus.

---

[1] *Letters*, p. 524.   [2] 25 January was a Monday.
[3] These three letters are all unpublished transcripts by E. H. Coleridge.
[4] Cf. i. 163–6, 168–74.
[5] *Diary*, etc. (1872), i. 140–1, note. The editor has searched in vain for the original manuscript of this report, in Robinson's miscellaneous papers, his reminiscences, his letters, and his diary. There is a slightly variant text in Miss Edith Morley's selections, *Blake, Coleridge, Wordsworth, Lamb, etc.* (Manchester, 1922).

'The Greek tragedies were the Biblical instruction for the people.

'Comedy arose from the natural sense of ridicule which expresses itself naturally in mimickry.

'Mr. Coleridge, in Italy, heard a quack in the street, who was accosted by his servant-boy smartly; a dialogue ensued which pleased the mob; the next day the quack, having perceived the good effect of an adjunct, hired a boy to talk with him. In this way a play might have originated.

'The modern Drama, like the ancient, originated in religion. The priests exhibited the miracles and splendid scenes of religion.

'Tragi-Comedy arose from the necessity of amusing and instructing at the same time.

'The entire ignorance of the ancient Drama occasioned the reproduction of it on the restoration of literature.

'Harlequin and the Clown are the legitimate descendants from the Vice and Devil of the ancient Comedy. In the early ages, very ludicrous images were mixed with the most serious ideas, not without a separate attention being paid to the solemn truths; the people had no sense of impiety; they enjoyed the comic scenes, and were yet edified by the instruction of the serious parts. Mr. Coleridge met with an ancient MS. at Helmstädt, in which God was represented visiting Noah's family. The descendants of Cain did not pull off their hats to the great visitor, and received boxes of the ear for their rudeness; while the progeny of Abel answered their catechism well. The Devil prompted the bad children to repeat the Lord's Prayer backwards.

'The Christian polytheism withdrew the mind from attending to the whisperings of conscience; yet Christianity in its worst state was not separated from humanity (except where zeal for Dogmata interfered). Mahometanism is an anomalous corruption of Christianity.

'In the production of the English Drama, the popular and the learned writers by their opposite tendencies contributed to rectify each other. The learned would have reduced Tragedy to oratorical declamation, while the vulgar wanted a direct appeal to their feelings. The many feel what is beautiful, but they also deem a great deal to be beautiful which is not in fact so: they cannot distinguish the counterfeit from the genuine. The vulgar love the Bible and also Hervey's 'Meditations.'

'The essence of poetry *universality*. The character of

Hamlet, &c., affects all men; addresses to personal feeling, the sympathy arising from a reference to individual sensibility spurious. [N.B. This applies to Kotzebue.]'

The next record which bears on the lectures is Coleridge's letter to Sir George Beaumont on 18 February. 'For many weeks,' Coleridge writes, 'with only two intervals, and these but day-long, I have been ill, very ill, confined mostly to my bed, altogether to my bedroom.'[1] The 'two intervals' are presumably 15 January and 5 February. Lamb is more explicit: 'Coleridge has delivered two lectures at the R. I.; two more were attended, but he did not come. It is thought he has gone sick upon them. He ain't well, that's certain. Wordsworth is coming to see him.'[2] Dorothy Wordsworth tells us that on 23 or 24 February Wordsworth left to see if he could help Coleridge.[3] Then, on Tuesday, 29 March, Coleridge writes to the Morgans, referring to 'tomorrow evening, after my Lecture (which I recommence).'[4] Presumably this promise was carried out, for Wordsworth writes to Beaumont on 8 April that he has just left Coleridge on Sunday (3 April) and that he has heard him lecture twice in the past week: 'he seemed to give great satisfaction; but he was not in spirits, and suffered much during the course of the week, both in body and mind.'[5]

The dates of the first four lectures, then, are as follows: I. Friday, 15 Jan.; II. Friday, 5 Feb.; III. Wednesday, 30 March; IV. Friday, 1 April. I assume that the Friday date was held for the fourth lecture, though Thursday, 31 March, and Saturday, 2 April, are possible dates.

The lectures probably went ahead on schedule from this time forward, but we know very little about them until we hear, from the minutes of the Royal Institution, 'that Mr. Coleridge had offered gratuitously to give a lecture on Education on Tuesday, May 3, proposing it to be twice the length of his other lectures.'[6] This lecture was given, and was reported by H. C. Robinson in a letter to Mrs Clarkson, which is here reproduced from the original manuscript.[7]

---

[1] *Memorials of Coleorton*, ii. 44.

[2] Campbell, Introduction to Coleridge's *Poetical Works*, p. lxxvi. I quote Campbell rather than Ainger because of Campbell's corrections from the original manuscript. Writing in March, Davy speaks also of Coleridge's missing two lectures through illness. *Life of Sir H. Davy*, by J. A. Paris (London, 1831), i. 294. On this point I have ignored De Quincey's utterly unreliable but very interesting recollections of Coleridge. *Works* (1889–90), ii. 188–90.

[3] *Letters of the Wordsworth Family*, i. 342. Dorothy's dates seem to be confused.

[4] Transcript by E. H. Coleridge of an unpublished letter.

[5] *Letters of the Wordsworth Family*, i. 347. See also iii. 464, note 1, for Wordsworth's movements and their dates.

[6] Bence Jones, *The Royal Institution*, p. 284.

[7] In Dr Williams's Library, Gordon Square, London. I have omitted the salutation, the signature, and Robinson's address, 56 Hatton Garden. Robinson's two letters on the lectures of 1808 have been previously printed, with slight alterations, by Mrs H. N. Coleridge in her edition of Coleridge's *Notes and Lectures upon Shakespeare* (1849), and by Miss Edith Morley in *Blake, Coleridge, Wordsworth, Lamb, etc.* (1922). They were not reprinted by Ashe.

May 7th, 1808.

On receiving your threatening letter I enclosed it in a note to Coleridge and on calling upon him before the lecture found a letter for me very civilly written, and for which I felt grateful to you, since it was written only in the confidence he has in your judgement, and was occasioned by your account of me.   He has offered to give me admission constantly, and I shall accept his offer whenever I can and give you a weekly letter on the subject. I shall not pretend to tell you what he says, but mention the topics he runs over.   Everything he observes on morals will be as familiar to you as all he says on criticism is to me; for he has adopted in all respects the German doctrines.   And it is a useful lesson to me how those doctrines are to be clothed with *original illustrations* adapted to an English audience.

The extraordinary lecture on Education was most excellent, delivered with great animation and *extorting* praise from those whose prejudices he was mercilessly attacking.   And he kept his audience on the rack of pleasure and offence two whole hours and ten minutes,[1] and few went away during the lecture.   He began by establishing a commonplace distinction neatly, between the *objects* and the *means* of education, which he observed to be 'perhaps almost the only safe way of being useful.'   Omitting a *tirade* which you can very well supply on the subject of E., I come to the means of forming the character, the cardinal rules of early education.   These are 1. to work by love and so generate love: 2. to habituate the mind to intellectual accuracy or truth: 3. to excite power.   1. He enforced a great truth strikingly: 'My experience tells me that little is taught or communicated by contest or dispute, but everything by sympathy and love. Collision elicits truth only from the hardest heads.'   'I hold motives to be of little influence compared with feelings.'   He apologised for early prejudices with a self-correction—'And yet what nobler judgement is there than that a child should listen with faith, the principle of all good things, to his father or preceptor?'   Digressing on Rousseau he told an anecdote pleasantly, *si non vero è ben trovato*.   A friend [2] had defended the negative education of Rousseau.   C. led him into his miserably neglected garden, choked with weeds.   'What is this?' said he. 'Only a garden,' C. replied, 'educated according to Rousseau's

---

[1] This was intended to be a lecture of double length, of course.
[2] Thelwall.   Cf. *Table-Talk*, 27 July 1830, and the seventh lecture at Bristol, *S.C.* ii. 291–2.

principles.' On punishment he pleaded the cause of humanity eloquently. He noticed the good arising from the corporal inflictions of our great schools—in the Spartan fortitude it excited—in the generous sympathy and friendship it awakened and in the point of honour it enforced.[1] Yet on the other hand he shewed this very reference to honour to be a great evil as a substitute for virtue and principle. School boys, he observed, lived in civil war with their masters. They are disgraced by a lie told to their fellows; it is an honour to impose on the common enemy. Thus the mind is prepared for every falsehood and injustice when the interest of the party, when honour requires it. On disgraceful punishments [2] such as fool's-caps he spoke with great indignation and declared that even now his life is embittered by the recollection of ignominious punishments he suffered when a child. It comes to him in disease and when his mind is dejected.—This part was delivered with fervour. Could all the pedagogues of the United Kingdom have been before him! 2. On truth, too, he was very judicious. He advised the beginning with enforcing great accuracy of assertion in young children. The parent, he observed, who should hear his child call a round leaf, 'long,' would do well to fetch it instantly. Thus tutored to render words conformable with ideas, the child would have the habit of truth without having any notion or thought of *moral truth*. 'We should not early begin with impressing ideas of virtue [or] goodness which the child could not comprehend.' [3] Then he digressed *à l'Allemagne*—on the distinction between obscure ideas and clear notions. Our notions resemble the index and hand of the dial; our feelings are the hidden springs which impel the machine, with this difference, that notions and feelings react on each other reciprocally. The veneration for the Supreme Being, sense of mysterious existence, not to be profaned by the intrusion of clear notions. Here he was applauded by those who do not pretend to understanding, while the Socinians of course felt profound contempt for the lecturer. I find from my notes that C. was not very methodical. You will excuse my not being more so. 1. and 2. 'Stimulate the heart to love, and the mind to be early accurate, and all other virtues will rise of their own accord and all vices will be thrown out.'—When treating of punishments he dared to represent the text, 'he that

---

[1] Cf. the seventh lecture at Bristol, *S.C.* ii. 293, and the sixth lecture of 1811–12, ii. 80.

[2] Cf. the seventh lecture at Bristol, *S.C.* ii. 294.

[3] Cf. the eighth lecture at Bristol, *S.C.* ii. 296, and *B.L.* ii. 611.

spareth the rod, spoileth the child,' as a source of much evil. He feelingly urged the repugnance of infancy to quiet and gloom and the duty of attending to such indications, observing that the severe notions entertained of religion, etc., were more pernicious than all that had been written by Voltaire and such '*paltry scribblers*.' Considering this phrase as the gilding of the pill, I let it pass. Coleridge is in the main right, but Voltaire is no paltry scribbler. *A propos* I could every twenty minutes rap the knuckles of the lecturer for little unworthy compliances for occasional conformity. But *n'importe*, he says such a number of things both good and useful at the same time that I can tolerate these draw-backs or rather make-weights. 3. In speaking of Education as a mean[s] of strengthening the character, he opposed our system of 'cramming' children. All this you know and feel already, as indeed you do what I have written above. He censured the practice of carrying the notion [a] of making learning easy much too far; and especially satirised the good books in Miss Edgeworth's style. 'I infinitely prefer the little books of "The Seven Champions of Christendom," "Jack the Giant Killer," etc., etc.—for at least they make the child forget himself [1]—to your moral tales where a good little boy comes in and says, "Mama, I met a poor beggar man and gave him the sixpence you gave me yesterday. Did I do right?"—"O, yes, my dear; to be sure you did." This is not virtue, but vanity; such books and such lessons do not teach goodness, but—if I might venture such a word—goodyness.' What goody he referred to I know not, for he praised Mrs. Trimmer afterwards. He afterwards added, 'The lesson to be inculcated should be, let the Child [be good?] [2] and know it not. Instructors should be careful not to let the intellect die of plethora.' The latter part of the lecture was taken up in a defence of education for the poor; it was very useful, but very trite. He said nothing worth quotation. He also lugged in most unnecessarily an attack upon Malthus; he was as unfair in his representation as Hazlitt in his answer. He also noticed Cobbett, etc. In conclusion, he eulogized Dr. Bell's plan of education and concluded by a severe attack upon Lancaster for having stolen from Dr. Bell all that is good in his plans. And [he] expatiated [with war [b]]mth on the

---

[a] MS. '*notice*.'
[b] *Hole in MS.*
[1] Cf. the seventh lecture at Bristol, *S.C.* ii. 293, and the fifth lecture of 1811–12, ii. 78–9. Cf. also Wordsworth's *Prelude* (Oxford, 1926), pp. 154, 155.
[2] The manuscript is torn here.

barbarous ignominious punishments Lancaster introduce[d [a]]. He also accused Lancaster of religious intolerance, but I susp[ect withou [a]]t knowing the fact that he on this point did not do justice to the Quaker.   He concluded by gratulating himself on living in this age; 'for I have seen what infinite good *one* man [can] do by persevering in his efforts to resist evil and spread good over human life.   And if I were called upon to say which two men in my own time had been most extensively useful and who had done most for humanity I should say Mr. Clarkson and Dr. Bell.'   I cannot answer for the terms of this sentence; the surprise I felt at the sudden introduction of your husband's name perhaps made me lose the immediate preceding words.

I could not go on Wednesday, and yesterday I went in late.[1] It was the least interesting lecture I have heard, tho' Milton was the subject.   But the word poetry was not used till the lecture was two-thirds over, nor Milton's name till ten minutes before the close.   The observation or two I may have to make on this lecture I will reserve till my next letter, for, as I said before, I mean to write weekly.   I am happy that I have thus formed Coleridge's acquaintance, for tho' we have not yet met, I feel we can meet.   He has given me a general invitation for evenings. Now my evenings are engaged; however, I shall contrive to see him now and then— . . .

Robinson attended in May at least two lectures of the regular course and reported these in another letter to Mrs Clarkson, which follows: [2]

May 15th, 1808.

. . . I have only two lectures [3] to speak about and shall not pretend to speak of them in the order in which Coleridge spoke, since there was no order in his speaking.   I came in late one day and found him in the midst of a deduction of the origin of the fine arts from the necessities of our being, which a friend who accompanied me could make neither head nor tail of, because he had not studied German metaphysics.   The first 'free art' of man (architecture) arose from the impulse to make his habitation

---

[a] *Hole in MS.*
[1] Wednesday would be 4 May; 'yesterday' would be Friday, 6 May.   It will be remembered that Robinson mentioned a previous lecture in the first sentence of this letter, probably that on Friday, 29 April.   We may assume, f.om the sentence above and from previous references (cf. ii. 6, 8) that the lectures were afternoon lectures, given Wednesdays and Fridays.
[2] Again from the original letter.
[3] These two lectures are perhaps those of Wednesday, 11 May, and Friday, 13 May, though one of them might be that of Friday, 6 May, which Robinson referred to in a previous letter.

beautiful; [the] 2d. arose from the instinct to provide himself food; the 3d [from] the love of dress. Here C. atoned for his metaphysics by his gallantry; he declared that the passion for dress in females has been the great cause of the civilization of mankind. 'When I behold the ornaments which adorn a beautiful woman, I see the mirror of that instinct which leads man not to be content with what is necessary or useful, but impels him to the beautiful.' 4. From the necessity of Self-defence, springs the military art, and this has produced the keenest sense of honour, the finest sensibility—the character of a gentleman. 5. The ornaments of speech are eloquence and poetry.[1] Here C. distinguished these arts by the characteristic that poetry is a *general* impulse; he might have said it gives the character of what is universal to what still remains particular. Eloquence impels to [a] particular act. Let us rise against Philip, said the Athenians when Demosthenes sat down, for D. had been eloquent. *A propos*, Kant observes that the orator treats an affair of business as if it were a thing of imagination, while the poet handles a work of fancy as if it were a matter of business.[2] Kant speaks (and Schiller [3] expatiates on this) of the method of the two artists. C. refers to the principle of the arts. But both assertions amount to the same thing. In this same lecture, Coleridge contrived to work into his speech Kant's admirably profound definition of the naive,[4] that it is *nature putting art to shame*. And he also digressed into a vehement but well merited declamation against those *soi disant* philosophers who deny the nobler powers of man, his idealizing poetic faculty, and degrade him to the beast, and declared he could not think of Buffon without horror—an assertion with which I sympathize and which is far less exceptionable than his vulgar and absurd abuse of Voltaire. But of this hereafter.

These are metaphysics enow for the present. Now for a critical remark or two. Of Shakespeare C. observed that he alone preserved the individuality of his characters without losing his own. High moral feeling is to be deduced from, tho' not in

---

[1] Brandl pointed out in his *Life of Coleridge* (Eng. trans. by Eastlake), p. 297, that these notes of Robinson's read almost like the index to Herder's *Kalligone*, Zweiter Theil, Kap. I. The plagiarism is obvious, for Coleridge certainly knew this work of Herder. His own copy, with marginalia, now rests in the British Museum.

[2] *Critique of Aesthetic Judgement* (ed. Meredith), pp. 184–5, 192. Robinson is obviously right in tracing this obligation to Kant.

[3] 'On the Necessary Limitations in the Use of Beauty of Form.' Cf. *Essays Aesthetical and Philosophical* (Bohn ed.), London, 1916, pp. 230–1.

[4] *Critique of Aesthetic Judgement* (ed. Meredith), p. 202.

Shakespeare, for the sentiment of his age was less pure than that of the preceding. Not a *vicious* passage in all Shakespeare, tho' there are many which are gross (for grossness depends on the age). Shakespeare surpasses all poets, first, in the purity of his female characters.[1] (N.B. he declared his conviction that no part of Richard the 3d except the character of Richard was written by S., doubtless with a silent reference to the disgusting character of Lady Anne.) They have no platonic refinements, but are perfect wives, mothers, etc.—2d. He is admirable for the close union of morality and passion. Shakespeare conceived that these should never be separated, in this differing from the Greeks, who reserved the *chorus* for the morality. The truths he teaches he told in character and with passion. They are the 'sparks from heated iron.' They have all an higher worth than their insulated sententious import bespeaks. (Would your worthy but most unpoetic friend Sarah Jane have been enlightened by C.'s statement? I doubt much). A third characteristic is this, that Shakespeare's observation was preceded by contemplation: 'he first conceived what the forms of things must be and then went humbly to the oracle of nature to ask whether he was right. He enquired of her as a sovereign; he did not gossip with her.' Shakespeare describes feelings which no observation could teach. Shakespeare made himself all characters; he left out parts of himself, and supplied what might have been in himself.[2] Nothing was given him but the canvas. ('This fact does honour to human nature for it shews that the seeds of all that is noble and good are in man; they require only to be developed.') This canvas which Shakespeare used, formed his stories. The absurdity of his tales has often been a reproach to Shakespeare from those who did not comprehend him (Johnson, Pope, etc.), but Shakespeare had nothing to do with the probability of the histories. It was enough for him that they had found their way among the people. Everybody admitted them to be true, tho' childish in the extreme. There was once upon a time a king who had three daughters and he said to them, 'tell me how you love me and I will give my kingdom to her that loves me best'; and so one daughter said, etc., etc. From such stuff as this Shakespeare has produced the most

---

[1] In his defence of Shakespeare's morality Schlegel comments on the 'tender maidenliness' of many of Shakespeare's women (*Werke*, vi. 172). Only coincidence is possible here, of course.

[2] This observation and that preceding again seem very near to similar remarks by Schlegel (*Werke*, vi. 187), though Schlegel's lectures were not yet in print.

wonderful work of human genius (as in *Othello* he produced the most perfect work). In the three first acts he carried human feelings to the utmost height; therefore, in the two following they seem to sink and become feeble, as after the bursting of the storm we behold the scattered clouds dispersed over the heavens.

Coleridge's digressions are not the worst parts of his lectures, or rather he is always digressing. He quoted Mrs. Barbauld under the appellation of an 'amiable lady' who had asked how Richardson was inferior to Shakespeare.[1] R., he allowed, evinces an exquisite perception of minute feeling but there is a want of harmony, a vulgarity in his sentiment. He is *only* interesting. Shakespeare, on the contrary, elevates and instructs. Instead of referring to our ordinary situations and common feelings, he emancipates us from them and, when most remote from ordinary life, is most interesting. I should observe this depreciation of *the interesting* in poetry is one of the most characteristic features of the new German criticism. It is always opposed by Schiller, etc., to the beautiful and is considered as a very subordinate merit indeed.[2] Hence the severity of the attacks on Kotzebue, who certainly is much more interesting to nineteen out of twenty than Shakespeare.—C. took occasion on mentioning R. to express his opinion of the *immorality* of his novels. 'The higher and lower passions of our nature are kept thro' seven or eight volumes in a hot-bed of interest. Fielding is far less pernicious, for the gusts of laughter drive away sensuality.'

Basta! I must bring up my arrears in my next letter, but C. has begged a week's holiday, as he is going to publish his lecture on education. His attack on Lancaster has given great offence. This was to be expected. . . .

P.S. Voltaire 'a paltry scribbler.' This is confounding aversion with contempt in a manner creditable to no man's understanding. I oppose to Coleridge's vulgar commonplace, Göthe's profound and cutting remark: 'It has been found that certain monarchs unite all the talents and powers of their race. It was

---

[1] Cf. the third lecture of 1811–12, ii. 49–50.

[2] Robinson should have referred to Friedrich Schlegel rather than to Schiller so far as the term 'interesting' is concerned, though Schlegel's discussion of the 'interesting' (*Über das Studium der griechischen Poesie*) is closely related with Schiller's definition of the sentimental in the essay 'On Naive and Sentimental Poetry.' And Schiller does not really disparage the 'sentimental,' but rather defends it, with a few concessions to the opposing point of view represented by Goethe. The 'interesting' is the 'subjective beautiful.' Coleridge may have obtained this term from reading Friedrich Schlegel himself, or indirectly through Schlegel's followers.

thus with Lewis the 14th, and it is so with authors.   In this
sense it may be said, that Voltaire is the greatest of all conceivable
*French*men.'   I abridge the remark because my paper obliges
me, but you will understand how much it says.   I abhor Bonaparte as the gates of hell, yet I smile at the drivellers who cry out,
C'est un bon caporal.   Damn 'em both if you will, but don't
despise them.

The next record is a letter of Coleridge to Wordsworth, which is
given by Campbell the very probable but rather vague date of May.[1]
Coleridge there says that he will soon, 'on next Tuesday,' give his 'first
lecture on Modern Poetry' which would be followed, 'on Friday
after next,' by a lecture on Wordsworth's 'system and compositions.' [2]
Whether these lectures were given may be doubted, for in *Biographia
Literaria* Coleridge refers to the lectures of 1808 quite clearly, and
asserts that he never lectured on his contemporaries, though he had at
first intended to do so.[3]   Certainly some of the later lectures announced
in his original plan were prevented by his illness.   On 13 June the
steward of the Royal Institution, Mr Savage, laid before the managers
a letter of Coleridge's explaining that he could not possibly continue
his course because of illness which seemed to threaten his death.[4]
The managers ordered that the lectures should be formally discon-
tinued and that a list of the actual lectures given should be prepared,
in order that a proportional payment might be made to Coleridge.
Campbell says that Coleridge received £100,[5] and this seems to agree
almost exactly with Coleridge's assertions in 1818 and 1819 that he had
delivered eighteen lectures,[6] if the order of the managers for a proportional payment was carried out.[7]

The only remaining comment upon these lectures is a letter of
Edward Jerningham's, which describes the course vividly, but
maliciously and inaccurately.[8]

---

[1] Campbell, Introduction to Coleridge's *Poetical Works*, p. lxxvii.

[2] Knight, *Life of William Wordsworth*, ii. 102.   [3] *B.L.* i. 38.

[4] Bence Jones, *The Royal Institution*, pp. 284–5.   This letter, which is
very interesting, seems to have escaped the notice both of Campbell and Wise.

[5] Campbell, Introduction to Coleridge's *Poetical Works*, p. lxxvii, note 4.

[6] Introductory note to *Hamlet*, January 1819, and letter to Mudford,
February 1818.   (Cf. i. 17; ii. 244.)

[7] Campbell's account of this matter contains several doubtful assertions for
which no evidence is given.   He speaks of 'the full contract number of
sixteen lectures,' while the minutes of Royal Institution record a plan for
twenty-five lectures (cf. ii. 5).   He says that £40 were 'advanced' in October
1808 (*after* the lectures, of course), while the minutes of the Royal Institution
say that the first payment was made in February 1808.   Bence Jones, *The
Royal Institution*, p. 284.

Allowing for the 'week's holiday' mentioned in Robinson's letter of 15
May, and presuming that the lectures were delivered twice a week, Coleridge
would have delivered twenty-two lectures by 13 June, rather than eighteen.
Probably he missed several lectures through illness before he resigned his
lectureship.   The letter of Edward Jerningham which is quoted below speaks
of a gap before Coleridge's last lecture of 'about three weeks.'

[8] *The Jerningham Letters* (London, 1896), vol. i, pp. 315–17

I attended at the Royal Institution the Lectures of Colleridge upon Shakespear and Milton: I need not observe to you that He is Southey's Friend.—My opinion as to the Lecturer is that He possesses a great reach of mind; That He is a wild Enthusiast respecting the objects of his Elogium; That He is sometimes very eloquent, sometimes paradoxical, sometimes absurd. His voice has something in it particularly plaintive and interesting. His person is short, Thick, his countenance not inspirited with any Animation. He spoke without any Assistance from a manuscript, and Therefore said several Things suddenly, struck off from the Anvil, some of which were entitled to high Applause and others Incurred mental disapprobation. He too often Interwove Himself into the Texture of his Lecture. I formed an Acquaintance with Him: that is, I generally spoke to Him at the End of the Lecture—with which He appeared much pleased. He was in some respect, I told Him one day, like Abelard: His Lectures were attended by Ladies of the first fashion, by Judges, and Bishops; and I could have added since another Resemblance to Abelard, by the Disgrace his course of Lectures concluded with. In one of his Lectures upon Milton, who wrote a short Treatise upon Education, He abandoned the Treatise of Milton [1] to abuse the plan of Education Instituted by Lancaster, of which plan He spoke in Terms of the utmost Asperity.

Being Ignorant of Lancaster's mode of Education I went along with the Lecturer and silently Approved. On the day, however, of the next Lecture He appeared much dejected; his voice assumed a more plaintive sound while he told us That his last had given great offence in speaking Truth. He cou'd hardly at Times refrain from Tears: long pauses sometimes Intervened— and he seemed as if He did not well know how to proceed.

I hastened to him immediately after the Lecture. He said that some of the proprietors of the Institution were much Displeased with his previous discourse; that Sir Henry Englefield had made an attack upon Him in company, without any preparation, and had said so many harsh Things, That He was obliged to Leave the room. Great Expectations were raised for the Day of the next Lecture and a crowd attended, but He had sent a Letter to the secretary to Inform him That coming out a Boat the Day before He fell back and hurt his head, and the Continuance of the Pain obliged Him to defer his Lecture. A common personage would have been satisfied with this Information that He

---

[1] It seems probable that this was the special lecture on education, 3 May, in which Milton's essay may well have served as a point of departure.

had convey'd to the Secretary; But Mr. Colleridge goes on in this manner (I read the Letter—and These are the very words):

'The pain however will soon subside, for it does not rise from so recent an Event as yesterday, but from a more distant period. It was when I was at Malta, Two years ago: a person rushed into my Apartment and abruptly announced to me the Death of a dear Friend, this occasioned my falling backwards and gave a contusion on my head which Brings back the pain occasionally upon any Exertion or Accident.' [1]

To continue the History of this Lecturer: He appeared among us again in about three weeks after—He looked sullen and told us that He previously had prepared and written down Quotations from different Authors to illustrate the present Lecture. These Quotations he had put among the Leaves of his Pocket Book which was stol'n as He was coming to the Institution. This narrative was not indulgently received, and He went thro' his Lecture heavily and without advancing any Thing that was spirited and animated—The next Day He received an Intimation from the Managers that his Lectures were no longer Expected.—

Jerningham's intimation that the Royal Institution had abruptly discharged Coleridge from his lectureship is of course flatly untrue. Coleridge himself requested that he be released from his engagement, and in terms that cannot be mistaken indicated the cause of his request; namely, extreme illness.   It is probable that Coleridge's attack on Lancaster aroused a good deal of criticism at the time, and malicious gossip would find in this the cause of the abrupt conclusion of the lectures, in default of more accurate knowledge.   As a matter of fact, in the annual meeting of the proprietors of the Royal Institution in 1809, a resolution was passed censuring Coleridge for introducing such personal animadversions into his lectures.[2]   But this was a year later, and the resolution would not have been offered and passed, had the managers already censured Coleridge for his partisanship.

Some of the manuscripts in the earlier part of this book seem to be intended for the lectures of 1808.   These are, chiefly, the fragments dealing with Milton's description of poetry (in part), Shakespeare's poetry, the judgment of Shakespeare (in part), the four kinds of readers, and the permanence of poetry.[3]   The evidence indicating the relation of these materials to the lectures of 1808, which should be consulted in the notes to the various fragments, consists partly of the date, 1808, on a later page of the notebook from which the manuscripts come, and partly of internal evidence, in Coleridge's references to his

---

[1] For another account of this incident see *A House of Letters*, ed. by E. Betham (London, 1905), pp. 107–8.   This undated letter belongs to the month of May, perhaps to the second week of that month.

[2] Bence Jones, *The Royal Institution*, p. 284, note.

[3] Cf. i. 148–9, 187–93, 194–5, 220–1, 223–6.

inexperience and the illness which interrupted his lectures almost at the very beginning.   In addition to this group of manuscripts one may count with safety 'The Definition of Taste,' 'The Origins of Drama,' and 'The Origins of Modern Drama,' [1] which have already been mentioned in connection with the lecture of 5 February 1808.   Aside from the interest attached to any new light upon Coleridge's first series of literary lectures, the chief value of dating these manuscripts is in the new evidence that Coleridge was expressing explicitly his faith in Shakespeare's judgment at the time of Schlegel's oral lectures in Vienna, three years before these lectures were published.

[1] Cf. i. 158–74.

THE LECTURES OF 1811–12

AFTER the lectures of 1808 Coleridge lectured no more for three years, years in which he was occupied with *The Friend*, with contributions to the *Courier*, and with painful dreams of lost friendship and lost hope. The care of the Wordsworth family had made possible *The Friend* in 1809–10; and now, after the rupture with Wordsworth, the Morgans took Coleridge under their care and brought him round to another period of productiveness, which resulted first in the journalistic work for the *Courier*, and then in the series of seventeen lectures which began 18 November 1811 (on time) and ended 27 January 1812. The lectures were announced for Monday and Thursday evenings of each week and were, therefore, delivered with great regularity, allowing for the intermission at Christmas. They did not, however, fulfil expectations with pedantic strictness: the fifteen lectures originally announced were not sufficient to carry out the promises of the prospectus, and Coleridge added two others. His inability to cover the ground in the allotted time was not due, one regrets to say, to a surplus of material but to repetition and digression, which were the result of lack of preparation and extemporaneous delivery, without or almost without notes.[1] To say that Coleridge was the lecturer is as much as to say that the lectures varied between the most superb literary criticism, as in Lectures VII and XII, and distinctly dull pulpit oratory, as in Lecture VIII, all the intermediate degrees being represented.

We are comparatively fortunate in the records of this course. Besides Crabb Robinson's memoranda in his *Diary* and various brief newspaper reports, shorthand reports of ten of the seventeen lectures are printed in the present edition.

Three of these—the third, fourth and fifth lectures—are by a Mr J. Tomalin, whose reports of the first eight lectures were known to James Dykes Campbell and Ernest Hartley Coleridge[2] but never published. The present editor found Campbell's transcript of three of these lectures among the papers of Ernest Hartley Coleridge and prints them in their proper place by the kind permission of the Reverend G. H. B. Coleridge, the great-grandson of the poet. The other reports cannot be found, but shorthand reports of J. P. Collier cover the same ground.

The present editor does not believe that there is any need of

---

[1] Cf. ii. 179, H. C. Robinson's letter of 13 December 1811.
[2] Campbell, Introduction to Coleridge's *Poetical Works*, p. lxxxiv, note 2; E. H. Coleridge, *Letters of Samuel Taylor Coleridge*, pp. 11, note; 575, note.

apologizing for or justifying at length his belief in the authenticity of these lectures. No one will believe that they are accurate in detail; nor does Collier claim that they are so. But that Collier could have manufactured out of whole cloth a body of reports so characteristic of Coleridge in his greatest excellences as well as his faults is to attribute to the great literary forger genius rather than dishonesty. We know that Collier attended the lectures and took notes; [1] and these notes correspond closely with the brief records of H. C. Robinson, which were not published until thirteen years after Collier's book. They show also occasional correspondences with manuscripts now published for the first time. The best examples of this are Collier's reports of the first and second lectures, [2] which closely resemble Coleridge's notes on 'Accidental and Permanent Causes of False Criticism,' 'Classes of Readers,' and 'The Use of General Terms' in the section of 'Miscellaneous Fragments.' [3] It would not be difficult to offer further evidence from cross-references, but this would merely be reviving a controversy which special students of Coleridge consider closed. In any case, no edition of Coleridge's Shakespearean criticism can be complete without the Collier reports so long as a majority, or even a minority of readers, consider the reports genuine.

Collier's full reports first appeared [4] in *Seven Lectures on Shakespeare and Milton*, published in 1856. They are best introduced by the following passages from Collier's Preface.

Collier's Preface.

I am fully aware that my memoranda, of forty-five years standing, are more or less imperfect: of some of the Lectures I appear to have made only abridged sketches: of others my notes are much fuller and more extended; but I am certain, even at this distance of time, that I did not knowingly register a sentence, that did not come from Coleridge's lips, although doubtless I missed, omitted, and mistook points and passages, which now I should have been most rejoiced to have preserved. In completing my transcripts, however, I added no word or syllable of my own. . . .

The series was delivered extemporaneously (almost without the assistance of notes) in a large room at what was called The Scot's Corporation Hall, in Crane Court, Fleet Street; and on applying for tickets, Coleridge sent us a copy of his prospectus, which, many years afterwards I was glad to see I had accidentally preserved, and which was in the following form:—

---

[1] Cf. ii. 166, 169, 181.   [2] Cf. ii. 32 ff.
[3] Cf. i. 217-22.
[4] They were first published in part in *Notes and Queries*, First Series, vol. x (1854), pp. 1, 21, 57, 106, 117.

LONDON PHILOSOPHICAL SOCIETY,

SCOT'S CORPORATION HALL,

CRANE COURT, FLEET STREET,

(ENTRANCE FROM FETTER LANE.)

MR. COLERIDGE

WILL COMMENCE

ON MONDAY, NOV. 18TH,

A COURSE OF LECTURES ON SHAKESPEAR AND MILTON,

IN ILLUSTRATION OF

THE PRINCIPLES OF POETRY,

AND THEIR

Application as Grounds of Criticism to the most popular Works of later English Poets, those of the Living included.

AFTER an introductory Lecture on False Criticism, (especially in Poetry,) and on its Causes: two thirds of the remaining course, will be assigned, 1st, to a philosophic Analysis and Explanation of all the principal *Characters* of our great Dramatist, as OTHELLO, FALSTAFF, RICHARD 3d, IAGO, HAMLET, &c.: and 2nd, to a critical *Comparison* of SHAKESPEAR, in respect of Diction, Imagery, management of the Passions, Judgment in the construction of his Dramas, in short, of all that belongs to him as a Poet, and as a dramatic Poet, with his contemporaries, or immediate successors, JONSON, BEAUMONT and FLETCHER, FORD, MASSINGER, &c. in the endeavour to determine what of SHAKESPEAR'S Merits and Defects are common to him with other Writers of the same age, and what remain peculiar to his own Genius.

The Course will extend to fifteen Lectures, which will be given on Monday and Thursday evenings successively. The Lectures to commence at $\frac{1}{2}$ past 7 o'clock.

Single Tickets for the whole Course, 2 Guineas; or 3 Guineas with the privilege of introducing a Lady: may be procured at J. Hatchard's, 190, Piccadilly; J. Murray's, Fleet Street; J. and A. Arch's, Booksellers and Stationers, Cornhill; Godwin's Juvenile Library, Skinner Street; W. Pople's, 67, Chancery Lane; or by Letter (post paid) to Mr. S. T. Coleridge, J. J. Morgan's, Esq. No. 7, Portland Place, Hammersmith.

W. Pople, Printer, Chancery Lane, London.

. . . My original notes, therefore, were taken at the close of 1811 and at the opening of 1812. I endeavoured in the interval between each lecture to transcribe them; but, from other avocations, I was unable to keep pace with the delivery, and at the termination of the course I must have been considerably in arrear: while I am writing I have two of my short-hand books (sheets of paper stitched together) before me, which remained undecyphered from 1812 until 1854,—a period of forty-two years. During the whole time I did not know what had become of any of them. I attended another course by the same lecturer in 1818, of which I had taken and preserved only a few scattered excerpts; and I cannot call to mind whether, even at that date, my notes of the previous lectures of 1811–12 were forthcoming. I know that I afterwards searched for them several times unsuccessfully; and with great diligence about the year 1842, when I was engaged in preparing a new edition of Shakespeare, to which I apprehended the opinions of Coleridge on the different plays would have been an important recommendation. I again failed to find them, and in 1850 I took up my residence in the country, carrying with me only such furniture as I required, and among it a double chest of drawers, in the highest part of which I subsequently discovered some of, but, I lament to say, by no means all, my lost notes. Even these were not brought to light until I was preparing to remove to my present residence, and was employing myself in turning out waste paper and worthless relics from every receptacle. . . .

These are what are now offered to the reader. I cannot but be sensible of their many and great imperfections: they are, I am sure, full of omissions, owing in some degree to want of facility on my part; in a greater degree, perhaps, to a mistaken estimate of what it was, or was not, expedient to minute; and in no little proportion to the fact, that in some cases I relied upon my recol-

lection to fill up chasms in my memoranda.   A few defects may
be attributed to the inconvenience of my position among other
auditors (though the Lectures were not always very fully
attended), and others to the plain fact, that I was not unfrequently so engrossed, and absorbed by the almost inspired look
and manner of the speaker, that I was, for a time, incapable of
performing the mechanical duty of writing.   I present my notes
merely as they are, doing, I know, great injustice to the man and
to the subject, but at the same time preserving many criticisms,
observations, and opinions, well worthy of attention from their
truth, their eloquence, and their originality.

[*Collier's Records of Coleridge's Conversation.*[1]]

My first note in which Coleridge is mentioned bears date on
the 13th October—as I presume 1811; [2] but I am without any
guide as to the year, beyond the fact that it appears to have been
the 13th October, immediately preceding the 18th November,
when Coleridge began his Lectures.   My entries are the
following:—

'*Sunday, 13th Oct.*—I mentioned, a few pages back, having
been in company with Godwin for several hours, and not having
heard him say a single word that I cared to remember.   Two or
three months ago I was in Coleridge's company for the first
time: I have seen him on various occasions since, to my great
delight and surprise.   I was delighted with his gentle manners
and unaffected good humour, and especially with his kindness
and considerateness for young people: I was surprised by the
variety and extent of his knowledge, displayed and enlivened by
so much natural eloquence.   All he says is without effort, but
not unfrequently with a sort of musical hum, and a catching of
his breath at the end, and sometimes in the middle, of a sentence,
enough to make a slight pause, but not so much as to interrupt
the flow of his language.   He never disdains to talk on the most
familiar topics, if they seem pleasing to others.

'In a conversation at my father's, a little while since, he gave
the following character of Falstaff, which I wrote down very soon
after it was delivered.

---

[1] These notes are also taken from Collier's Preface.   I have not attempted
to indicate my occasional omission of Collier's footnotes, either here or in the
reports of lectures which follow.   All unsigned notes are by the present
editor.
[2] The week-days which Collier records belong to the year 1811.

'Falstaff was no coward, but pretended to be one merely for the sake of trying experiments on the credulity of mankind: he was a liar with the same object, and not because he loved false-hood for itself.   He was a man of such pre-eminent abilities, as to give him a profound contempt for all those by whom he was usually surrounded, and to lead to a determination on his part, in spite of their fancied superiority, to make them his tools and dupes.   He knew, however low he descended, that his own talents would raise him, and extricate him from any difficulty. While he was thought to be the greatest rogue, thief, and liar, he still had that about him which could render him not only respect-able, but absolutely necessary to his companions.   It was in characters of complete moral depravity, but of first-rate wit and talents, that Shakespeare delighted; and Coleridge instanced Richard the Third, Falstaff, and Iago.[1]

'As Coleridge is a man of genius and knowledge, he seems glad of opportunities of display: being a good talker, he likes to get hold of a good listener: he admits it. . . .

'Coleridge was recently asked his opinion as to the order in which Shakespeare had written his plays? [2]   His answer was to this effect, as well as I can remember:—that although Malone had collected a great many external particulars regarding the age of each play, they were all, in Coleridge's mind, much less satis-factory than the knowledge to be obtained from internal evidence. If he were to adopt any theory upon the subject, it would rather be physiological and pathological than chronological.   There appeared to be three stages in Shakespeare's genius; it did not seem as if in the outset he thought his ability of a dramatic kind, excepting perhaps as an actor, in which, like many others, he had been somewhat mistaken, though by no means so much as it was the custom to believe.[3]   Hence his two poems, "Venus and

---

[1] For more or less similar remarks on this subject cf. i. 206; ii. 141, 165, 237; and *B.L.* ii. 189.

[2] Cf. this list with 'The Order of Shakespeare's Plays,' i. 208–14, and with ii. 60–1, 67, note.

[3] I have a separate note of what Coleridge once said on the subject of the acting powers of Shakespeare, to which I can assign no date, but which I may appropriately add here: it is in these words:—

'It is my persuasion—indeed my firm conviction—so firm that nothing can shake it—the rising of Shakespeare's spirit from the grave, modestly con-fessing his own deficiencies, could not alter my opinion—that Shakespeare, in the best sense of the word, was a very great actor; nothing can exceed the judgment he displays upon that subject.   He may not have had the physical advantages of Burbage or Field; but they would never have become what they were without his most able and sagacious instructions; and what would either of them have been without Shakespeare's plays?   Great dramatists make

Adonis" and "Lucrece," both of a narrative character, which must have been written very early: the first, at all events, must have been produced in the country, amid country scenes, sights and employments; but the last had more the air of a city, and of society.

'With regard to his dramas, they might easily be placed in groups. "Titus Andronicus" would, in some sort, stand alone, because it was obviously intended to excite vulgar audiences by its scenes of blood and horror—to our ears shocking and disgusting. This was the fashion of plays in Shakespeare's youth; but the taste, if such indeed it were, soon disappeared, as it was sure to do with a man of his character of mind; and then followed, probably, that beautiful love-poem "Romeo and Juliet," and "Love's Labour's Lost," made up entirely of the same passion. These might be succeeded by "All's Well that Ends Well," not an agreeable story, but still full of love; and by "As You Like It," not Shakespeare's invention as to plot, but entirely his own as to dialogue, with all the vivacity of wit, and the elasticity of youth and animal spirits. No man, even in the middle period of life, he thought, could have produced it. "Midsummer Night's Dream" and "Twelfth Night" hardly appeared to belong to the complete maturity of his genius: Shakespeare was then ripening his powers for such works as "Troilus and Cressida," "Coriolanus," "Julius Caesar," "Cymbeline," and "Othello." Coleridge professed that he could not yet make up his mind to assign a period to "The Merchant of Venice," to "Much Ado about Nothing," nor to "Measure for Measure"; but he was convinced that "Antony and Cleopatra," "Hamlet," "Macbeth," "Lear," "The Tempest," and "The Winter's Tale," were late productions,—especially "The Winter's Tale." These belonged to the third group.

---

great actors. But looking at him merely as a performer, I am certain that he was greater as *Adam*, in "As You Like It," than Burbage, as *Hamlet*, or *Richard the Third*. Think of the scene between him and *Orlando*; and think again, that the actor of that part had to carry the author of that play in his arms! Think of having had Shakespeare in one's arms! It is worth having died two hundred years ago to have heard Shakespeare deliver a single line. He must have been a great actor.'

Here the enthusiasm of the poet may be said to have overwhelmed the sobriety of the critic; for on Sunday, 13th October, Coleridge admitted that Shakespeare had been 'somewhat mistaken' in his own powers as an actor.— [J. P. C.]

It may be remarked that Schlegel also thought that Shakespeare must have been an excellent actor (*Werke*, vi. 324). This, perhaps, may be set down as merely coincidence.

'When asked what he would do with the historical plays, he replied that he was much at a loss. Historical plays had been written and acted before Shakespeare took up those subjects; and there was no doubt whatever that his contributions to the three parts of Henry VI. were very small; indeed he doubted, in opposition to Malone, whether he had had anything to do with the first part of Henry VI.: if he had, it must have been extremely early in his career. "Richard II." and "Richard III."—noble plays, and the finest specimens of their kind—must have preceded the two parts of "Henry IV."; and "Henry VIII." was decidedly a late play. Dramas of this description ought to be treated by themselves; they were neither tragedy nor comedy, and yet at times both. Though far from accurate as to events, in point of character they were the essential truth of history. "Let no man (said Coleridge) blame his son for learning history from Shakespeare."

I felt that this last sentence was so very applicable to myself, that it will always be impressed upon my mind, and I never shall forget the peculiarly emphatic tone, and rich voice in which Coleridge delivered it. He continued in this strain:—

'He did not agree with some Germans (whom he had heard talk upon the subject) that Shakespeare had had much to do with the doubtful plays imputed to him in the third folio: on the contrary, he was sure that, if he had touched any of them, it was only very lightly and rarely. Being asked whether he included the "Two Noble Kinsmen," among the doubtful plays, he answered, "Decidedly not: there is the clearest internal evidence that Shakespeare importantly aided Fletcher in the composition of it. Parts are most unlike Fletcher, yet most like Shakespeare, while other parts are most like Fletcher, and most unlike Shakespeare. The mad scenes of the Jailor's daughter are coarsely imitated from "Hamlet": those were by Fletcher, and so very inferior, that I wonder how he could so far condescend. Shakespeare would never have imitated himself at all, much less so badly.[1] There is no finer, or more characteristic dramatic writing than some scenes in "The Two Noble Kinsmen."' [2]

The above is what I registered under the date of 13th October, but I find from my Diary that I was again in Coleridge's

---

[1] Schlegel gives almost exactly the same argument against the Shakespearean authorship of these scenes (*Werke*, vi. 350). The dates preclude Schlegel's influence.

[2] 'I have no doubt whatever that the first act and the first scene of the second act of *The Two Noble Kinsmen* are Shakspeare's' (*Table-Talk*, 17 February 1833). See also *M.C.*, pp. 92–3.

company at Charles Lamb's on the 16th October, and the next day I wrote as follows:—

'Thursday, 17th Oct.—Yesterday, at Lamb's, I met Coleridge again. I expected to see him there, and I made up my mind that I would remember as much as possible of what he said. I went into the apartment, where he and others were assembled, at 8, and before 9 my recollection was so burdened that I was obliged to leave the room for some time, that I might lighten the weight. However, I could not prevail upon myself to stay away long, and returned to the company with a resolution to take the matter more easily. Few others talked, although Hazlitt, Lloyd, Rickman, Dyer, and Burney, with Lamb and his sister, now and then interposed a remark, and gave Coleridge, as it were, a bottom to spin upon: they all seemed disposed to allow him sea-room enough, and he availed himself of it, and, spreading canvas, sailed away majestically. The following is the bare skeleton, and mere bone of what fell from him. He was speaking of Shakespeare when I entered the room:

'He said that Shakespeare was almost the only dramatic poet, who by his characters represented a class, and not an individual: other writers for the stage, and in other respects good ones too, had aimed their satire and ridicule at particular foibles and particular persons, while Shakespeare at one stroke lashed thousands: Shakespeare struck at a crowd; Jonson picked out an especial object for his attack. Coleridge drew a parallel between Shakespeare and a geometrician: the latter, when tracing a circle, had his eye upon the centre as the important point, but included also in his vision a wide circumference; so Shakespeare, while his eye rested upon an individual character, always embraced a wide circumference of others, without diminishing the separate interest he intended to attach to the being he pourtrayed. Othello was a personage of this description; but all Shakespeare's chief characters possessed, in a greater or less degree, this claim to our admiration. He was not a mere painter of portraits, with the dress, features, and peculiarities of the sitter; but a painter of likenesses so true that, although nobody could perhaps say they knew the very person represented, all saw at once that it was faithful, and that it must be a likeness.

'Lamb led Coleridge on to speak of Beaumont and Fletcher: he highly extolled their comedies in many respects, especially for the vivacity of the dialogue, but he contended that their tragedies were liable to grave objections. They always proceeded upon something forced and unnatural; the reader never can reconcile the plot with probability, and sometimes not with possibility.[1]   One of their tragedies [2] was founded upon this:— A lady expresses a wish to possess the heart of her lover, terms which that lover understands, all the way through, in a literal sense; and nothing can satisfy him but tearing out his heart, and having it presented to the heroine, in order to secure her affections, after he was past the enjoyment of them.   Their comedies, however, were much superior, and at times, and excepting in the generalization of humour and application, almost rivalled those of Shakespeare.   The situations are sometimes so disgusting, and the language so indecent and immoral, that it is impossible to read the plays in private society.   The difference in this respect between Shakespeare and Beaumont and Fletcher (speaking of them in their joint capacity) is, that Shakespeare always makes vice odious and virtue admirable, while Beaumont and Fletcher do the very reverse—they ridicule virtue and encourage vice: they pander to the lowest and basest passions of our nature.

'Coleridge afterwards made some remarks upon more modern dramatists, and was especially severe upon Dryden, who could degrade his fine intellect, and debase his noble use of the English language in such plays as "All for Love," and "Sebastian," down to "Limberham," and "The Spanish Friar."   He spoke also of Moore's "Gamester," and applauded warmly the acting of Mrs. Siddons.   He admitted that the situations were affecting, but maintained that the language of the tragedy was below criticism: it was about upon a par with "Kotzebue."   It was extremely natural for any one to shed tears at seeing a beautiful woman in the depths of anguish and despair, when she beheld her husband, who had ruined himself by gambling, dying of poison at the very moment he had come into a large fortune, which would have paid all his debts, and enabled him to live in affluence and happiness.   "This (said Coleridge) reminds one of the modern termination of 'Romeo and Juliet,'—I mean the way in which Garrick, or somebody else, terminated it,—so that Juliet should revive before the death of Romeo, and just in time to be not in time, but to find that he had swallowed a mortal poison.   I know that this conclusion is consistent with the old

---

[1] Schlegel (*Werke*, vi. 345–7) coincides with Coleridge in preferring the comedies of Beaumont and Fletcher to their tragedies, in censuring their improbabilities and their licentiousness.   The supposed dates of Collier's reports preclude the possibility of an influence from Schlegel; and, in any case, the parallels are almost too general to be worth citing.

[2] *The Mad Lover*.   (Cf. i. 53.)

novel upon which the tragedy is founded, but a narrative is one thing and a drama another, and Shakespeare's judgment revolted at such situations on the stage. To be sure they produce tears, and so does a blunt razor shaving the upper lip."" [1]

---

[1] Cf. i. 181.   In *S.C.* (1930) I added at this point twenty pages of Collier's records of Coleridge's literary conversation on non-Shakespearean subjects, which I must omit here because of my limits of space.

LECTURES ON SHAKESPEARE AND MILTON

THE FIRST LECTURE

[*Collier Report.*]

I CANNOT avoid the acknowledgment of the difficulty of the task I have undertaken; yet I have undertaken it voluntarily, and I shall discharge it to the best of my abilities, requesting those who hear me to allow for deficiencies, and to bear in mind the wide extent of my subject. The field is almost boundless as the sea, yet full of beauty and variety as the land: I feel in some sort oppressed by abundance; *inopem me copia fecit.*

What I most rely upon is your sympathy; and, as I proceed, I trust that I shall interest you: sympathy and interest are to a lecturer like the sun and the showers to nature—absolutely necessary to the production of blossoms and fruit.

May I venture to observe that my own life has been employed more in reading and conversation—in collecting and reflecting, than in printing and publishing; for I never felt the desire, so often experienced by others, of becoming an author. It was accident made me an author in the first instance: I was called a poet almost before I knew I could write poetry. In what I have to offer I shall speak freely, whether of myself or of my contemporaries, when it is necessary: conscious superiority, if indeed it be superior, need not fear to have its self-love or its pride wounded; and contempt, the most absurd and debasing feeling that can actuate the human mind, must be far below the sphere in which lofty intellects live and move and have their being.

On [1] the first examination of a work, especially a work of fiction and fancy, it is right to inquire to what feeling or passion it addresses itself—to the benevolent, or to the vindictive? whether it is calculated to excite emulation, or to produce envy, under the common mask of scorn? and, in the next place, whether the pleasure we receive from it has a tendency to keep us good, to make us better, or to reward us for being good.

It will be expected of me, as my prospectus indicates, that I should say something of the causes of false criticism, particularly

[1] From this point the lecture may be compared with the manuscript printed on i. 217–20, on which the oral lecture was based.

32

as regards poetry, though I do not mean to confine myself to that only: in doing so, it will be necessary for me to point out some of the obstacles which impede, and possibly prevent, the formation of a correct judgment.   These are either—

1. Accidental causes, arising out of the particular circumstances of the age in which we live; or—

2. Permanent causes, flowing out of the general principles of our nature.

Under the first head, accidental causes, may be classed— 1. The events that have occurred in our own day, which, from their importance alone, have created a world of readers.   2. The practice of public speaking, which encourages a too great desire to be understood at once, and at the first blush.   3. The prevalence of reviews, magazines, newspapers, novels, &c.

Of the last, and of the perusal of them, I will run the risk of asserting, that where the reading of novels prevails as a habit, it occasions in time the entire destruction of the powers of the mind: it is such an utter loss to the reader, that it is not so much to be called pass-time as kill-time.[1]   It conveys no trustworthy information as to facts; it produces no improvement of the intellect, but fills the mind with a mawkish and morbid sensibility, which is directly hostile to the cultivation, invigoration, and enlargement of the nobler faculties of the understanding.

Reviews are generally pernicious, because the writers determine without reference to fixed principles—because reviews are usually filled with personalities; and, above all, because they teach people rather to judge than to consider, to decide than to reflect: thus they encourage superficiality, and induce the thoughtless and the idle to adopt sentiments conveyed under the authoritative WE, and not, by the working and subsequent clearing of their own minds, to form just original opinions.   In older times writers were looked up to almost as intermediate beings, between angels and men; afterwards they were regarded as venerable and, perhaps, inspired teachers; subsequently they descended to the level of learned and instructive friends; but in modern days they are deemed culprits more than benefactors: as culprits they are brought to the bar of self-erected and self-satisfied tribunals.[2]   If a person be now seen reading a new book, the most usual question is—'What trash have you there?' I admit that there is some reason for this difference in the estimate; for in these times, if a man fail as a tailor, or a shoemaker,

---

[1] Cf. B.L. i. 34, Coleridge's note, and M.C., pp. 195–6.
[2] Cf. i. 219 and B.L. i. 41, for similar passages.

and can read and write correctly (for spelling is still of some consequence) he becomes an author.[1]

The crying sin of modern criticism is that it is overloaded with personality. If an author commit an error, there is no wish to set him right for the sake of truth, but for the sake of triumph—that the reviewer may show how much wiser, or how much abler he is than the writer. Reviewers are usually people who would have been poets, historians, biographers, &c., if they could: they have tried their talents at one or at the other, and have failed; therefore they turn critics, and, like the Roman emperor, a critic most hates those who excel in the particular department in which he, the critic, has notoriously been defeated. This is an age of personality and political gossip, when insects, as in ancient Egypt, are worshipped in proportion to the venom of their stings—when poems, and especially satires, are valued according to the number of living names they contain; and where the notes, however, have this comparative excellence, that they are generally more poetical and pointed than the text. This style of criticism is at the present moment one of the chief pillars of the Scotch professorial court; and, as to personality in poems, I remember to have once seen an epic advertised, and strongly recommended, because it contained more than a hundred names of living characters.

How derogatory, how degrading, this is to true poetry I need not say. A very wise writer has maintained that there is more difference between one man and another, than between man and a beast: I can conceive of no lower state of human existence than that of a being who, insensible to the beauties of poetry himself, endeavours to reduce others to his own level. What Hooker so eloquently claims for law [2] I say of poetry—'Her seat is the bosom of God, her voice the harmony of the world; all things in heaven and on earth do her homage.' It is the language of heaven, and in the exquisite delight we derive from poetry we have, as it were, a type, a foretaste, and a prophecy of the joys of heaven.

Another cause of false criticism is the greater purity of morality in the present age, compared even with the last. Our notions upon this subject are sometimes carried to excess, particularly among those who in print affect to enforce the value of a high

---

[1] Here my shorthand note informs me that Coleridge made a quotation from Jeremy Taylor, but from what work, or of what import, does not appear. He observed, that 'although Jeremy Taylor wrote only in prose, according to some definitions of poetry he might be considered one of our noblest poets.'—J. P. C.   [2] Hooker's *Ecclesiastical Polity*, I. xvi. 8.

standard.   Far be it from me to depreciate that value; but let me ask, who now will venture to read a number of the Spectator, or of the Tatler, to his wife and daughters, without first examining it to make sure that it contains no word which might, in our day, offend the delicacy of female ears, and shock feminine susceptibility?   Even our theatres, the representations at which usually reflect the morals of the period, have taken a sort of domestic turn, and while the performances at them may be said, in some sense, to improve the heart, there is no doubt that they vitiate the taste.   The effect is bad, however good the cause.

Attempts have been made to compose and adapt systems of education; but it appears to me something like putting Greek and Latin grammars into the hands of boys, before they understand a word of Greek or Latin.   These grammars contain instructions on all the minutiæ and refinements of language, but of what use are they to persons who do not comprehend the first rudiments?   Why are you to furnish the means of judging, before you give the capacity to judge?   These seem to me to be among the principal accidental causes of false criticism.

Among the permanent causes, I may notice—

First, the great pleasure we feel in being told of the knowledge we possess, rather than of the ignorance we suffer.   Let it be our first duty to teach thinking, and then what to think about.   You cannot expect a person to be able to go through the arduous process of thinking, who has never exercised his faculties.   In the Alps we see the Chamois hunter ascend the most perilous precipices without danger, and leap from crag to crag over vast chasms without dread or difficulty, and who but a fool, if unpractised, would attempt to follow him? it is not intrepidity alone that is necessary, but he who would imitate the hunter must have gone through the same process for the acquisition of strength, skill, and knowledge: he must exert, and be capable of exerting, the same muscular energies, and display the same perseverance and courage, or all his efforts will be worse than fruitless: they will lead not only to disappointment, but to destruction.   Systems have been invented with the avowed object of teaching people how to think; but in my opinion the proper title for such a work ought to be 'The Art of teaching how to think without thinking.'   Nobody endeavours to instruct a man how to leap, until he has first given him vigour and elasticity.

Nothing is more essential—nothing can be more important, than in every possible way to cultivate and improve the thinking powers: the mind as much requires exercise as the body, and no man can fully and adequately discharge the duties of whatever station he is placed in without the power of thought. I do not, of course, say that a man may not get through life without much thinking, or much power of thought; but if he be a carpenter, without thought a carpenter he must remain: if he be a weaver, without thought a weaver he must remain.—On man God has not only bestowed gifts, but the power of giving: he is not a creature born but to live and die: he has had faculties communicated to him, which, if he do his duty, he is bound to communicate and make beneficial to others. Man, in a secondary sense, may be looked upon in part as his own creator, for by the improvement of the faculties bestowed upon him by God, he not only enlarges them, but may be said to bring new ones into existence. The Almighty has thus condescended to communicate to man, in a high state of moral cultivation, a portion of his own great attributes.

A second permanent cause of false criticism is connected with the habit of not taking the trouble to think: it is the custom which some people have established of judging of books by books.— Hence to such the use and value of reviews. Why has nature given limbs, if they are not to be applied to motion and action; why abilities, if they are to lie asleep, while we avail ourselves of the eyes, ears, and understandings of others? As men often employ servants, to spare them the nuisance of rising from their seats and walking across a room, so men employ reviews in order to save themselves the trouble of exercising their own powers of judging: it is only mental slothfulness and sluggishness that induce so many to adopt, and take for granted the opinions of others.

I may illustrate this moral imbecility by a case which came within my own knowledge. A friend of mine had seen it stated somewhere, or had heard it said, that Shakespeare had not made Constance, in 'King John,' speak the language of nature, when she exclaims on the loss of Arthur,

> 'Grief fills the room up of my absent child,
> Lies in his bed, walks up and down with me;
> Puts on his pretty looks, repeats his words,
> Remembers me of all his gracious parts,
> Stuffs out his vacant garments with his form:
> Then have I reason to be fond of grief.'

King John, Act iii, Scene 4.

Within three months after he had repeated the opinion, (not thinking for himself) that these lines were out of nature, my friend died. I called upon his mother, an affectionate, but

ignorant woman, who had scarcely heard the name of Shakespeare, much less read any of his plays. Like Philip, I endeavoured to console her, and among other things I told her, in
the anguish of her sorrow, that she seemed to be as fond of grief
as she had been of her son. What was her reply? Almost a
prose parody on the very language of Shakespeare—the same
thoughts in nearly the same words, but with a different arrangement. An attestation like this is worth a thousand criticisms.

As a third permanent cause of false criticism we may notice the
vague use of terms. And here I may take the liberty of impressing upon my hearers, the fitness, if not the necessity, of employing the most appropriate words and expressions, even in
common conversation, and in the ordinary transactions of life.
If you want a substantive do not take the first that comes into
your head, but that which most distinctly and peculiarly conveys
your meaning: if an adjective, remember the grammatical use of
that part of speech, and be careful that it expresses some quality
in the substantive that you wish to impress upon your hearer.
Reflect for a moment on the vague and uncertain manner in
which the word 'taste' has been often employed; and how such
epithets as 'sublime,' 'majestic,' 'grand,' 'striking,' 'picturesque,' &c. have been misapplied, and how they have been used
on the most unworthy and inappropriate occasions.

I was one day admiring one of the falls of the Clyde; and
ruminating upon what descriptive term could be most fitly
applied to it, I came to the conclusion that the epithet 'majestic'
was the most appropriate. While I was still contemplating the
scene a gentleman and a lady came up, neither of whose faces
bore much of the stamp of superior intelligence, and the first
words the gentleman uttered were 'It is very majestic.' I was
pleased to find such a confirmation of my opinion, and I complimented the spectator upon the choice of his epithet, saying that
he had used the best word that could have been selected from our
language: 'Yes, sir,' replied the gentleman, 'I say it is very
majestic: it is sublime, it is beautiful, it is grand, it is picturesque.'—'Ay (added the lady), it is the prettiest thing I ever
saw.' I own that I was not a little disconcerted.[1]

---

[1] (Cf. i. 162, 220.) This anecdote has still more point if we remember
Coleridge's interest in Kant's fundamental distinction between the sublime
and the beautiful (*Critique of Aesthetic Judgement*), and in other discussions by
aestheticians of the same subject. The most accurate form of this anecdote
is surely that in Dorothy Wordsworth's 'Recollections of a Tour made in
Scotland' (*Journals*, London, 1897, vol. i, p. 195). Other versions are those in
B.L. ii. 224–5, and *Table-Talk*, 24 June 1827.

You will see, by the terms of my prospectus, that I intend my lectures to be, not only 'in illustration of the principles of poetry,' but to include a statement of the application of those principles, 'as grounds of criticism on the most popular works of later English poets, those of the living included.' If I had thought this task presumptuous on my part, I should not have voluntarily undertaken it; and in examining the merits, whether positive or comparative, of my contemporaries, I shall dismiss all feelings and associations which might lead me from the formation of a right estimate. I shall give talent and genius its due praise, and only bestow censure where, as it seems to me, truth and justice demand it. I shall, of course, carefully avoid falling into that system of false criticism, which I condemn in others; and, above all, whether I speak of those whom I know, or of those whom I do not know, of friends or of enemies, of the dead or of the living, my great aim will be to be strictly impartial. No man can truly apply principles, who displays the slightest bias in the application of them; and I shall have much greater pleasure in pointing out the good, than in exposing the bad. I fear no accusation of arrogance from the amiable and the wise: I shall pity the weak, and despise the malevolent.

THE SECOND LECTURE

[Collier Report.]

READERS may be divided into four classes:

1. Sponges, who absorb all they read, and return it nearly in the same state, only a little dirtied.

2. Sand-glasses, who retain nothing, and are content to get through a book for the sake of getting through the time.

3. Strain-bags, who retain merely the dregs of what they read.

4. Mogul diamonds, equally rare and valuable, who profit by what they read, and enable others to profit by it also.[1]

I adverted in my last lecture to the prevailing laxity in the use of terms: this is the principal complaint to which the moderns are exposed; but it is a grievous one, inasmuch as it inevitably tends to the misapplication of words, and to the corruption of language. I mentioned the word 'taste,' but the remark applies not merely to substantives and adjectives, to things and their epithets, but to verbs: thus, how frequently is the verb 'indorsed' strained from its true signification, as given by Milton in the expression—'And elephants indorsed with towers.' Again, 'virtue' has been equally perverted: originally it signified merely strength; it then became strength of mind and valour, and it has now been changed to the class term for moral excellence [2]

[1] Coleridge's source is evidently the tractate Ābhōth (v. 18) of the Mishnāh: 'There are four qualities among those that sit before the wise: they are like a sponge, a funnel, a strainer, or a sieve: a sponge, which sucks up everything; a funnel, which lets in at one end and out at the other; a strainer, which lets the wine pass out and retains the lees; a sieve, which lets out the bran and retains the fine flour.' For Coleridge's knowledge of the Mishnāh and his interest in Hebrew, see his *Letters*, p. 667, note. The parallel passage quoted in this note was pointed out by the Rev. S. R. Maitland in a private letter to J. P. Collier, after seeing part of Collier's reports printed in *Notes and Queries*, 22 July 1854. The present editor has discarded Collier's note in order to correct his faulty reference and to quote the English translation of the Mishnāh. The manuscripts of the introductory part of this lecture are evidently those on i. 220–2.

[2] My shorthand note of this part of the sentence strongly illustrates the point adverted to in the Preface, viz., how easy it is for a person, somewhat mechanically taking down words uttered *viva voce*, to mishear what is said. I am confident that Coleridge's words were 'moral excellence'—there cannot be a doubt about it—but in my note it stands '*modern* excellence.' My ear deceived me, and I thought he said *modern*, when in fact he said 'moral.'— J. P. C.

in all its various species.   I only introduce these as instances by the way, and nothing could be easier than to multiply them.

At the same time, while I recommend precision both of thought and expression, I am far from advocating a pedantic niceness in the choice of language: such a course would only render conversation stiff and stilted.   Dr. Johnson used to say that in the most unrestrained discourse he always sought for the properest word,—that which best and most exactly conveyed his meaning: to a certain point he was right, but because he carried it too far, he was often laborious where he ought to have been light, and formal where he ought to have been familiar.   Men ought to endeavour to distinguish subtilely, that they may be able afterwards to assimilate truly.

I have often heard the question put whether Pope is a great poet, and it has been warmly debated on both sides, some positively maintaining the affirmative, and others dogmatically insisting upon the negative; but it never occurred to either party to make the necessary preliminary inquiry—What is meant by the words 'poet' and 'poetry'?   Poetry is not merely invention: if it were, Gulliver's Travels would be poetry; and before you can arrive at a decision of the question, as to Pope's claim, it is absolutely necessary to ascertain what people intend by the words they use.   Harmonious versification no more makes poetry than mere invention makes a poet; and to both these requisites there is much besides to be added.   In morals, politics, and philosophy no useful discussion can be entered upon, unless we begin by explaining and understanding the terms we employ.   It is therefore requisite that I should state to you what I mean by the word 'poetry,' before I commence any consideration of the comparative merits of those who are popularly called 'poets.'

Words are used in two ways:—

1. In a sense that comprises everything called by that name. For instance, the words 'poetry' and 'sense' are employed in this manner, when we say that such a line is bad poetry or bad sense, when in truth it is neither poetry nor sense.   If it be bad poetry, it is not poetry; if it be bad sense, it is not sense.   The same of 'metre': bad metre is not metre.

2. In a philosophic sense, which must include a definition of what is essential to the thing.   Nobody means mere metre by poetry; so, mere rhyme is not poetry.   Something more is required, and what is that something?   It is not wit, because we may have wit where we never dream of poetry.   Is it the just

observation of human life? Is it a peculiar and a felicitous selection of words? This, indeed, would come nearer to the taste of the present age, when sound is preferred to sense; but I am happy to think that this taste is not likely to last long.

The Greeks and Romans, in the best period of their literature, knew nothing of any such taste. High-flown epithets and violent metaphors, conveyed in inflated language, is not poetry. Simplicity is indispensable, and in Catullus it is often impossible that more simple language could be used; there is scarcely a word or a line, which a lamenting mother in a cottage might not have employed.[1] That I may be clearly understood, I will venture to give the following definition of poetry.

It is an art (or whatever better term our language may afford) of representing, in words, external nature and human thoughts and affections, both relatively to human affections, by the production of as much immediate pleasure in parts, as is compatible with the largest sum of pleasure in the whole.

Or, to vary the words, in order to make the abstract idea more intelligible:—

It is the art of communicating whatever we wish to communicate, so as both to express and produce excitement, but for the purpose of immediate pleasure; and each part is fitted to afford as much pleasure, as is compatible with the largest sum in the whole.

You will naturally ask my reasons for this definition of poetry, and they are these:—

'It is a representation of nature'; but that is not enough: the anatomist and the topographer give representations of nature; therefore I add:

'And of the human thoughts and affections.' Here the metaphysician interferes: here our best novelists interfere likewise,— excepting that the latter describe with more minuteness, accuracy, and truth, than is consistent with poetry. Consequently I subjoin:

'It must be relative to the human affections.' Here my chief point of difference is with the novel-writer, the historian, and all those who describe not only nature, and the human affections, but relatively to the human affections: therefore I must add:

'And it must be done for the purpose of immediate pleasure.'

---

[1] It appears by my shorthand note that Coleridge here named some particular poem by Catullus; but what it was is not stated. . . .—J. P. C.

Collier here leaves the reader to his own conjectures, and after some reading of Catullus the present editor has decided to do likewise.

In poetry the general good is to be accomplished through the pleasure, and if the poet do not do that, he ceases to be a poet to him to whom he gives it not.   Still, it is not enough, because we may point out many prose writers to whom the whole of the definition hitherto furnished would apply.   I add, therefore, that it is not only for the purpose of immediate pleasure, but—

'The work must be so constructed as to produce in each part that highest quantity of pleasure, or a high quantity of pleasure.' There metre introduces its claim, where the feeling calls for it. Our language gives to expression a certain measure, and will, in a strong state of passion, admit of scansion from the very mouth. The very assumption that we are reading the work of a poet supposes that he is in a continuous state of excitement; and thereby arises a language in prose unnatural, but in poetry natural.

There is one error which ought to be peculiarly guarded against, which young poets are apt to fall into, and which old poets commit, from being no poets, but desirous of the end which true poets seek to attain.   No: I revoke the words; they are not desirous of that of which their little minds can have no just conception.   They have no desire of fame—that glorious immortality of true greatness—

> 'That lives and spreads aloft by those pure eyes,
>   And perfect witness of all judging Jove;'
>
>   MILTON'S *Lycidas*.

but they struggle for reputation, that echo of an echo, in whose very etymon its signification is contained.   Into this error the author of 'The Botanic Garden' has fallen, through the whole of which work, I will venture to assert, there are not twenty images described as a man would describe them in a state of excitement. The poem is written with all the tawdry industry of a milliner anxious to dress up a doll in silks and satins.   Dr. Darwin laboured to make his style fine and gaudy, by accumulating and applying all the sonorous and handsome-looking words in our language.   This is not poetry, and I subjoin to my definition—

That a true poem must give 'as much pleasure in each part as is compatible with the greatest sum of pleasure in the whole.' We must not look to parts merely, but to the whole, and to the effect of that whole.   In reading Milton, for instance, scarcely a line can be pointed out which, critically examined, could be called in itself good: the poet would not have attempted to produce merely what is in general understood by a good line; he sought to produce glorious paragraphs and systems of harmony, or, as he himself expresses it,

> 'Many a winding bout
> Of linked sweetness long drawn out.'
>
> *L'Allegro.*

Such, therefore, as I have now defined it, I shall consider the sense of the word 'Poetry': pleasurable excitement is its origin and object; pleasure is the magic circle out of which the poet must not dare to tread. Part of my definition, you will be aware, would apply equally to the arts of painting and music, as to poetry; but to the last are added words and metre, so that my definition is strictly and logically applicable to poetry, and to poetry only, which produces delight, the parent of so many virtues. When I was in Italy, a friend of mine, who pursued painting almost with the enthusiasm of madness, believing it superior to every other art, heard the definition I have given, acknowledged its correctness, and admitted the pre-eminence of poetry.

I never shall forget, when in Rome, the acute sensation of pain I experienced on beholding the frescoes of Raphael and Michael Angelo, and on reflecting that they were indebted for their preservation solely to the durable material upon which they were painted. There they are, the permanent monuments (permanent as long as walls and plaster last) of genius and skill, while many others of their mighty works have become the spoils of insatiate avarice, or the victims of wanton barbarism. How grateful ought mankind to be, that so many of the great literary productions of antiquity have come down to us—that the works of Homer, Euclid, and Plato, have been preserved—while we possess those of Bacon, Newton, Milton, Shakespeare, and of so many other living-dead men of our own island. These, fortunately, may be considered indestructible: they shall remain to us till the end of time itself—till time, in the words of a great poet of the age of Shakespeare, has thrown his last dart at death, and shall himself submit to the final and inevitable destruction of all created matter.[1]

---

[1] Alluding, of course, to Ben Jonson's epitaph on the Countess of Pembroke:

> 'Underneath this sable herse
> Lies the subject of all verse,
> Sidney's sister, Pembroke's mother.
> Death! ere thou hast slain another,
> Learn'd, and fair, and good as she,
> Time shall throw a dart at thee.'
>
> *Ben Jonson's Works; edit. Gifford,* viii. 337.—J. P. C.

A second irruption of the Goths and Vandals could not now endanger their existence, secured as they are by the wonders of modern invention, and by the affectionate admiration of myriads of human beings.   It is as nearly two centuries as possible since Shakespeare ceased to write, but when shall he cease to be read? When shall he cease to give light and delight?   Yet even at this moment he is only receiving the first-fruits of that glory, which must continue to augment as long as our language is spoken. English has given immortality to him, and he has given immortality to English.   Shakespeare can never die, and the language in which he wrote must with him live for ever.

Yet, in spite of all this, some prejudices have attached themselves to the name of our illustrious countryman, which it will be necessary for me first to endeavour to overcome.   On the continent, we may remark, the works of Shakespeare are honoured in a double way—by the admiration of the Germans, and by the contempt of the French.

Among other points of objection taken by the French, perhaps, the most noticeable is, that he has not observed the sacred unities, so hallowed by the practice of their own extolled tragedians.   They hold, of course after Corneille and Racine, that Sophocles is the most perfect model for tragedy, and Aristotle its most infallible censor; and that as Hamlet, Lear, Macbeth, and other dramas by Shakespeare are not framed upon that model, and consequently not subject to the same laws, they maintain (not having impartiality enough to question the model, or to deny the rules of the Stagirite) that Shakespeare was a sort of irregular genius—that he is now and then tasteful and touching, but generally incorrect; and, in short, that he was a mere child of nature, who did not know any better than to write as he has written.

It is an old, and I have hitherto esteemed it a just, Latin maxim, *Oportet discentem credere, edoctum judicare*; but modern practice has inverted it, and it ought now rather to stand, *Oportet discentem judicare, edoctum credere.*   To remedy this mistake there is but one course, namely the acquirement of knowledge.   I have often run the risk of applying to the ignorant, who assumed the post and province of judges, a ludicrous, but not inapt simile: they remind me of a congregation of frogs, involved in darkness in a ditch, who keep an eternal croaking, until a lantern is brought near the scene of their disputation, when they instantly cease their discordant harangues.   They may be more politely resembled to night-flies, which flutter round the glimmering of a feeble taper, but are overpowered by the dazzling splendour of noon-day. Nor can it be otherwise, until the prevalent notion is exploded, that knowledge is easily taught, and until the conviction is general, that the hardest thing learned is that people are ignorant. All are apt enough to discover and expose the ignorance of their friends, but their blind faith in their own sufficiency is something more than marvellous.

Some persons have contended that mathematics ought to be taught by making the illustrations obvious to the senses. Nothing can be more absurd or injurious: it ought to be our never-ceasing effort to make people think, not feel; and it is very much owing to this mistake that, to those who do not think, and have not been made to think, Shakespeare has been found so difficult of comprehension. The condition of the stage, and the character of the times in which our great poet flourished, must first of all be taken into account, in considering the question as to his judgment. If it were possible to say which of his great powers and qualifications is more admirable than the rest, it unquestionably appears to me that his judgment is the most wonderful; and at this conviction I have arrived after a careful comparison of his productions with those of his best and greatest contemporaries.[1]

If indeed 'King Lear' were to be tried by the laws which Aristotle established, and Sophocles obeyed, it must be at once admitted to be outrageously irregular; and supposing the rules regarding the unities to be founded on man and nature, Shakespeare must be condemned for arraying his works in charms with which they ought never to have been decorated. I have no doubt, however, that both were right in their divergent courses, and that they arrived at the same conclusion by a different process.[2]

[1] This emphasis upon Shakespeare's judgment antedates Coleridge's acquaintance with Schlegel and is, therefore, noteworthy. (Cf. i. 194–5; ii. 109.) The tendency was well established in English criticism before the day of Coleridge; but Coleridge goes further in this direction than his English predecessors. He does not seem to know much of their work, which might have otherwise given him ideas which he seems to owe chiefly to Lessing. These points have been already discussed in the Introduction to the present edition (vol. i).

[2] The statement of the historical point of view in this and the preceding paragraph may very possibly be due to the influence of Herder's essay on Shakespeare (*Von deutscher Art und Kunst*). Heyne, under whom Coleridge studied at Göttingen, was a friend of Herder's, and may have introduced Coleridge to Herder's writings, some of which Coleridge certainly knew. There is no evidence that he read the essay on Shakespeare, but he may have done so; and certainly he would have become acquainted with the historical point of view in Heyne's own teaching.

Without entering into matters which must be generally known to persons of education, respecting the origin of tragedy and comedy among the Greeks, it may be observed, that the unities grew mainly out of the size and construction of the ancient theatres: the plays represented were made to include within a short space of time events which it is impossible should have occurred in that short space. This fact alone establishes, that all dramatic performances were then looked upon merely as ideal. It is the same with us: nobody supposes that a tragedian suffers real pain when he is stabbed or tortured; or that a comedian is in fact transported with delight when successful in pretended love.

If we want to witness mere pain, we can visit the hospitals: if we seek the exhibition of mere pleasure, we can find it in ball-rooms.[1] It is the representation of it, not the reality, that we require, the imitation, and not the thing itself; and we pronounce it good or bad in proportion as the representation is an incorrect, or a correct imitation. The true pleasure we derive from theatrical performances arises from the fact that they are unreal and fictitious. If dying agonies were unfeigned, who, in these days of civilisation, could derive gratification from beholding them?

Performances in a large theatre made it necessary that the human voice should be unnaturally and unmusically stretched, and hence the introduction of recitative, for the purpose of rendering pleasantly artificial the distortion of the face, and straining of the voice, occasioned by the magnitude of the building. The fact that the ancient choruses were always on the stage made it impossible that any change of place should be represented, or even supposed.

The origin of the English stage is less boastful than that of the Greek stage: like the constitution under which we live, though more barbarous in its derivation, it gives more genuine and more diffused liberty, than Athens in the zenith of her political glory ever possessed. Our earliest dramatic performances were religious, founded chiefly upon Scripture history; and, although countenanced by the clergy, they were filled with blasphemies and ribaldry, such as the most hardened and desperate of the

---

[1] As A. C. Dunstan points out, Schiller complains of German tragedy that 'instead of imitating real nature, [it] achieves only an insipid and ignoble expression of the *actual*, so that after such a banquet of tears, we feel as if we had paid a visit to a hospital.' *Werke* (Säkular-Ausgabe), xii. 237; Schiller's *Essays* (Bohn), p. 324. This parallel (from the essay 'On Naïve and Sentimental Poetry') probably indicates an influence rather than a coincidence.

present day would not dare to utter.   In these representations vice and the principle of evil were personified; and hence the introduction of fools and clowns in dramas of a more advanced period.[1]

While Shakespeare accommodated himself to the taste and spirit of the times in which he lived, his genius and his judgment taught him to use these characters with terrible effect, in aggravating the misery and agony of some of his most distressing scenes.   This result is especially obvious in 'King Lear': the contrast of the Fool wonderfully heightens the colouring of some of the most painful situations, where the old monarch in the depth and fury of his despair, complains to the warring elements of the ingratitude of his daughters.

> ' . . . . Spit, fire! spout, rain!
> Nor rain, wind, thunder, fire, are my daughters:
> I tax not you, you elements, with unkindness,
> I never gave you kingdom, call'd you children;
> You owe me no subscription: then, let fall
> Your horrible pleasure; here I stand, your slave,
> A poor, infirm, weak, and despis'd old man.'
>
> *King Lear*, Act iii, Scene 2.

Just afterwards, the Fool interposes, to heighten and inflame the passion of the scene.

In other dramas, though perhaps in a less degree, our great poet has evinced the same skill and felicity of treatment; and in no instance can it be justly alleged of him, as it may be of some of the ablest of his contemporaries, that he introduced his fool, or his clown, merely for the sake of exciting the laughter of his audiences.   Shakespeare had a loftier and a better purpose, and in this respect availed himself of resources, which, it would almost seem, he alone possessed.[2]

---

[1] Cf. i. 168–74 (from the lectures of 1808) for an extended treatment of the subject of this paragraph.   The lecture which Collier heard was probably delivered in part from these earlier notes.

[2] I most deeply regret, that I have not recovered any of my notes of the third, fourth, and fifth Lectures.—J. P. C.

THE THIRD LECTURE

24th Nov^r.   [*Tomalin Report.*]

UNDERSTANDING [1] that the definition or rather description he had given of poetry in [the] last lecture had left no definite idea in the minds of his auditors, and as the whole of the fabric he should raise in a manner rested *a* upon laying the foundation firmly and distinctly, he thought it necessary to add something to what he had before said.   It was easy to define gold so as to distinguish it from any of the earths, or to show the difference between a circle and a square; but in poetry it was as if he were verbally to give to an American a distinction between the English sycamore and the American maple,—the points of similarity were so numerous that it would require much explanation and attention to show the points of distinction.   The intelligibility of almost everything he had to say on the subject of poetry would depend [on] his being perspicuous in his definition, because, as he had before said, it often happened that differences between men of good sense arose solely from having attached different ideas to the same words.[2]   He had been supposed in the former lecture by some persons to have spoken disrespectfully of that great and admirable writer, Pope.   He had not perhaps determined whether or not he deserves the name of a poet, but in many cases he thought that if the words 'excellent and delightful writer' were substituted, persons disputing as to the merits of individual authors would agree in confessing [in] the instance of Pope that they never looked into his writings without pleasure or laid them down without instruction.[3]

Coleridge begged first to be permitted to say that in his view poetry was no proper antithesis to prose.   In truth, the correct opposite of poetry was science, and the correct antithesis of prose

---

a *MS. 'rested of upon.'*
[1] J. D. Campbell enriched his transcript with marginal cross-references of the most exact and copious kind.   Though these were not in a form suitable for publication and are too long for the purposes of this edition, most of them are essentially reproduced in the cross-references of the present editor, who here wishes to acknowledge his obligation to Campbell.
[2] Cf. *B.L.* ii. 10.
[3] Cf. i. 221–2; ii. 39–40, 212.

was metre.[1] The immediate object of science was the communication and acquirement of truth; the immediate object of poetry is the communication of pleasure.[2] Yet it would be acknowledged by all that when they read Newton's *Principia* or Locke's works the immediate object was not pleasure, but to obtain truth which might hereafter enlighten the pursuit of pleasure, or something [a] nobler, for which we have not a name, but distinct altogether from what in the ordinary language of common sense can be brought under the name of pleasure, but which was expressed in the sacred writings as a peace that passeth all understanding, the delight of which could never be known but by experience, which, consisting of no difference of parts, but being in itself entire, must be altogether unknown, or fully known.

So on the other hand, with regard to poetry, he doubted not but that the most important moral truths might be impressed by poetry; but such is not the immediate object of the poet. His immediate object was pleasure; [3] and it was that which constituted a poet, to what [ever ?] purpose he employed his means,— it was that which constituted him a bad or a good man. He therefore defined poetry to be, the *communication of immediate pleasure*.

This definition would be useful, inasmuch as it would distinguish it from science, but it would be inadequate, inasmuch as it would include novels, romances, and other works of fiction,[3] not called poems. Therefore, there must be some additional characters to poetry distinguishing it from those modes of composition which, though similar, are yet different.

How, he inquired, was this to be effected? In animated prose the beauties of nature, the passions and accidents of human life, including all that was comprized under the names of the heart and the head, are often expressed in the natural language which may be dictated by the incidents. Yet still neither the reader nor the writer called the work a poem, though no work could deserve the title of poem which did not include those circumstances—but *together with something else*.[4]

What is that something? One amiable female writer [5] of the

[a] *MS. 'of something.'*
[1] Cf. Wordsworth's Preface to *L.B.*, and i. 147, note 2. The latter part of this antithesis seems to be borrowed from the *Monthly Magazine* of 1796 (ii. 456).
[2] Cf. Wordsworth's Preface to *L.B.*, and i. 147.   [3] Cf. *B.L.* ii. 9.
[4] Cf. the two preceding paragraphs with i. 147.
[5] Mrs Barbauld. (Cf. H. C. Robinson's letter of 15 May 1808, ii. 15.

present day, speaking of Richardson, wondered why we should hesitate to call him a *great poet* and place him in the same class with Shakespeare and Milton.   The first answer would be that mankind has not so placed him and there must be some reason for it.   This we all felt, though it required great thought and patient investigation to discover causes—for nature had gifted us with a large portion of knowledge which might be called the rude stock which we were to work upon; and our intellectual life was passed not so much in acquiring new facts, as in acquiring a distinct consciousness,—in making a mere gift of nature, as it were, our own, so that it was no longer a something which we now had and now was lost, but continuing with our thoughts, a regular series of cause and effect, it becomes, in the truest sense, our own—the possession of the present, and the dowry of our future nature.

What then is this something?   With much diffidence, he would answer that

It is that pleasurable emotion, that peculiar state and degree of excitement that arises in the poet himself in the act of composition.

And in order to understand this we must combine under the notion of true poet more than ordinary sensibility, occasioning a more than ordinary sympathy with the objects of nature or the incidents of human life.   This, again, united with a more than ordinary activity of mind in general, but more particularly of those faculties of the mind we class under the names of fancy and imagination—faculties (I know not how I shall make myself intelligible) that are rather spontaneous than voluntary.   They excite great activity, but such as is greatly beyond all proportion to the effects occasioned by them.[1]

All persons, he observed, were aware of the difference between our moral feelings, faculties, etc., being called forth and gratified when a soft piece of music by Cimarosa or Handel, or a fine picture by Raphael or Michael Angelo, are contemplated.   In both instances the faculties are called forth, but, in one also a painful effort, unless the prospect of what we are to gain interfered and still urged us on.   That which excites us to all the activity of which our nature is capable and yet demands no painful effort, and occasions no sense of effort—this [2] is the state of mind (for he wished to impress particularly that it is the pleasure

---

[1] Cf. the two preceding paragraphs with i. 147–8.
[2] Cf. with i. 148 the remainder of this paragraph and the two following paragraphs (the definition of poetry).   Evidently these materials have the same manuscript source.   Cf. the definition also with *B.L.* ii. 10, and with ii. 68, below.

derived from the spontaneous activity, and our best faculties not accompanied by painful efforts) which admits the production of a highly favourable whole, but of which each part shall communicate a distinct and common pleasure.   Hence arose the definition that

Poetry is a species of composition opposed to science as having intellectual pleasure for its object and not truth—and attaining that end by the language natural to all persons in a stage of excitement.[1]

So far it was opposed to science, but distinguished from other species of *composition* not excluded by this criticism by [a] admitting pleasure from the whole, consistent with a consciousness of pleasurable excitement from the component parts, and the perfection of which is the acquirement from each part of the greatest immediate pleasure compatible with the largest sum of pleasure in the whole.

This would vary with the different modes of poetry [2] in all that which distinguishes poetry from all other classes of composition—is [3] in truth the poet himself.   We expect from him all the faculties we are possessed of: accurate observation and meditation, in what he has observed; sympathy in the sufferings and joys he either witnesses or imagines.   And besides, we look for an activity of those faculties which justify at each moment his writing in metre.

Physicians asserted that each passion has its proper pulse. So it was with metre when rightly used.   A state of excitement produced is, in truth, an analogy of the language of strong passion—not that strong passion always speaks in metre, but it has a language more measured than is employed in common speaking.

In reading a poem, we look not only for a just description of material objects, or human affections, but we expect to find them represented in such constant activity of mind, arising from the poet himself, as shall give a greater pleasure to that which is already pleasurable, and shall bring within the bounds of pleasure that which otherwise would be painful.[4]

---

[a] *MS. 'but.'*

[1] 'On the blank page opposite is written in a totally different hand: "Poetry is a species of composition having intellectual pleasure for its object, but opposed to science as not necessarily including truth, and attaining that end by the language natural to all persons in states of excitement."'. . .— J. D. Campbell.

[2] Cf. i. 148.

[3] Read 'as,' or perhaps 'that which is.'

[4] Cf. the two preceding paragraphs with *B.L.* ii. 50.

He would even venture to give the definition of poetry as being
That which, from the always present, though always conscious
idea that it is poetry in the mind of the reader, allows a greater
attention to each particular part of a composition the greater
power of giving pleasure and attracting attention from each part
than would be permitted in ordinary language or ordinary
writing, though writing a fiction.   And the great rule by which a
poet is to be judged is the balance between them: Is there more
pleasure in the particular lines than is consistent with the whole?
Is the sense of totality injured, or not injured, by the splendour
of particular passages?   For the great object of the poet must be
to produce the great total effect.[1]

So closely connected, he continued, was metre with passion
that many of the finest passages we read in prose are in themselves, in point of metre, poetry—only they are forms of metre
which we have not been familiarized to and [are] not brought
forward to us and other English readers in the shape of metre.
Coleridge had paid particular attention to the language of the
Bible and had found that all persons had been affected with a
sense of their high poetic character, not merely from the thoughts
conveyed in them, but from the language enclosing those
thoughts—from the stately march of the words, which had
affected them in a degree and kind altogether different from that
of common writing, and different from the narrative and pre-
ceptive parts of the same books.   It had been his business to
discover the cause, and he found that in almost every passage
brought before him, as having produced a particular effect, there
was metre and very often poetry—not, indeed, regular,—not
such as could be scanned on the fingers; but in some cases fragments of hexameter verses,—not like the line of Pope—

'Awake, my St. John, leave all meaner things'—[2]

where the line consisted nearly entirely of iambics, but regularly
of dactyls and spondees, forming sometimes a complete hexameter verse; e.g.,

'God went / up with a / shout, our /
Lord with the / sound of the / trumpet'[3]

---

[1] Cf. the end of this paragraph with i. 148 and *B.L.* ii. 10.
[2] *Essay on Man*, i. 1.
[3] Psa. xlvii. 5:
'God is gone up with a shout, the Lord with the sound of a trumpet.'

forming a line exactly similar with the first of Homer and Virgil.
In another it was equally evident—

'There is a river the flowing whereof,' [1] etc.

Thus taking the first chapter of Isaiah,[2] without more than
four or five transpositions and no alteration of words, he had
reduced it to complete hexameters—so true it is that wherever
passion was, the language became a sort of metre.

It would be necessary for him, in the first place, to enquire
whether poetry ought to be a *copy*, or only an *imitation* of what is
true nature? [3]   According to every effect he had been able to
trace, he was of opinion that the pleasure we receive arose, not
from its being a *copy*, but from its being an imitation; and the
word imitation itself means always a combination of a certain
degree of dissimilitude with a certain degree of similitude.   If
it were merely the same as looking at a glass reflection, we should
receive no pleasure.   A waxen image after once it had been seen
pleased no longer, or very little, but when the resemblance of a
thing was given upon canvas or a flat surface, then we were
delighted.

In poetry it is still more so; the difference there is of a higher
character.   We take the purest parts and combine them [a] with
our own minds, with our own hopes, with our own inward
yearnings after perfection, and, being frail and imperfect, we
wish to have a shadow, a sort of prophetic existence present to us,
which tells us what we are not, but yet, blending in us much that
we are, promises great things of what we may be.   It is the truth
(and poetry results from that instinct—the effort of perfecting
ourselves), the conceiving that which is imperfect to be perfect
and blending the nobler mind with the meaner object.

Thus, of [b] Shakespeare he had often heard it said that he was a
close copier of nature, that he was a child of nature, like a Dutch
painter copying exactly the object before him.   He was a child
of nature, but it was of human nature and of the most important
of human nature.   In the meanest characters, it was still Shakespeare; it was not the mere Nurse in *Romeo and Juliet*, or the
Dogberry in *Much Ado about Nothing*, or the blundering Constable in *Measure for Measure*, but it was this great and mighty

[a] MS. 'it.'   [b] MS. 'in.'
[1] Psa. xlvi. 4: 'There is a river the streams whereof'. . . .
[2] Cited in *B.L.* ii. 11.
[3] Cf. i. 177, etc.

being changing himself into [a] the Nurse or the blundering Constable, that gave delight.   We know that no Nurse talked exactly in that way, tho' particular sentences might be to that purpose. He might compare it to Proteus,[1] who now flowed, a river; now raged, a fire; now roared, a lion—he assumed all changes, but still in the stream, in the fire, in the beast, it was not only the resemblance, but it was the divinity that appeared in it, and assumed the character.

Coleridge included music and painting under the great genus of poetry, and we could not understand those unless we first impressed upon the mind that they are ideal, and not the mere copy of things, but the contemplation of mind upon things. When you look upon a portrait, you must not compare it with the face when present, but with the recollection of the face.   It refers not so much to the senses, as to the ideal sense of the friend not present.[2]

Hitherto the lecturer had judged of Shakespeare by the ancients.   In his last lecture, he [b] endeavoured to detect the error of this mode of judging.   When he [said] the Grecian theatre, he alluded to the great works of Euripides and Aeschylus and Sophocles, which had been held out as models, not of what is essential to the drama in all possible states, but as ideal of the construction of the drama.   He had tried to show that the construction of the Greek drama was owing to pure accident and that of those accidents they made the best possible use.   The origin of it was the song of the goat, and at first the principal part was the chorus.   Then dialogue was introduced; and then they sought to make the two consistent with each other.   The size of the theatre rendered it impossible to make the human voice intelligible without artificial means; and being resolved that it should be delightful[ly] artificial [c] they introduced music.   But as in a good picture, it is necessary that all things should be in keeping; and as the chorus was always present, it enforced the preservation of the unities, for it would have been too great an extravagation from nature to have had the same men and characters on the stage when the scene was totally different.   As the chorus was always on the stage, there was no dropping of curtains; the same men could not be at the same time at Thebes and at Rome.   It therefore became necessary that the same scene

---

[a] MS. 'into into.'   [b] MS. 'he he.'   [c] MS. 'delightful, artificial.'
[1] Cf. i. 193 and *B.L.* ii. 20.
[2] For a repetition of this penetrating remark see Coleridge's essay 'On Poesy or Art,' *B.L.* ii. 259.

should be presented to the eye, constituting the *unity of place*, and that the piece should be acted nearly within the time that the events could have occurred in. And, lastly, they had, what is common to all dramas, a *unity of interest* [1] *and action*.

The two first [2] he had shewn to be mere effect of accident in the Grecian drama, and he would venture to add, that they were most unfortunate effects, because in the very best of their plays, they [a] involved the authors in absurdities. It frequently happened that seventy or eighty plays were [b] written on the same subject and with the same characters, so few were the subjects which could be represented consistently with the preservation of the unities. In our earliest youth there were none who had not listened to the 'tale divine of Troy,' [3] and Pope's popular translation was in the hand, nay, in the mouth, of every person; while the translations of Sophocles, of Aeschylus, or Euripides, were found only in the libraries of those who did not want them, scarcely making any impression on the community at large.

He had thus attempted to show that the unities of time and place were not essential to the drama, and that to suppose them necessary was to suppose as evident a falsehood as that the drama impresses with pleasure only as it is supposed to be reality. The truth is, it is never believed to be real.[4] In a farce written to ridicule ancient plays the chorus is represented as lamenting for some crime which a man who had just escaped had committed, when one of the characters comes in and exclaims, 'Why don't you run for a constable; why do [you] remain there doing nothing?' The height of delusion, the utmost point to which it can arrive, is that we do not think about its being real or false, but are affected only by the vividness of the impression, independent of the thought of reality. This difference between a sense of reality and falsehood admitted of various degrees, from the domestic tragedy, which is too real to be compatible with pleasure, to Shakespeare, who seems to have taken the due medium, and to gratify our senses from the imitation of reality,

---

[a] *MS. 'it'*   [b] *MS. 'were were.'*

[1] (Cf. i. 4, 45.) This reference to the unity of interest is evidence that Coleridge knew the first two volumes of Schlegel's lectures, which were published in 1809, before he became acquainted with the third (the 'second part of the second volume') which discussed Shakespeare. (Cf. ii. 168, note 1, and 203, note 2.) This does not agree with his own account (ii. 126, 188–9), but we know that he applied to H. C. Robinson for Schlegel's works before the lectures of 1811–12 began (cf. ii. 176).

[2] The unities of time and place.

[3] Milton's *Il Penseroso*, 100. Read 'the tale of Troy divine.' (Cf. ii. 82.)

[4] For other discussions of dramatic 'illusion' cf. i. 114–18, 176–83; ii. 257–8.

and down to the mere dance at an opera, which is yet capable of giving us the highest pleasure, and which, with music and harmonious motions of the body, can, by thus explaining some tale, deeply affect and delight an audience.[1]

Coleridge did not blame the authors of the French drama that they had less reality, but that many of their thoughts were painfully false in logic, and never could have occurred to [the] mind of men placed in the same situation. He never dreamed that Lear could think what he said according to Shakespeare; but it was the language of nature, and such language that while we wept it mingle[d] wisdom with our tears. It might give pain, but not such pain as was inconsistent with pleasure.[2]

Shakespeare had advantages as well as disadvantages in forming the class of writing which he took, and it had been truly said that it was a magic circle in which he himself could only tread. This remark had been applied to his magic [3] characters only, and it had been added that in this alone Shakespeare succeeded; but it would be found equally true that in the whole scheme of his drama, he invented a work which was peculiar to himself, and not to be compared with the productions of any writer of any nation,—in which he had neither follower nor second.

How was he able to effect this?

He lived in an age in which from the religious controversies, carried on in a way of which we have no conception, there was a general energy of thinking, a pleasure in hard thinking and an expectation of it from those who came forward to solicit public praise, of which, in this day, we are equally [4] ignorant. Consequently the judges were real amateurs. The author had to deal with a learned public, and he had no idea of a mixed public; it was divided, in truth, between those who had no taste at all and who went merely to amuse themselves, and those who were deeply versed in the literature to which they gave encouragement.

Altho' the piety of the times narrowed the numbers of those who attended the theatre, it made those who did visit it especially conversant with what they ought to expect. The theatre itself had no artificial, extraneous inducements—few scenes, little music—and all that was to excite the senses in a high degree was

---

[1] Cf. Coleridge's lecture, 'On Poesy or Art,' *B.L.* ii. 256.
[2] Cf. this sentence with i. 181.
[3] '[*Sic*—"tragic"?].'—J. D. Campbell.
[4] Perhaps 'entirely' is the correct reading.

wanting. Shakespeare himself said, 'We appeal to your imaginations; by your imagination you can conceive this round O to
be a mighty field of monarchs [1] and if you do not, all must seem
absurd.' [2]

The circumstances of acting were altogether different from
ours; it was much more of recitation, or rather a medium
between recitation and what we now call recitation. The idea
of the poet was always present, not of the actors, not of the
thing to be represented. It was at that time more a delight
and employment for the intellect, than [an] amusement for the
senses.[3]

It was natural that Shakespeare should avail himself of all
that imagination afforded. If he had lived in the present day
and had seen one of his plays represented, he would the first
moment have felt the shifting of the scenes. Now, there is so
much to please the senses in the performance and so much to
offend them in the play, that he would have constructed them no
doubt on a different model. 'We are grateful,' said Coleridge,
'that he did not, since there can be no comparative pleasure
between having a great man in our closet and on the stage.[4] All
may be delighted that Shakespeare did not anticipate, and write
his plays with any conception of that strong excitement of
the senses, that inward endeavour to make everything appear
reality which is deemed excellent as to the effort of the present
day.

'Surely, we may be grateful that we may take Shakespeare
out of the rank of mere stage-writers to place him among the
Miltons, the Homers, the Dantes, the Ariostos, and the great
men of all nations and of all ages.'

He added that it was a very bad criterion indeed of what had
pleased a former age—what gave delight to the present. He
further confirmed this opinion by reading a quotation from
Webster containing the following sentence:

[1] Cf. ii. 215.
[2] Prologue to *Henry V*.
> '. . . can this cockpit hold
> The vasty fields of France? or may we cram
> Within this wooden O the very casques
> That did affright the air at Agincourt?'

[3] Cf. i. 176; ii. 68.
[4] Cf. ii. 68, 230; Gillman's *Life*, p. 280; Introduction to this book, vol. i,
p. xlvi; Lamb's essay 'On the Tragedies of Shakespeare'; Hazlitt's essay on
Hamlet, etc., in *The Characters of Shakespeare's Plays*. This antipathy to
the performance of Shakespeare's plays on the stage was characteristic of
romantic criticism.

'In other words, the learned would have had English trage-dians to be mere reflections of the Greek, or of the oratorical declamation in dialogue under the name of Seneca.'[1]

Hence (he continued), the excellence of the English drama was that it possessed that which delighted both classes, but in different ways. One man would carry away nothing but the jokes and what was externally ludicrous, while the other would be pleased that his fellow-citizens had received an innocent enjoyment, which had been to him a profitable employment. He saw that which gave him a deeper knowledge of his own heart and of the actions of his fellow-creatures, and he wonders that this great man could at the same time excite the admiration of the most profound metaphysician and draw tears or awake laughter from the most ignorant.

There was, in truth, an energy in the age, an energy of think-ing, which gave writers of the reigns of Elizabeth and James, the same energy. At the present, the chief object of an author was to be intelligible at the first view; then, it was to make the reader think—not to make him understand at once, but to show him rather that he did not understand, or to make him to review, and re-meditate till he had placed himself upon a par with the writer.

With regard to his education, it was little more than might be expected from his character. Conceive a profound meta-physician and a great poet, intensely occupied in thinking on all subjects, on the least as well as the greatest—on all the operations of nature and of man, and feeling the importance of all the sub-jects presented to him—conceive this philosophical part of his character combined with the poetic, the twofold energy con-stantly acting; the poet and the philosopher embracing, but, as it were, in a warm embrace, when if both had not been equal, one or the other must have been strangled.[2]

With this rule the reader might go through what was really Shakespeare's, and distinguish him from every man that ever lived.[3]

His education was the combination of the poet and the philo-sopher—a rapid mind, impatient that the means of communica-tion were so few and defective compared with what he possessed to be communicated.

From this cause, his images followed upon each other and if

---

[1] The editor has sought for this reference in vain.
[2] Cf. *B.L.* ii. 19.
[3] Cf. *Table-Talk*, 7 April 1833.

his genius had not guided him to the stage, Shakespeare would by them have been rendered a writer rather to be wondered at than admired.

Therefore it was, that in all the great characters, it was still Shakespeare,—now imitating this, now imitating that—now displaying the operations of a mind under the influence of strong intellect—sometimes without, and sometimes against the moral feeling.

Mr Coleridge concluded by apologizing for speaking what he conceived to be the truth, etc.[1]

[1] 'Copied by J. D. C., 23-10-88 (from Tomalin's report).'—J. D. Campbell.

THE FOURTH LECTURE ^a

[*Tomalin Report.*]

VARIOUS attempts, he said, had been made to arrange Shakespeare's plays in the order in which they had been written. How these endeavours had failed might be easily shown from the different results different commentators had come to,—rising ^b in some instances from a want of learning, and in more from the unsatisfactory nature of the facts and dates themselves. At that time the press was chiefly occupied with practical and systematic divinity, and the law and the church occupied all honour, while poetry and poets were despised; and it was deemed a sort of disgrace which needed pardon even to sport with the muse in private,—much more to adopt it as a profession—

'Levior quaedam infamia[e] inimica.' ¹

This fact might be proved from a letter of Dr. Donne ² where[in] he expressed his mortification that any of his poems should have been published and he thereby have incurred the disgrace of being a poet.

Another cause of the obscurity hanging over the works of Shakespeare was the poverty of the poet, who could not even bear the expense of printing, which was generally defrayed by the liberality of a patron.

The greater part of the works of our renowned poet Spenser and the poets more approved by the best judges of the day remained in MS. many years and in all [probability] perished. Half his *Fairy Queen*, his comedies, his Hymn, and a number of his Epistles were thus lost to the world.³

The religious zeal of the age rendered, besides, the frequenters of the theatre few, and those only amateurs known to and familiar with each other. This was another cause. And lastly, it would

^a MS. '*Coleridge's 4th Lecture.*'   ^b MS. '*writing.*'
¹ Read 'macula.' (Cf. i. 208.)
² Edmund Gosse, *The Life and Letters of John Donne* (London, 1899), i. 302–4; ii. 68. A general discussion of this subject may be found in ch. vii. of *The Literary Profession in the Elizabethan Age* (Manchester, 1909) by Phoebe Sheavyn.
³ F. I. Carpenter, *A Reference Guide to Edmund Spenser* (Chicago, 1923), i. 125–7, gives a convenient short list of these lost works of Spenser.

be remembered that the plays of Shakespeare even, during and after his life, were the property of the stage of which he became a manager and were published by the players as their own property, with a view only to their popularity.

In the absence, therefore, of external evidence, he would proceed to the internal evidence, guiding himself as he proceeded by the few certain data that were known of an external kind which tended to corroborate the internal testimony.

It was known from the author's own dedication that the *Venus and Adonis* was the first of his works, and that the *Lucrece* was published the year afterwards; yet they were not printed till he was twenty-nine years old, altho' there can be no doubt that they had been by him many years. According to Malone, Shakespeare became a writer for the stage at twenty-seven years old,[1] in 1591. There was a strong circumstance to prove that it must have been in MS. some years, because it was difficult to imagine that a mind like Shakespeare's could have permitted him to remain until he was near thirty before he wrote any poems; and it seemed probable that between *Venus and Adonis* and *Lucrece*, there must have intervened some other drama or poem before the tragedy of *Romeo and Juliet*.[2]

Coleridge paid little attention to the anecdotes, or rather, hearsay stories, regarding Shakespeare's having held horses, snuffed candles at the theatre, etc.; the facts of his history confuted them. Those offices were wholly unworthy of his birth and inconsistent with the circumstances of his having so soon purchased himself a share in the theatre, and retired at so early an age with an independent fortune. He rather thought that Shakespeare early felt an impulse for a species of poetry different from that he first attempted, and the very imperfections of which seemed to imply a dormancy and yet at the same time a powerful prompting of his powers to the drama.

We shall be better able to judge of the facts after contemplating the characteristics of Shakespeare's first poem, the *Venus and Adonis*.[3]

The subject was one which few with Shakespeare's mind

---

[1] Malone's 'Essay on the Chronology of Shakespeare's Plays.' See Boswell-Malone edition of Shakespeare (1821), ii. 298.

[2] From the beginning of the lecture to this point Coleridge is evidently lecturing from the manuscript ultimately published as 'The Order of Shakespeare's Plays.' (Cf. i. 208–9.)

[3] This lecture on Shakespeare's poetry is evidently the basis of ch. xv. in *B.L.*, and it should also be compared with the fragments of lectures printed on i. 187–93, and with the conclusion of the sixth lecture at Bristol (ii. 238).

would have chosen, and which none but a mind like Shake-speare's could have treated as he did. It appealed not to the senses—it placed it[self] out[side] of the ordinary feelings, and on reading it, the loves of Venus and Adonis, as far as our passions were concerned, as little affected us as the amours of the fairy queen with Nick Bottom.

The object of Coleridge in making these remarks was not so much to illustrate the character of Shakespeare as to illustrate the principles of poetry. We should then see what principles in this work had led us to more intimate knowledge of our great poet, and to form a foundation of a rational system concerning poetry in general.

The first thing which struck Coleridge on reading the *Venus and Adonis* was the perfect sweetness of the versification, so well adapted to the subject, without possessing more majestic rhythm than the subject required; and the propriety of preserving the melody. There was a delightful sweetness of sound, even to faulty excess, at the same time that it was completely distinguish-able from that mechanic metre, where, in truth, there was no richness or sweetness, but, being scanned by the fingers, could by such scansion be learnt. If we put this sort of poetry out of our minds in reading the *Venus and Adonis*, we should find it possessed that delight, that richness and sweetness which could not but be regarded as a highly favourable promise of future excellence.

He was not certain that 'the man who hath not music in his soul' would be liable to all that Shakespeare had charged him with, but he was well assured that such a being could never be a poet. Images might be copied from works of voyages and travels, or of natural history, and even from nature herself. In like manner, affecting incidents might be obtained from observa-tion, or from reading, and curiosity might be kept up in the detail. Domestic feelings themselves of the best and tenderest kind might be borrowed not only from books, but even from the heart, and all might be so happily combined by wit as to make a pleasing work—and yet the man not be a *poet*.[1] He might have talent, and a good education, and yet have mistaken (perhaps, for his own interest, wisely) an intense desire for poetic reputation for a natural genius and poetic powers. He might mistake, as we all too often did, the strong thirst for the end, for a natural capability of the means.

[1] Cf. i. 193.

That gift of true Imagination, that capability of reducing a multitude into unity of effect, or by strong passion to modify series of thoughts into one predominant thought or feeling [1] —those were faculties which might be cultivated and improved, but could not be acquired.   Only such a man as possessed them deserved the title of *poeta* who *nascitur non fit*—he was that child of Nature, and not the creature of his own efforts. [2]

The second sure promise of genius was the choice of the subject remote from the private interests, circumstances, and feelings of the poet himself. [3]   Coleridge himself had been more than once deluded and led into a false expectation of genius from the perusal of very affecting poems in which the poet had described those incidents and passions which misfortune, disease, or any other cause had made the poet himself possess. Grant to such a man knowledge of language, and what would follow?   A lively description,—yet he is not a *poet*.   He will not be the man, who, tho' happy in his domestic and conjugal relations, can yet paint a noble and generous mind under the pangs of jealously loving to desperation a being whom he be-lieves unworthy of that love.   He never can be the man who from a handkerchief can weave a dreadful tissue of human calamity.   He never can be the being who could paint a Lear or Othello.

If it were not that it fell too much below the subject, he could relate a tale told by one of the ancients more illustrative of the truth of his position, than consistent with the feelings of his auditory. [4]   There was said to be a statuary in ancient Greece whose figures were awkward and unideal in every respect but one—he had gained much praise from the beautiful feet and ankles of Venus.   His name was introduced in a company of which his wife formed a part, and with as much delicacy as possible the merits of the husband were discussed.   One person dwelt with much warmth of praise on the symmetry and grace of the feet and ankles of the Venus he had just completed.   The wife was so transported at the compliment that she interrupted the eulogist by observing that her husband always took her for his model, and she was always reckoned to have a most beautiful foot and ankle.   As little could a poet by profession become a poet by nature, because he had happily succeeded in painting

---

[1] Cf. i. 188.

[2] Cf. the three preceding paragraphs with their redaction in *B.L.* ii. 14.

[3] Cf. i. 188, 190, 193.

[4] In *B.L.* ii. 15 this anecdote is again related.   There 'ankles' become 'legs.'

those circumstances and scenes which were not created by him, but by which he was possessed and employed no creative faculty.

This excellence was perhaps carried too far in the *Venus and Adonis*, but not too far if we regarded it as a fragment in the history of the mind of Shakespeare. It appeared to him as if Shakespeare in this instance had been a mere passive being, not actuated by the passions and feelings he displayed under the agency of some superior spirit,—had represented every look and action and feeling, without himself participating. He thought or should have conjectured from this poem and *Lucrece* that, even then, the impulse to the drama was secretly working in him. The scenes of unbroken images, unbroken, and therefore minute and as picturesque as language was capable of, and of a far higher order than any other poet had produced, seemed to fit him admirably for the line of composition he afterwards pursued. His *Venus and Adonis* seemed at once the characters themselves, but more, the representations of those characters by the most consummate actors. Throughout you seemed to be told nothing, and to hear and see everything.

The poem was certainly unfit for public recitation, but never was any work written that was less dangerous in a moral point of view. Instead of doing as Ariosto, or, in a still more offensive way, Wieland had done—degrading the struggles of passion into a low animal feeling, Shakespeare had dissipated the reader's attention by a thousand outward images, which formed the drapery and scenery of his tale, or diverted us by sallies of wit and bursts of profound reflection, which the active mind of the poet had diffused thro' and blended with the images and incidents. The reader's thoughts were forced into too much action to sympathise with what was merely passion in our nature. As little could the noisome mist hang over our northern Windermere, when a strong and invigorating gale was driving the lake in foam and billows before it.[1]

He had said that images taken from nature and accurately described did not characterize *the poet*. They must be blended or merged with other images, the offspring of imagination, and blended, besides, with the passions or other pleasurable emotions which contemplation has awakened in the poet himself. Many had witnessed the rising of the sun without any poetic sensations, but who would not feel the beauty of this passage—

---

[1] The four preceding paragraphs are the basis of *B.L.* ii. 14–16. The next paragraph begins the third point made in *B.L.* ii. 16–18. The differences of the two versions are considerable.

> 'Full many a glorious morning have I seen
> Flatter the mountain-tops with sovereign eye.' [1]

Here is a union of thoughts, [so] that, bringing all into one, you see not only the sun rising over the mountains, but you have also the moral feeling with which the rapidity of the poet's mind had connected it. You behold the sun the sovereign of the world, the elation [a] of the high mountain flattered by a glance of his beams, and the activity of the poet's mind, which, in one image, has merged so many associations. You feel him to be a poet, inasmuch as, for a time, he has made you one—an active creative being.

Coleridge here introduced another instance of the same kind,[2] beginning—

> 'Since I left you, my [b] eye is in my mind'

and terminating

> 'My most true mind thus makes my eye [c] untrue.'

That blending of thoughts into each other, or, rather, into one passion, at the time it contemplates, was one of the greatest criterions of a true poet, because it was impossible excepting to a true poet,—which implied three constituent parts, namely, sensibility, imagination, and the powers of association.

Lastly, the metaphor must be combined with the poetic feeling itself, so that the pleasure of the reader, as well as the vividness of the description, is in part derived from the force and fervour of the describer. The latter excellence was, he admitted, though the least of a great poet, still an excellent [d] characteristic and indispensable excellence.

In the instances he should now give from Shakespeare, the auditors would recollect that they must consider him as a young poet presented to their promise just rising into notice at the age of twenty-three or twenty-four years.

Coleridge here read the description of the horse of Adonis from the line—

> 'Imperiously he leaps, he neighs, he bounds' [3]

to the line—

> 'Fanning the hairs who wave like feather'd wings.' [4]

[a] MS. 'relation.'   [b] Read 'mine.'
[c] Read 'maketh mine.'   Capell MS. and Malone conj. 'makes mine eye.
[d] MS. 'excellence.'
[1] Sonnet XXXIII.   [2] Sonnet CXIII.   [3] V. and A., 265.
[4] Ibid., 306.   Tomalin reads 'which heave.'

The lecturer also read the description of the hare. In these quotations the auditors would perceive that there was accuracy of description blended with the fervour of the poet's mind, thereby communicating pleasure to the reader. In the description where Adonis flies from Venus prior to the hunt in which he lost his life, there seemed to be all that could be expected from imagination. It was a complete picture [in]formed with all the passions of the person viewing it.

It was here read—

'With this he breaketh,' etc.

to

'So glides he in the night,' [1] etc.

The suddenness, beauty, and fancifulness of the image, all joined with the characters, exemplified what he was advancing better than any other passage Coleridge remembered.[2]

He then proceeded to the poem of *Lucrece*. The *Venus and Adonis* did not allow the lofty and moral mind to display its deeper and nobler qualities. He therefore took this well-known story *Lucrece*, altho' the lecturer confessed *there was nothing in the poem* highly pathetic or dramatic. The same minuteness of imagery, with a more profound display of reflection, with dominion—sometimes even a domination—over the whole world of language, were to be found in it. What then, he enquired, shall we say of Shakespeare? That he was not a mere child of nature, and that he was possessed of a feeling that he had no power to control? No! but that, like a great man, he first studied deeply, read and thoroughly understood every part of human nature, which he joined with his poetical feeling, till at length it gave him that wonderful power in which he had no equal—not even a second in his own class.

It was this which entitled him to occupy one of the two golden thrones of the English Parnassus—Milton on the one and Shakespeare on the first. He, darting himself forth, and passing himself into all the forms of human character and human passion; the other attracted all forms and all things to himself into the unity of his own grand ideal.

Shakespeare became all things well into which he infused himself, while all forms, all things became Milton—the poet ever

[1] *V. and A.*, 811–16. For this quotation see also i. 189.
[2] With the next paragraph begins an equivalent to the fourth point in *B.L.* ii. 18–20.

present to our minds and more than gratifying us for the loss of the distinct individuality of what he represents.

In speaking of the dramas of Shakespeare, Coleridge said he should be inclined to pursue a psychological, rather than a historical mode of reasoning. He should take them as they seemed naturally to flow from the progress and order of his mind. As the first of his poems, or rather, amongst the first, he should place the *Love's Labour['s] Lost* together with the *All's Well That Ends Well, Romeo and Juliet, Midsummer Night's Dream, As You Like It, The Tempest, Winter's Tale, Twelfth Night*—all, in short, in which the poet still blends with the dramatist, but in which the dramatist still seems to press forward and never loses his own being in the character he represents to us.

In the next class he should present him as on his journey to the last and most complete forms of his genius, when he was growing towards it with some of the awkwardness of growth. He would then take *Troilus and Cressida, Cymbeline, Merchant of Venice, Much Ado about Nothing*.

Finally, he should comment upon the plays which might be considered as the greatest works of our immortal poet; viz., *Macbeth, King Lear, Hamlet*.[1] He should afterwards, and in conclusion, [treat] Shakespeare's historical dramas as a distinct class, in order to state his reasons, not only for rejecting whole plays hitherto considered as Shakespeare's, but also many scenes in his other works; likewise to point out this as one species of composition in which Shakespeare alone succeeded, and which, he would fain prove, was his, and his only—neither imitated with success by his followers, nor anticipated by his predecessors.[2]

The lecturer, having proceeded thus far, reverted to what he had alluded to in the second lecture; viz., the accidents of the Greek stage which gave rise to the ancient unities—the accidents

---

[1] '*Measure for Measure* he omitted to mention' [Tomalin's note]. '*Othello* is not named [to] follow Hamlet in MS.—J. D. C.'

[2] The three preceding paragraphs should be compared with the 'Classification attempted, 1810,' i. 211—a fragment which shows close verbal correspondences with Tomalin's record. J. P. Collier's mother preserved a memorandum of Coleridge's chronological classification of the plays in this lecture. Its differences from Tomalin's report are probably due to the superior correctness of Tomalin's shorthand. I summarize Mrs Collier's list, abbreviating the names of the plays: Youthful plays—L.L.L., R. and J., All's Well; Manly Plays—M.N.D., A.Y.L.I., T. Night, Measure, Much Ado; Mature Plays—Merchant of V., T. and C., Cymb., Mac., Lear, Ham., Oth., Tempest, W. T. Historical plays to be taken separately.—This list is from J. P. Collier's Preface to *Coleridge's Seven Lectures on Shakespeare and Milton*, p. xix.

of the English stage which gave rise to Shakespeare's dramas.[1]
These latter accidents left Shakespeare to rely on his own
imagination, and to speak not to the senses, as was now done,
but to the mind.   He found the stage as near as possible a closet,
and in the closet only could it be fully and completely enjoyed.[2]
He asserted that those who went to the theatre in our own day,
when any of our poets' works were represented, went to see Mr.
Kemble in *Macbeth*, or Mrs. Siddons' Isabel, to hear speeches
usurped by fellows who owed their very elevation to dexterity in
snuffing candles, since all the inferior characters, thro' which our
poet shone no less conspicuously and brightly, were given them
to deliver.

Coleridge then, in the warmest language, censured those who
had attempted to alter the works of Shakespeare in order to
accommodate him to modern ears.   It would scarcely be
believed that a man like [   ] had transformed the purity
of Milton's Adam and Eve into such a shape as imagination,
even memory, turned aside from loathing.[3]

Coleridge then proceeded to correct the definition he had
given of poetry, and substituted the following: [4]

It is that species of composition which, being together with
some others opposed to science, as having for its immediate
object the communication of pleasure, not of truth, is yet distinguished from all others by proposing to itself such a delight from
the whole as is compatible with the distinct gratification from
each component part, and thence enables us to place the perfection of a poem in the power of communicating the greatest degree
of pleasurable excitement from each part as is consistent with the
largest possible portion of pleasurable excitement from the whole.

After adverting to the delight received from a passage in Burns
alluding to the transitoriness of pleasure—

> 'Like snow that falls upon a river,
>   A moment white, then gone for ever,' [5]

Coleridge went on to describe what a poet was.

---

[1] Cf. ii. 54.   [2] Cf. ii. 57, 230, etc.
[3] Perhaps Coleridge referred to Dryden's 'opera,' *The State of Innocence
and Fall of Man* (1677), an imitation or adaptation of *Paradise Lost* in heroic
couplets.   But Tomalin would probably not have missed so well known a
name as that of Dryden.   For certain other adaptations, see R. D. Havens,
The Influence of Milton on English Poetry (1922), pp. 34–5.
[4] Cf. i. 148; ii. 41, 50–1; and *B.L.* ii. 10.
[5] 'Tam o' Shanter,' 61–2.
>   'Or like the snow falls in the river,
>   A moment white—then melts forever.'

He was a person who balances sameness with difference, and triteness with novelty; who reconciles judgement with enthusiasm, and vehemence with feeling, art with nature, the manner with the matter, and our admiration of the poet with the sympathy with the characters and incidents of the poem.[1]

The importance of this observation would be seen in comparing the works of our dramatist with French plays, and with those of the Greeks, from which the French were little better than translations. The lecturer concluded by quoting the following passage from Sir John Davies [2] where he speaks of the mind, which was equally applicable to the mind in its highest state of perfection in a great poet.

> Doubtless this could not be but that she turns
> Bodies to spirits by sublimation strange;
> As fire commutes to fire the thing[s] it burns
> As we [our food] into our nature change.
> From their gross matter she abstracts their forms
> And draws a kind of quintessence from things;
> Which to her proper nature she transforms
> To [bear them light] on her celestial wings
> This doth she when from individual [states]
> She doth abstract the universal kind[s];
> Which then [re-clothed] in divers names [and fates]
> [Steal access through our senses to our minds.[3]]

[1] This paragraph is developed and expanded on i. 150, and in *B.L.* ii. 12. Both versions quote the passage from Davies which here follows after an intervening sentence.

[2] Sir John Davies, *Nosce Teipsum*, Section 4, altered to suit the purpose. Cf. i. 150 and *B.L.* ii. 12–13.

[3] The bracketed interpolations are from *B.L.* ii. 12–13, to fill gaps in Tomalin's text.

THE FIFTH LECTURE

[Tomalin Report.]

AMONG the strange differences between our ancestors and their descendants of latter days was the wide difference between the feelings and language of commentators on great classical works. At the restoration of letters, when men discovered the MSS. of the great ancients, as some long hidden treasure, the editor of even the most trivial work was exuberant in phrases of panegyric, and superlatives of praise seemed to be almost their only terms. In the editing of modern writers, on the contrary, we found the commentator everywhere assuming a sort of critical superiority over the author he edited. Which of the two was to be blamed? Coleridge confessed that the former (even admitting him more deficient in judgement, which he was by no means prepared to allow) was more congenial with the moral feelings, and better suited to all purposes of instruction, for tho' too much love for an author was like a mist which magnified unduly, it brought forward objects that would otherwise have passed unnoticed.[1]

Never would he cease to deprecate that haughty insolence of the modern critic whose name would pass unknown were it not for the great and awful being on whom he exercises his art—like a monkey who had seated himself on the top of a rock, it was the rock which enabled him to reach the eminence where he was making his grimaces. In the course of the lectures it would be necessary to point out many instances of this kind.

It might be proper here to examine what had been the causes of this remarkable change—and to understand the matter it would be necessary to look back into history. There perhaps never was a time in civilized and christianized Europe which would be called an age of universal and complete darkness. When we spoke of the dark ages, we ought often rather to say ages in which we were in the dark,[2] for there was always a chain

---

[1] Cf. this paragraph and that following with the similar ideas in i. 219; ii. 34; and *B.L.* i. 41–2.
[2] Cf. ii. 213.

along which the bright electric spark was conveyed,[1] from the periods of its pristine brightness even to our own day.

During the reign of Henry VI. and within a short time afterwards, when the art of printing was discovered, the ancient MSS. were chiefly found.

In Russia we had seen monarch after monarch encouraging men of learning and placing them at the head of literary societies, and endeavouring to bring man in from his state of first being, neither angel nor animal, but which, according to circumstances, was capable of rising to [a] the one or sinking to the other. What had been the consequences? Travellers told us that men of talents and fine understandings in Russia were like the plants of tropical climates [taken] thither. They could only flourish under glasses, with the utmost care and attention. They were wells, from which water could be drawn by those who could discover the well, but the people at large, from the nobleman down to the peasant, were without interest or enthusiasm. If any desire of improvement were shown, it was that of the ape—a mere imitation of those around them. They copied the wit, the genius, and the philosophy of the French, who, in truth, were ignorant of philosophy, incapable of poetry, and had never soared as high as religion.[2] It was an undoubted fact that since the days of Descartes and Malebranche they had not had a philosopher among them.

Contrast the progress of the sciences in Russia with its advance in other parts of Europe at the first restoration of letters, when learning sounded throughout Christendom like a trumpet, when all classes, headed even by kings, hurried forward as if it were the moment of their redemption; when fifty thousand from different parts of Europe were collected to attend a single teacher; when an Erasmus, or a Melanchton, the children of boors, hastened to drink at the fountain of knowledge; when they could starve for the sake of learning and read their folios by moonlight, because they could not afford tapers; when they pursued the carriages of the great exclaiming 'Date obolum pauperio discipulo.' [3]

The result of this eagerness was afterwards an abasement

---

[a] MS. 'rising to rising to.

[1] Cf. i. 170.

[2] This was the period of the Napoleonic wars. Coleridge's temperament was, moreover, incompatible with French thought, which he needed, and only too much open to the German influence which encouraged his weaknesses.

[3] Cf. ii. 213; The Prelude, iii. 449–81; and Schlegel, Werke, v. 7–8.

of mind under authority.   Authority was substituted for reason
and the *ipse dixit* of a philosopher for a due appreciation of those
grounds which justified the philosopher in the formation of his
judgement.

Thence arose another race of men; and, how, he enquired,
could it be otherwise?   For if ignorance is to begin to judge of
the highest points to which knowledge had been carried, that
knowledge must appear absurd of necessity, because the ignorant
could not understand all the prior knowledge, all the previous
process in which the most perfect exemplification of the human
mind was built.

They then began, as a new discovery, with the last point of
the human mind: viz., the simple observation of facts—facts,
taken as the senses recorded them without even a psychological
connection; and finding that the more learned talked without
applying them in the spirit, they understood and used those
words as incapable of conveying anything else, and, therefore,
where they could not find a distinct image which could be
touched as well as seen, they rejected it.

With such persons a shoemaker might have been the admiration of mankind while the name of Shakespeare was consigned
to oblivion, not knowing that our passions, the mere passivity
of our nature, must diminish in proportion as our intellectual
faculties became alive.

Hence naturally arose a general contempt for the ancients;
but when a great man arose among them, it was a new source of
delusion, and this was of the utmost importance to be explained,
in order to the true understanding of the merits of Shakespeare.

All things that had been highly admired by mankind at any
time, or which have gone into excess, must have been originally
applicable to some part or other of our nature.   They had
become ridiculous only in the excess; but great geniuses having
used them with the truth of nature and the force of passion, have
extorted from all mankind praise, or, rather, won it by their
instant sympathy.   Men, afterwards, most desirous of the end,
and mistaking the desire of the end for a capacity of the means,
have mechanically, and devoid of that spirit of life, employed the
terms.   They enquired what pleased or struck us?   It was this
or that—and they imitated it without knowing what it was that
made them excellent, or that, excellent as they were, they would
be ridiculous in another form.   Such was the nature of metaphors, apostrophes, and what were called conceits.

He would venture to say, though it might excite a smile—

punning. There were states in all our passions when even punning is no longer ridiculous, but is strictly, in a philosophical sense, a natural expression of natural emotion.

It was known that all deviations from ordinary language— by which the lecturer meant such language as is used, by a man speaking without emotion, to express anything simply—not that he was quite correct in using the last phrase, because all language arose out of passion—the only difference was in the figure that was employed, old or new; thus we said, the tops of trees, or the heads of mountains, which expressions, with innumerable others in common use, were figurative, and originally used in a state of emotion, but they were now worn out. Passion was the true parent of every word in existence in every language.

But in the present state of language, in expressing an abstract idea, such as virtue, or a particular thing, such as a table, all deviations from ordinary language must be justified by some passion which renders it natural. How ridiculous would it seem in a stage of comparative insensibility to employ a figure used only by a person under *a* the highest emotion, such as the impersonation of an abstract being, and an apostrophe to it as [if] it were not only in existence, but actually present. What if this were to be used as a vulgar artifice of poetic connection, just as he had heard in a Methodist meeting the minister in his prayer, at a loss for an idea, and when there seemed to be no natural connection, he would unite his thoughts by a new string of epithets applied to the Supreme Being, thus degrading the highest exertion of the human faculties to a mere art to give a pretence of connection where none exists.

In the poems produced in modern days he had observed the same thing. He had seen works which had acquired great fame, or at least what was called fame, such as *The Pleasures of Tea-drinking*; *The Pleasures of Wine-drinking*; *The Pleasures of Hope*; *The Pleasures of Fear*,[1] and so on—which were mere abstract ideas, and which poems were made up by heaping together a certain number of images and a certain number of thoughts, and

---

a MS. '*only by a person only under.*'

[1] Mark Akenside, *The Pleasures of Imagination* (1744); Thomas Warton, *The Pleasures of Melancholy* (1747); Samuel Rogers, *The Pleasures of Memory* (1792); Thomas Campbell, *The Pleasures of Hope* (1799). This is rather harsh ridicule of predecessors and contemporaries so distinguished, but Coleridge's criticism will scarcely be questioned to-day.

Cf. Byron's comment in his letter to Hobhouse, 15 December. 'Coleridge has attacked "The Pleasures of Hope," and all other pleasures whatsoever.' *Correspondence* (1922), i. 66.

then merely tying [them] together with a string as if it had [been] bought at a penny the yard. What was the consequence? When the artist had come to the end of one thought, another must arise with [a] which there was not the least connection of mind, or even of logic (which was the least connection of a poet), or of passions, frequently acting by contrast, but always justifying themselves—no, there was no such connection, but a full pause ensues and the reader must begin again.

'Oh Hope! likewise,' etc.

The conceits which had been so rudely treated arose, one and all, from this circumstance, that language is not, was not, and never will be, the mere vehicle of representing external objects or simple information.

Horne Tooke had called his book *Epea Pteroenta*,[1] 'winged words.' In Coleridge's judgment it might have been much more fitly called *Verba Viventia*, or 'living words,' for words are the living products of the living mind and could not be a due medium between the thing and the mind unless they partook of both. The word was not to convey merely what a certain thing is, but the very passion and all the circumstances which were conceived as constituting the perception of the thing by the person who used the word.

Hence the gradual progression of language—for could it be supposed that words should be no object of the human mind? If so, why was style cultivated in order to make the movement of words correspond with the thoughts and emotions they were to convey, so that the words themselves are a part of the emotion? And in Coleridge's opinion it would be no ill compliment to call [an] author 'a man of words,' if the term were used in all the force and sublimity it [b] naturally contained.

The general desire of knowledge, and its diffusion, which in the first instance must produce shallowness, had rendered necessary a set of men called *reviewers*. With them Plato and Bacon talked nonsense, and *Locke* was the only man who understood anything. The others were fellows who talked of *ideas* as distinguished from *images*—true knowledge only began with Mr. John Locke. These reviewers might be compared with the Roman *praegustatores* whose business it was to tell you what was fit to be eaten, and like the *praegustatores* the reviewers gave their

---

[a] MS. 'between.'   [b] MS. 'they.'

[1] *ΕΠΕΑ ΠΤΕΡΟΕΝΤΑ* or *The Diversions of Purley*, 1786, 1798. Coleridge used these remarks (expanded) for his preface to *Aids to Reflection*. *Works* (Shedd), i. 114.

opinions, but carefully concealed all the reasons for such judge-
ments. They were incapable, in the first place, of writing themselves and, therefore, had more time to criticize others. Besides,
according to them, all the noblest faculties of the human mind
were incompatible with each other. Had a man imagination,
fancy, or a power of exciting emotion, he must necessarily be
devoid of judgement; but if they saw a man stripped of all those
faculties—as in point of charity, they were bound to clothe the
naked—they decree him to be *judicious*. If they reviewed one
man who had neither heart, fancy, nor sympathy, derived from
the relations of life, or from the instincts and yearnings of our
nature, he was declared to be *profound*, for he was quite below all
others; he was said to be beyond all sight, simply because there
was nothing to be seen.

He owned that he bore *reviewers* no good will, altho' for one
scratch they had given him, they had bestowed twenty plasters
of basilicon [1] flattery; but he deemed the business degrading from
the beginning; and he was convinced that to be connected with a
review was below a gentleman and a man of honour.

The reviewers had produced more superficiality, more bad
feelings, and had put a more complete stop to the progress of
knowledge than any other causes.

Let it be granted they had written books; they were generally
bad ones, and they were therefore more acquainted with the
means of manufacturing such things. It was a hint he had taken
from a German writer,[2] that anciently when a [certain St.
Nepomuc] was thrown over a bridge, he was constituted immediately guardian of all bridges. This was very applicable to
reviewers. They attempted to pass the bridge of Literary
Reputation; they were thrown into the stream of Oblivion, which
in its buffeting against piers produced a coarse imitation of
laughter; then they were dragged [out] by some reanimating
power, restored to their senses (not to their wits), and were
appointed a sort of literary toll-gatherers from all who afterwards attempted to pass.

In the opinion of such persons, *Shakespeare* was an ignorant
man, a child of nature, a wild genius, a strange medley [3]—at
least as the most admired critics, such as Dr. Johnson, thought.

---

[1] 'Name given to several ointments, supposed to possess "sovereign"
[βασιλικός] virtues.'—*O.E.D.*
[2] Jean Paul Richter, the fifth chapter of *Blumen- Frucht- und Dornen-
stücke*. For a later use of this story from Richter, see *B.L.* i. 42. The
application of the story to critics is Richter's.
[3] Cf. i. 194–5.

He was indeed such a mixture of contraries, that Coleridge could only compare him to a chess-board, with here a white square, there a black square. Here Shakespeare was below contempt; there he rose above all praise. Here he displayed an utter ignorance of human nature; there a most profound acquaintance with it—so proceeding with one sentence giving the lie to the anterior that he trusted in the next lecture he should be able to produce a table of their opinions which if read across would contradict itself in every line. They, in short, had made him here white and there black, and the only wonder was that after so much trampling they had not made him black and blue.

The reason why he considered *Love's Labour['s] Lost* as the first of Shakespeare's plays was that it afforded the strongest possible presumption that Shakespeare was not an ignorant man, and that the former part of his life had been passed in scholastic pursuits, because when a man began to write, his first work will bear a colour or tincture of his past life, provided he be a man of genius. The earliest plays of Lessing, the German dramatist, were drawn from the university—from prizes bestowed, or [such] other similar incidents and feelings as were natural to young students. Ben Jonson, who had served as a soldier in Flanders, in his excellent works depicted the manners of soldiers, and one of his most popular characters, his Captain Bobadil, was the mockery of an officer.[1]

What was the *Love's Labour['s] Lost*? Was it the production of a person accustomed to stroll as a vagabond about the streets, or to hold horses at a playhouse door, and who had contented himself with making observations on human nature? No such thing! There is scarcely a trace of any observation of nature in Shakespeare's earliest works. The dialogue consisted either of remarks upon what is grotesque in language,[2] or mistaken in literature; all bore the appearance of being written by a man of reading and learning, and the force of genius early saw what was excellent, or what was ridiculous. Hence the wonderful activity of this kind in the first scene of *Love's Labour['s] Lost*. Such thoughts would never have occurred to a man ignorant and merely an observer of nature.

The King says to Biron—

> 'These be the stops that hinder study quite,
> And train our intellects to vain delight.'

[1] (Cf. i. 87.) This paragraph corresponds closely with the manuscript printed by H. N. C.
[2] Cf. this remark with i. 83.

Biron replies—

> 'Why! all delights are vain—and [a] that most vain,
> Which, with pain purchased, doth inherit pain:
> As painfully to pore upon a book
> To seek the light of Truth, while Truth the while
> Doth falsely blind the eye-sight of his look:
> Light seeking light, doth light of light beguile.' [1]

Coleridge would venture to say that the two first lines of Biron's answer contain a complete confutation of Malthus's theory. Truly we had delights which pain alone could purchase, the continuance of pain, without giving the most distant prospect of good to be obtained from it. The concluding sentiment also received his highest eulogium, which compared the light of truth to the light of the sun, the gazing at which destroyed the sight.

This play in reality contained in itself very little character. The *dramatis personæ* were only the embryos of characters. Biron was afterwards seen more perfectly in Benedict and Mercutio, and Rosaline in Beatrice, the beloved of Benedict. The old man Boyet came forward afterwards in Lafeu in *All's Well That Ends Well*.[2] The poet in this play [*L.L.L.*] was always uppermost, and little was drawn from real life. His judgement only was shewn in placing the scenes at such a period when we could imagine the transactions of the play natural.

In former ages [existed] the courts of Love,[3] which are now entirely forgotten and appear in themselves improbable; but in Shakespeare's time they were not so far removed, and it was only a pleasing effort on his part to revive the recollection of something not far distant.

But the play was most interesting as it exemplified Shakespeare's mind, when one of the characters, Longueville, objects to Biron—

> 'Biron is like an envious sneaking [b] frost
> That bites the first-born infants of the spring.' [4]

A thousand times had the answer of Biron occurred to Coleridge in this age of prodigies, when the young Roscii of the times had been followed as superior beings, wonderment always taking

---

[a] *Q1* 'but'; *Ff Q2* 'and.' [b] Read 'sneaping.'
[1] *L.L.L.*, I. i. 70–8.
[2] Cf. i. 82; *Table-Talk*, 7 April 1833, for repetitions of these remarks.
[3] The Courts of Love are mentioned also on i. 84.
[4] *L.L.L.* I. 100–1.

place of sense.   Nothing was valued according to the moral feeling it produced, but only according to its strangeness, just as if a rose could have no sweetness unless it grew upon a thorn, or a bunch of grapes could afford no delight to the taste unless it grew by some miracle from a mushroom.

Biron's reply was—

> 'Well! say I am; why should proud summer boast
> Before the birds have any power *a* to sing?
> Why should I joy in an *b* abortive birth?
> At Christmas I no more desire a rose
> Than wish a snow in May's new fangled shows *c*
> But like of each thing that in season grows.' [1]

Coleridge wished the last line to be impressed on every parent in this wonder-loving age—*but like of each thing that in season grows.*

But if they attended to it, he should not have seen so many miserable little beings taught to think before they had the means of thinking.   One of them he had once seen walking about a room, and enquiring why she did so, she answered, 'I do it for exercise, not for pleasure, but too much study will injure my health.'   This young old lady was aged about four years!

If parents constantly kept the last line in their view, they would not delight in hearing their infants reason when patience ought to be exercised in listening to their natural infantile prattle. 'Children,' a friend of his had truly said, 'did not consider themselves children.   They delighted in that which they were not, they took pleasure in the pursuits of men, and all that gratified their vigorous activity.   Instead of attending to this circumstance, what were the books given to children?   Little Fanny is to read the story of little Billy.   A child is to come home and tell its mother, 'The sixpence you gave me I gave to a poor beggar. Did I do right, Mamma?'—'O! yes, my dear,' cries the mother, kissing him; 'you did,'—thus blending one of the first virtues, charity, with one of the basest passions of the human heart, the love of hearing oneself praised.[2]

'Give me,' cried Coleridge, with enthusiasm, 'the works which delighted my youth.   Give me the *History of St. George* and the *Seven Champions of Christendom*, which at every leisure

---

a Read 'cause.'   *b Read 'any.'*
c Ff Qq, Camb. ed., 'shows'; Globe ed. (S. Walker conj.), 'mirth.'
[1] *L.L.L.* I. i. 102–7.
[2] Cf. the 1808 lecture on education, ii. 11, the seventh lecture at Bristol, *S.C.* ii. 293, and Wordsworth's *Prelude*, v. 293–346.

moment I used to hide myself in a corner to read. Give me the *Arabian Nights Entertainments*, which I used to watch till the sun shining on the bookcase approached it, and glowing full upon it gave me courage to take it from the shelf.[1] I heard of no little Billies, and sought no praise for giving to beggars, and I trust that my heart is not the worse, or the less inclined to feel sympathy for all men, because I first learnt the powers of my nature, and to reverence that nature—for who can feel and reverence the nature of man and not feel deeply for the afflictions of others possessing like powers and like nature.[2]

He trusted that what he had thus said in the ardour of his feelings would not be entirely lost, but would awaken in his audience those sympathies without which it was vain to proceed in his criticism of Shakespeare.

The shifting of the scenes could add nothing to the delusion [3] and only destroy [it], by arousing [us] from that delightful dream of our inner nature which was in truth more than a dream. It was a vision of what we might be hereafter—which was the endeavour of the moral being to exert, and at the same time to express itself in the infinite.

Above all it should be recollected that he had taken the great names of Milton and Shakespeare rather for the purpose of illustrating great principles than for any minute examination of their works. In the next lecture, however, he hoped that he should be able to go thro' the *Love's Labour['s] Lost*, from thence proceed to *Romeo and Juliet*, and afterwards, if time permitted, to all those plays of Shakespeare in which was a gradual growth of character, but in which still the *poet* was predominant over the *dramatist*.

---

[1] Cf. *The Friend*, *Works* (Shedd ed.), vol. ii, pp. 137–8, note.
[2] This paragraph was quoted from the manuscript of the Tomalin reports by E. H. Coleridge in his edition of his grandfather's *Letters*, p. 11, note.
[3] '*Illusion*'?—J. D. Campbell.

THE SIXTH LECTURE

[Collier Report.]

THE recollection of what has been said by some of his biographers, on the supposed fact that Milton received corporal
punishment at college, induces me to express my entire dissent
from the notion, that flogging or caning has a tendency to
degrade and debase the minds of boys at school.   In my opinion
it is an entire mistake; since this species of castigation has not
only been inflicted time out of mind, but those who are subjected
to it are well aware that the very highest persons in the realm,
and those to whom people are accustomed to look up with most
respect and reverence, such as the judges of the land, have
quietly submitted to it in their pupilage.

I well remember, about twenty years ago, an advertisement
from a schoolmaster, in which he assured tender-hearted and
foolish parents, that corporal punishment was never inflicted,
excepting in cases of absolute necessity; and that even then the
rod was composed of lilies and roses, the latter, I conclude,
stripped of their thorns.[1]   What, let me ask, has been the consequence, in many cases, of the abolition of flogging in schools?
Reluctance to remove a pimple has not unfrequently transferred
the disease to the vitals: sparing the rod, for the correction of
minor faults, has ended in the commission of the highest crimes.
A man of great reputation [2] (I should rather say of great noto-
riety) sometimes punished the pupils under his care by suspending
them from the ceiling in baskets, exposed to the derision of their
school-fellows; at other times he pinned upon the clothes of the
offender a number of last dying speeches and confessions, and
employed another boy to walk before the culprit, making the
usual monotonous lamentation and outcry.

On one occasion this absurd, and really degrading punishment was inflicted because a boy read with a tone, although, I

---

[1] Cf. the seventh lecture at Bristol, *S.C.* ii. 293.
[2] Joseph Lancaster.   See the 1808 lecture on education (ii. 12) and the
seventh lecture at Bristol, *S.C.* ii. 294.

may observe in passing, that reading with intonation is strictly natural, and therefore truly proper, excepting in the excess.[1]

Then, as to the character and effect of the punishment just noticed, what must a parent of well regulated and instructed mind think of the exhibition of his son in the manner I have described? Here, indeed, was debasement of the worst and lowest kind; for the feelings of a child were outraged, and made to associate and connect themselves with the sentence on an abandoned and shameless criminal. Who would not prefer the momentary, but useful, impression of flogging to this gross attack upon the moral feelings and self-respect of a boy? Again, as to the proper mode of reading: why is a tone in reading to be visited as a criminal offence, especially when the estimate of that offence arises out of the ignorance and incompetence of the master? Every man who reads with true sensibility, especially poetry, must read with a tone, since it conveys, with additional effect, the harmony and rhythm of the verse, without in the slightest degree obscuring the meaning. That is the highest point of excellence in reading, which gives to every thing, whether of thought or language, its most just expression. There may be a wrong tone, as a right, and a wrong tone is of course to be avoided; but a poet writes in measure, and measure is best made apparent by reading with a tone, which heightens the verse, and does not in any respect lower the sense. I defy any man, who has a true relish of the beauty of versification, to read a canto of 'the Fairy Queen,' or a book of 'Paradise Lost,' without some species of intonation.

In various instances we are hardly sensible of its existence, but it does exist, and persons have not scrupled to say, and I believe it, that the tone of a good reader may be set to musical notation. If in these, and in other remarks that fall from me, I appear dogmatical, or dictatorial, it is to be borne in mind, that every man who takes upon himself to lecture, requires that he should be considered by his hearers capable of teaching something that is valuable, or of saying something that is worth hearing. In a mixed audience not a few are desirous of instruction, and some require it; but placed in my present situation I consider myself, not as a man who carries moveables into an

---

[1] This was the Lecturer's own mode of reading verse, and even in prose there was an approach to intonation. I have heard him read Spenser with such an excess (to use his own word) in this respect, that it almost amounted to a song. In blank verse it was less, but still apparent. . . .—J. P. C.
Cf. the seventh lecture at Bristol, *S.C.* ii. 294, and *B.L.* ii. 45–6, note.

empty house, but as a man who entering a generally well furnished dwelling, exhibits a light which enables the owner to see
what is still wanting.   I endeavour to introduce the means of
ascertaining what is, and is not, in a man's own mind.

Not long since,[1] when I lectured at the Royal Institution, I
had the honour of sitting at the desk so ably occupied by Sir [2]
Humphry Davy, who may be said to have elevated the art of
chemistry to the dignity of a science; who has discovered that
one common law is applicable to the mind and to the body, and
who has enabled us to give a full and perfect Amen to the great
axiom of Lord Bacon, that knowledge is power.   In the delivery
of that course I carefully prepared my first essay, and received for
it a cold suffrage of approbation: from accidental causes I was
unable to study the exact form and language of my second
lecture, and when it was at an end, I obtained universal and
heart-felt applause.   What a lesson was this to me not to elaborate my materials, not to consider too nicely the expressions I
should employ, but to trust mainly to the extemporaneous
ebullition of my thoughts.   In this conviction I have ventured
to come before you here; and may I add a hope, that what I offer
will be received in a similar spirit?   It is true that my matter
may not be so accurately arranged: it may not dovetail and fit at
all times as nicely as could be wished; but you shall have my
thoughts warm from my heart, and fresh from my understanding: you shall have the whole skeleton, although the bones
may not be put together with the utmost anatomical skill.

The immense advantage possessed by men of genius over men
of talents can be illustrated in no stronger manner, than by a
comparison of the benefits resulting to mankind from the works
of Homer and of Thucydides.   The merits and claims of
Thucydides, as a historian, are at once admitted; but what care
we for the incidents of the Peloponnesian War?   An individual
may be ignorant of them, as far as regards the particular narrative
of Thucydides; but woe to that statesman, or, I may say, woe to
that man, who has not availed himself of the wisdom contained
in 'the tale of Troy divine!'

Lord Bacon has beautifully expressed this idea,[3] where he

---

[1] In 1808.   I fear that Coleridge is using an undeserved reward for delin-
quency as an excuse for further transgressions.

[2] Evidently Collier has altered his notes here, since Davy only received this
title in April 1812.   This alteration was noticed by the anonymous author
[A. E. Brae] of Collier, Coleridge, and Shakespeare (1860), who used it as one
of his futile arguments against the authenticity of these reports.

[3] Advancement of Learning, the conclusion of Bk I.   (Cf. i. 225–6.)

talks of the instability and destruction of the monuments of the greatest heroes, and compares them with the everlasting writings of Homer, one word of which has never been lost since the days of Pisistratus. Like a mighty ship, they have passed over the sea of time, not leaving a mere ideal track, which soon altogether disappears, but leaving a train of glory in its wake, present and enduring, daily acting upon our minds, and ennobling us by grand thoughts and images: to this work, perhaps, the bravest of our soldiery may trace and attribute some of their heroic achievements. Just as the body is to the immortal mind, so are the actions of our bodily powers in proportion to those by which, independent of individual continuity,[1] we are governed for ever and ever; by which we call, not only the narrow circle of mankind (narrow comparatively) as they now exist, our brethren, but by which we carry our being into future ages, and call all who shall succeed us our brethren, until at length we arrive at that exalted state, when we shall welcome into Heaven thousands and thousands, who will exclaim—'To you I owe the first development of my imagination; to you I owe the withdrawing of my mind from the low brutal part of my nature, to the lofty, the pure, and the perpetual.'

Adverting to the subject more immediately before us, I may observe that I have looked at the reign of Elizabeth, interesting on many accounts, with peculiar pleasure and satisfaction, because it furnished circumstances so favourable to the existence, and to the full development of the powers of Shakespeare. The Reformation, just completed, had occasioned unusual activity of mind, a passion, as it were, for thinking, and for the discovery and use of words capable of expressing the objects of thought and invention. It was, consequently, the age of many conceits, and an age when, for a time, the intellect stood superior to the moral sense.[2]

The difference between the state of mind in the reign of

---

[1] I give this passage exactly as I find it on my notes; but it strikes me that something explanatory must have been accidentally omitted, and perhaps that the word I have written 'continuity' ought to be *contiguity*. I might have left out the whole from 'Just as the body' down to 'the pure and the perpetual,' but I preferred showing my own imperfectness to omitting what may be clear to others, though, at this distance of time, not so evident to me. The general point and bearing of what Coleridge said will be easily understood.—J. P. C.

[2] In marking coincidences between Schlegel and Coleridge's criticism which could not possibly be evidences of Schlegel's influence, their common enthusiasm for the Renaissance and defence of the period against classical critics, should be emphasized. See Schlegel, *Werke*, vi. 168–70.

Elizabeth, and in that of Charles I. is astonishing. In the former period there was an amazing development of power, but all connected with prudential purposes—an attempt to reconcile the moral feeling with the full exercise of the powers of the mind, and the accomplishment of certain practical ends. Then lived Bacon, Burghley, Sir Walter Raleigh, Sir Philip Sidney, and a galaxy of great men, statesmen, lawyers, politicians, philosophers, and poets; and it is lamentable that they should have degraded their mighty powers to such base designs and purposes, dissolving the rich pearls of their great faculties in a worthless acid, to be drunken by a harlot. What was seeking the favour of the Queen, to a man like Bacon, but the mere courtship of harlotry?

Compare this age with that of the republicans: that indeed was an awful age, as compared with our own. England may be said to have then overflowed from the fulness of grand principle —from the greatness which men felt in themselves, abstracted from the prudence with which they ought to have considered, whether their principles were, or were not, adapted to the condition of mankind at large. Compare the revolution then effected with that of a day not long past, when the bubbling-up and overflowing was occasioned by the elevation of the dregs— when there was a total absence of all principle, when the dregs had risen from the bottom to the top, and thus converted into scum, founded a monarchy to be the poisonous bane and misery of the rest of mankind.

It is absolutely necessary to recollect, that the age in which Shakespeare lived was one of great abilities applied to individual and prudential purposes, and not an age of high moral feeling and lofty principle, which gives a man of genius the power of thinking of all things in reference to all. If, then, we should find that Shakespeare took these materials as they were presented to him, and yet to all effectual purposes produced the same grand result as others attempted to produce in an age so much more favourable, shall we not feel and acknowledge the purity and holiness of genius—a light, which, however it might shine on a dunghill, was as pure as the divine effluence which created all the beauty of nature?

One of the consequences of the idea prevalent at the period when Shakespeare flourished, viz., that persons must be men of talents in proportion as they were gentlemen, renders certain characters in his dramas natural with reference to the date when they were drawn: when we read them we are aware that they are not of our age, and in one sense they may be said to be of no age. A friend of mine well remarked of Spenser, that he is out of space: the reader never knows where he is, but still he knows, from the consciousness within him, that all is as natural and proper, as if the country where the action is laid were distinctly pointed out, and marked down in a map. Shakespeare is as much out of time, as Spenser is out of space; yet we feel conscious, though we never knew that such characters existed, that they might exist, and are satisfied with the belief in their existence.

This circumstance enabled Shakespeare to paint truly, and according to the colouring of nature, a vast number of personages by the simple force of meditation: he had only to imitate certain parts of his own character, or to exaggerate such as existed in possibility, and they were at once true to nature, and fragments of the divine mind that drew them. Men who see the great luminary of our system through various optical instruments declare that it seems either square, triangular, or round, when in truth it is still the sun, unchanged in shape and proportion. So with the characters of our great poet: some may think them of one form, and some of another; but they are still nature, still Shakespeare, and the creatures of his meditation.

When I use the term meditation, I do not mean that our great dramatist was without observation of external circumstances: quite the reverse; but mere observation may be able to produce an accurate copy, and even to furnish to other men's minds more than the copyist professed; but what is produced can only consist of parts and fragments, according to the means and extent of observation. Meditation looks at every character with interest, only as it contains something generally true, and such as might be expressed in a philosophical problem.[1]

---

[1] The variations and developments of this fundamental idea deserve careful comparison from the reader who is interested in Coleridge's aesthetics. Cf. i. 201, 203, 205, 206; ii. 14, 51, 98–102, 130, and *Works* (Shedd), ii. 428; iv. 257; *B.L.* ii. 64, *Anima Poetae* (London, 1895), pp. 166–7; Allsop's *Letters, etc., of Coleridge* (1858), p. 225. Cf. also Coleridge's distinction of copy and imitation, i. 177, note. Striking parallels may be found in Richter's *Vorschule der Aesthetik* (1804), Section 57, and in Schelling's lecture 'Über das Verhältniss der bildenden Künste zu der Natur' (1807), *Werke* (1856–61), vii. 301. The dates permit either to be Coleridge's source, and Coleridge is known to have read both books, at least before 1818. To the present editor, however, the evidence does not seem to be entirely conclusive, for Coleridge was thinking along these lines at a very early date. On 11 May 1804 he wrote in his notebook this extremely romantic definition of poetry: 'Poetry is rationalized dreaming, dealing to manifold forms our own feelings, that never perhaps were attached by us consciously to our own personal selves. What is the *Lear*, the *Othello*, but a divine dream, all Shakespeare;—and

Shakespeare's characters may be reduced to a few—that is to say, to a few classes of characters. If you take his gentlemen, for instance, Biron is seen again in Mercutio, in Benedick, and in several others. They were men who combine the politeness of the courtier with the faculties of high intellect—those powers of combination and severance which only belong to an intellectual mind. The wonder is how Shakespeare can thus disguise himself, and possess such miraculous powers of conveying what he means without betraying the poet, and without even producing the consciousness of him.

In the address of Mercutio regarding Queen Mab, which is so well known that it is unnecessary to repeat it, is to be noted all the fancy of the poet; and the language in which it is conveyed possesses such facility and felicity, that one would almost say that it was impossible for it to be thought, unless it were thought as naturally, and without effort, as Mercutio repeats it. This is the great art by which Shakespeare combines the poet and the gentleman throughout, borrowing from his most amiable nature that which alone could combine them, a perfect simplicity of mind, a delight in all that is excellent for its own sake, without reference to himself as causing it, and by that which distinguishes him from all other poets, alluded to by one of his admirers in a short poem, where he tells us that while Shakespeare possessed all the powers of a man, and more than a man, yet he had all the feelings, the sensibility, the purity, innocence, and delicacy of an affectionate girl of eighteen.

Before I enter upon the merits of the tragedy of 'Romeo and Juliet,' it will be necessary for me to say something of the language of our country. And here I beg leave to observe, that although I have announced these as lectures upon Milton and Shakespeare, they are in reality, as also stated in the prospectus, intended to illustrate the principles of poetry: therefore, all must not be regarded as mere digression which does not immediately

---

nothing Shakespeare.' (Notebook 15, in the British Museum.) Cf. also *Anima Poetae* (London, 1895), p. 136, dated 1805. For later and fuller discussions see the essay 'On Poesy or Art,' *B.L.* ii. 257–9, and *The Friend* (Section 2, Essays V–VI). Whatever Coleridge's indebtedness to Richter and Schelling, there is a previous debt to the apriorism of the Platonists—to Plato himself, to the Neo-Platonists, and to the Cambridge Platonists. See A. E. Powell, *The Romantic Theory of Poetry*, ch. iv, and C. Howard, *Coleridge's Idealism* (1924). An important essay bearing indirectly but significantly on this point is that on 'Kant and the English Platonists' (especially pp. 265–80), by A. O. Lovejoy, in *Essays Philosophical and Psychological in Honor of William James* (1908).

and exclusively refer to those writers.[1]   I have chosen them, in order to bring under the notice of my hearers great general truths; in fact, whatever may aid myself, as well as others, in deciding upon the claims of all writers of all countries.

The language, that is to say the particular tongue, in which Shakespeare wrote, cannot be left out of consideration.   It will not be disputed, that one language may possess advantages which another does not enjoy; and we may state with confidence, that English excels all other languages in the number of its practical words.   The French may bear the palm in the names of trades, and in military and diplomatic terms.   Of the German it may be said, that, exclusive of many mineralogical words, it is incomparable in its metaphysical and psychological force: in another respect it nearly rivals the Greek,

> 'The learned Greek, rich in fit epithets,
>   Blest in the lovely marriage of pure words;' [2]

I mean in its capability of composition—of forming compound words.   Italian is the sweetest and softest language; Spanish the most majestic.   All these have their peculiar faults; but I never can agree that any language is unfit for poetry, although different languages, from the condition and circumstances of the people, may certainly be adapted to one species of poetry more than to another.

Take the French as an example.   It is, perhaps, the most perspicuous and pointed language in the world, and therefore best fitted for conversation, for the expression of light and airy passion, attaining its object by peculiar and felicitous turns of phrase, which are evanescent, and, like the beautifully coloured dust on the wings of a butterfly, must not be judged by the test of touch.   It appears as if it were all surface and had no substratum, and it constantly most dangerously tampers with morals, without positively offending decency.   As the language for what is called modern genteel comedy all others must yield to French.

Italian can only be deemed second to Spanish, and Spanish to Greek, which contains all the excellences of all languages. Italian, though sweet and soft, is not deficient in force and

---

[1] Cf. ii. 82 and note 1.
[2] From Act I, Scene 1, of 'Lingua, or the Combat of the Tongue and the Five Senses.'   This drama is reprinted in Dodsley's Old Plays, vol. v (last edition), and the lines may be found on p. 107 of that volume.—[J. P. C.]
Collier refers to the 1825 edition.

dignity; and I may appeal to Ariosto, as a poet who displays to the utmost advantage the use of his native tongue for all purposes, whether of passion, sentiment, humour, or description.

But in English I find that which is possessed by no other modern language, and which, as it were, appropriates it to the drama. It is a language made out of many, and it has consequently many words, which originally had the same meaning; but in the progress of society those words have gradually assumed different shades of meaning. Take any homogeneous language, such as German, and try to translate into it the following lines:—

> 'But not to one, in this benighted age,
>   Is that diviner inspiration given,
> That burns in Shakespeare's or in Milton's page,
>   The pomp and prodigality of heaven.'
>
> GRAY'S *Stanzas to Bentley*.

In German it would be necessary to say 'the pomp and *spendthriftness* of heaven,' because the German has not, as we have, one word with two such distinct meanings, one expressing the nobler, the other the baser idea of the same action.

The monosyllabic character of English enables us, besides, to express more meaning in a shorter compass than can be done in any other language. In truth, English may be called the harvest of the unconscious wisdom of various nations, and was not the formation of any particular time, or assemblage of individuals. Hence the number of its passionate phrases—its metaphorical terms, not borrowed from poets, but adopted by them. Our commonest people, when excited by passion, constantly employ them: if a mother lose her child she is full of the wildest fancies, and the words she uses assume a tone of dignity; for the constant hearing and reading of the Bible and Liturgy clothes her thoughts not only in the most natural, but in the most beautiful forms of language.

I have been induced to offer these remarks, in order to obviate an objection often made against Shakespeare on the ground of the multitude of his conceits. I do not pretend to justify every conceit, and a vast number have been most unfairly imputed to him; for I am satisfied that many portions of scenes attributed to Shakespeare were never written by him. I admit, however, that even in those which bear the strongest characteristics of his mind, there are some conceits not strictly to be vindicated. The notion against which I declare war is, that when ever a conceit is met with it is unnatural. People who entertain this opinion forget, that had they lived in the age of Shakespeare, they would have deemed them natural. Dryden in his translation of Juvenal has used the words 'Look round the world,' which are a literal version of the original; but Dr. Johnson has swelled and expanded this expression into the following couplet:—

> 'Let observation, with extensive view,
>   Survey mankind from China to Peru';
>
> Vanity of Human Wishes.

mere bombast and tautology; as much as to say, 'Let observation with extensive observation observe mankind extensively.' [1]

Had Dr. Johnson lived in the time of Shakespeare, or even of Dryden, he would never have been guilty of such an outrage upon common sense and common language; and if people would, in idea, throw themselves back a couple of centuries, they would find that conceits, and even puns, were very allowable, because very natural. Puns often arise out of a mingled sense of injury, and contempt of the person inflicting it, and, as it seems to me, it is a natural way of expressing that mixed feeling.[2] I could point out puns in Shakespeare, where they appear almost as if the first openings of the mouth of nature—where nothing else could so properly be said. This is not peculiar to puns, but is of much wider application: read any part of the works of our great dramatist, and the conviction comes upon you irresistibly, not only that what he puts into the mouths of his personages might have been said, but that it must have been said, because nothing so proper could have been said.

In a future lecture I will enter somewhat into the history of conceits, and shew the wise use that has heretofore been made of them. I will now, (and I hope it will be received with favour) attempt a defence of conceits and puns, taking my examples mainly from the poet under consideration. I admit, of course, that they may be misapplied; but throughout life, I may say, I never have discovered the wrong use of a thing, without having previously discovered the right use of it. To the young I would remark, that it is always unwise to judge of anything by its defects: the first attempt ought to be to discover its excellences.[3]

---

[1] Cf. ii. 170.

[2] Schlegel makes a similar remark, *Werke*, vi. 192. Since Coleridge had not yet seen Schlegel's book, this parallel is a coincidence. See also *Werke*, vi. 170, 193–5.

[3] This is a favourite idea of Coleridge's. See, for example, *B.L.* i. 43, ii. 94; *Anima Poetae* (London, 1895), p. 30.

If a man come into my company and abuse a book, his invectives coming down like water from a shower bath, I never feel obliged to him: he probably tells me no news, for all works, even the best, have defects, and they are easily seen; but if a man show me beauties, I thank him for his information, because, in my time, I have unfortunately gone through so many volumes that have had little or nothing to recommend them.   Always begin with the good—*à Jove principium*—and the bad will make itself evident enough, quite as soon as is desirable.

I will proceed to speak of Shakespeare's wit, in connexion with his much abused puns and conceits; because an excellent writer,[1] who has done good service to the public taste by driving out the nonsense of the Italian school, has expressed his surprise, that all the other excellences of Shakespeare were, in a greater or less degree, possessed by his contemporaries: thus, Ben Jonson had one qualification, Massinger another, while he declares that Beaumont and Fletcher had equal knowledge of human nature, with more variety.[2]   The point in which none of them had approached Shakespeare, according to this writer, was his wit.   I own, I was somewhat shocked to see it gravely said in print, that the quality by which Shakespeare was to be individualised from all others was, what is ordinarily called, wit.   I had read his plays over and over, and it did not strike me that wit was his great and characteristic superiority.   In reading Voltaire, or (to take a standard and most witty comedy as an example) in reading 'The School for Scandal,' I never experienced the same sort of feeling as in reading Shakespeare.

That Shakespeare has wit is indisputable, but it is not the same kind of wit as in other writers: his wit is blended with the other qualities of his works, and is, by its nature, capable of being so blended.   It appears in all parts of his productions, in his tragedies, comedies, and histories: it is not like the wit of Voltaire, and of many modern writers, to whom the epithet 'witty' has been properly applied, whose wit consists in a mere combination of words; but in at least nine times out of ten in Shakespeare, the wit is produced not by a combination of words, but by a combination of images.

It is not always easy to distinguish between wit and fancy. When the whole pleasure received is derived from surprise at an

---

[1] William Gifford, whose *Baviad* and *Maeviad* exposed the 'Della Cruscan' poets to ridicule.   Coleridge refers to Gifford's edition of Massinger in 1805, Introduction, p. li.   Cf. *M.C.*, pp. 41–2.

[2] 'Beaumont is as sublime, Fletcher as pathetick, and Jonson as nervous.' *Plays of Massinger*, Introduction, p. li.

unexpected turn of expression, then I call it wit; but when the pleasure is produced not only by surprise, but also by an image which remains with us and gratifies for its own sake, then I call it fancy. I know of no mode so satisfactory of distinguishing between wit and fancy. I appeal to the recollection of those who hear me, whether the greater part of what passes for wit in Shakespeare, is not most exquisite humour, heightened by a figure, and attributed to a particular character? Take the instance of the flea on Bardolph's nose, which Falstaff compares to a soul suffering in purgatory. The images themselves, in cases like this, afford a great part of the pleasure.

These remarks are not without importance in forming a judgment of poets and writers in general: there is a wide difference between the talent which gives a sort of electric surprise by a mere turn of phrase, and that higher ability which produces surprise by a permanent medium, and always leaves something behind it, which satisfies the mind as well as tickles the hearing. The first belongs to men of cleverness, who, having been long in the world, have observed the turns of phrase which please in company, and which, passing away the moment, are passed in a moment, being no longer recollected than the time they take in utterance. We must all have seen and known such people; and I remember saying of one of them that he was like a man who squandered his estate in farthings: he gave away so many, that he must needs have been wealthy. This sort of talent by no means constitutes genius, although it has some affinity to it.

The wit of Shakespeare is, as it were, like the flourishing of a man's stick, when he is walking, in the full flow of animal spirits: it is a sort of exuberance of hilarity which disburdens, and it resembles a conductor, to distribute a portion of our gladness to the surrounding air. While, however, it disburdens, it leaves behind what is weightiest and most important, and what most contributes to some direct aim and purpose.

I will now touch upon a very serious charge against Shakespeare—that of indecency and immorality.[1] Many have been those who have endeavoured to exculpate him by saying, that it was the vice of his age; but he was too great to require exculpation from the accidents of any age. These persons have appealed to Beaumont and Fletcher, to Massinger, and to other less eminent dramatists, to prove that what is complained of was

---

[1] Schlegel also defends the morality of Shakespeare against the neo-classical critics. See *Werke*, vi. 172, 195. There is no particular similarity between his arguments and those of Coleridge.

common to them all. Oh! shame and sorrow, if it were so: there is nothing common to Shakespeare and to other writers of his day—not even the language they employed.

In order to form a proper judgment upon this point, it is necessary to make a distinction between manners and morals; and that distinction being once established, and clearly comprehended, Shakespeare will appear as pure a writer, in reference to all that we ought to be, and to all that we ought to feel, as he is wonderful in reference to his intellectual faculties.

By manners I mean what is dependent on the particular customs and fashions of the age. Even in a state of comparative barbarism as to manners, there may be, and there is, morality. But give me leave to say that we have seen much worse times than those—times when the mind was so enervated and degraded, that the most distant associations, that could possibly connect our ideas with the basest feelings, immediately brought forward those base feelings, without reference to the nobler impulses; thus destroying the little remnant of humanity, excluding from the mind what is good, and introducing what is bad to keep the bestial nature company.

On looking through Shakespeare, offences against decency and manners may certainly be pointed out; but let us examine history minutely, and we shall find that this was the ordinary language of the time, and then let us ask, where is the offence? The offence, so to call it, was not committed wantonly, and for the sake of offending, but for the sake of merriment; for what is most observable in Shakespeare, in reference to this topic, is that what he says is always calculated to raise a gust of laughter, that would, as it were, blow away all impure ideas, if it did not excite abhorrence of them.

Above all, let us compare him with some modern writers, the servile imitators of the French, and we shall receive a most instructive lesson. I may take the liberty of reading the following note, written by me after witnessing the performance of a modern play at Malta, about nine years ago [1]:—'I went to the theatre, and came away without waiting for the entertainment. The longer I live, the more I am impressed with the exceeding immorality of modern plays: I can scarcely refrain from anger and laughter at the shamelessness, and the absurdity of the presumption which presents itself, when I think of their pretences to superior morality, compared with the plays of Shakespeare.'

[1] Read 'six or seven years ago.' Coleridge was in Malta from 18 May 1804 to 21 September 1805.

Here let me pause for one moment; for while reading my note I call to mind a novel, on the sofa or toilet of nearly every woman of quality, in which the author gravely warns parents against the indiscreet communication to their children of the contents of some parts of the Bible, as calculated to injure their morals.[1] Another modern author, who has done his utmost to undermine the innocence of the young of both sexes, has the effrontery to protest against the exhibition of the bare leg of a Corinthian female. My note thus pursues the subject:—

'In Shakespeare there are a few gross speeches, but it is doubtful to me if they would produce any ill effect on an unsullied mind; while in some modern plays, as well as in some modern novels, there is a systematic undermining of all morality: they are written in the true cant of humanity, that has no object but to impose; where virtue is not placed in action, or in the habits that lead to action, but, like the title of a book I have heard of, they are "a hot huddle of indefinite sensations." In these the lowest incitements to piety are obtruded upon us; like an impudent rascal at a masquerade, who is well known in spite of his vizor, or known by it, and yet is allowed to be impudent in virtue of his disguise. In short, I appeal to the whole of Shakespeare's writings, whether his grossness is not the mere sport of fancy, dissipating low feelings by exciting the intellect, and only injuring while it offends? Modern dramas injure in consequence of not offending. Shakespeare's worst passages are grossnesses against the degradations of our nature: those of our modern plays are too often delicacies directly in favour of them.'

Such was my note, made nine years ago, and I have since seen every reason to adhere firmly to the opinions it expresses.

In my next lecture I will proceed to an examination of 'Romeo and Juliet'; and I take that tragedy, because in it are to be found all the crude materials of future excellence. The poet, the great dramatic poet, is throughout seen, but the various parts of the composition are not blended with such harmony as in some of his after writings. I am directed to it, more than all, for this reason, —because it affords me the best opportunity of introducing Shakespeare as a delineator of female character, and of love in all its forms, and with all the emotions which deserve that sweet and man-elevating name.

It has been remarked, I believe by Dryden,[2] that Shakespeare wrote for men only, but Beaumont and Fletcher (or rather 'the

[1] Cf. *M.C.*, pp. 374–5, and *The Friend, Works* (Shedd ed.), ii. 38, 537.
[2] Preface to *Troilus and Cressida*.

gentle Fletcher') for women.   I wish to begin by shewing, not
only that this is not true, but that, of all writers for the stage, he
only has drawn the female character with that mixture of the real
and of the ideal which belongs to it; and that there is no one
female personage in the plays of all his contemporaries, of whom
a man, seriously examining his heart and his good sense, can say
'Let that woman be my companion through life: let her be the
object of my suit, and the reward of my success.' [1]

i. 106.)   William Richardson, Professor of Humanity at
es the credit of anticipating Coleridge in this appreciation
women.   *Essays on Shakespeare's Dramatic Character of
and on his Imitation of Female Characters*, London, 1789.

THE SEVENTH LECTURE

[*Collier Report.*]

IN a former lecture I endeavoured to point out the union of the Poet and the Philosopher, or rather the warm embrace between them, in the 'Venus and Adonis' and 'Lucrece' of Shakespeare. From thence I passed on to 'Love's Labour's Lost,' as the link between his character as a Poet, and his art as a Dramatist; and I shewed that, although in that work the former was still predominant, yet that the germs of his subsequent dramatic power were easily discernible.

I will now, as I promised in my last, proceed to 'Romeo and Juliet,' not because it is the earliest, or among the earliest of Shakespeare's works of that kind, but because in it are to be found specimens, in degree, of all the excellences which he afterwards displayed in his more perfect dramas, but differing from them in being less forcibly evidenced, and less happily combined: all the parts are more or less present, but they are not united with the same harmony.

There are, however, in 'Romeo and Juliet' passages where the poet's whole excellence is evinced, so that nothing superior to them can be met with in the productions of his after years. The main distinction between this play and others is, as I said, that the parts are less happily combined, or to borrow a phrase from the painter, the whole work is less in keeping. Grand portions are produced: we have limbs of giant growth; but the production, as a whole, in which each part gives delight for itself, and the whole, consisting of these delightful parts, communicates the highest intellectual pleasure and satisfaction, is the result of the application of judgment and taste. These are not to be attained but by painful study, and to the sacrifice of the stronger pleasures derived from the dazzling light which a man of genius throws over every circumstance, and where we are chiefly struck by vivid and distinct images. Taste is an attainment after a poet has been disciplined by experience, and has added to genius that talent by which he knows what part of his genius he can make acceptable, and intelligible to the portion of mankind for which he writes.

In my mind it would be a hopeless symptom, as regards genius, if I found a young man with anything like perfect taste. In the earlier works of Shakespeare we have a profusion of double epithets, and sometimes even the coarsest terms are employed, if they convey a more vivid image; but by degrees the associations are connected with the image they are designed to impress, and the poet descends from the ideal into the real world so far as to conjoin both—to give a sphere of active operations to the ideal, and to elevate and refine the real.

In 'Romeo and Juliet' the principal characters may be divided into two classes: in one class passion—the passion of love—is drawn and drawn truly, as well as beautifully; but the persons are not individualised farther than as the actor appears on the stage.[1]   It is a very just description and development of love, without giving, if I may so express myself, the philosophical history of it—without shewing how the man became acted upon by that particular passion, but leading it through all the incidents of the drama, and rendering it predominant.

Tybalt is, in himself, a common-place personage.   And here allow me to remark upon a great distinction between Shakespeare, and all who have written in imitation of him.   I know no character in his plays (unless indeed Pistol be an exception) which can be called the mere portrait of an individual: while the reader feels all the satisfaction arising from individuality, yet that very individual is a sort of class character, and this circumstance renders Shakespeare the poet of all ages.

Tybalt is a man abandoned to his passions—with all the pride of family, only because he thought it belonged to him as a member of that family, and valuing himself highly, simply because he does not care for death.   This indifference to death is perhaps more common than any other feeling: men are apt to flatter themselves extravagantly, merely because they possess a quality which it is a disgrace not to have, but which a wise man never puts forward, but when it is necessary.

Jeremy Taylor in one part of his voluminous works, speaking of a great man, says that he was naturally a coward, as indeed most men are, knowing the value of life, but the power of his reason enabled him, when required, to conduct himself with uniform courage and hardihood.   The good bishop, perhaps, had in his mind a story, told by one of the ancients, of a

---

[1] The second class is explained by Coleridge's references to Hamlet and Mercutio on p. 98, though Coleridge (or Collier reporting him) failed to indicate the transition.   (Cf. ii. 160, 217–18.)

Philosopher and a Coxcomb, on board the same ship during a storm: the Coxcomb reviled the Philosopher for betraying marks of fear: 'Why are you so frightened? I am not afraid of being drowned: I do not care a farthing for my life.'—'You are perfectly right,' said the Philosopher, 'for your life is not worth a farthing.'

Shakespeare never takes pains to make his characters win your esteem, but leaves it to the general command of the passions, and to poetic justice. It is most beautiful to observe, in 'Romeo and Juliet,' that the characters principally engaged in the incidents are preserved innocent from all that could lower them in our opinion, while the rest of the personages, deserving little interest in themselves, derive it from being instrumental in those situations in which the more important personages develope their thoughts and passions.

Look at Capulet—a worthy, noble-minded old man of high rank, with all the impatience that is likely to accompany it. It is delightful to see all the sensibilities of our nature so exquisitely called forth; as if the poet had the hundred arms of the polypus, and had thrown them out in all directions to catch the predominant feeling. We may see in Capulet the manner in which anger seizes hold of everything that comes in its way, in order to express itself, as in the lines where he reproves Tybalt for his fierceness of behaviour, which led him to wish to insult a Montague, and disturb the merriment.—

> 'Go to, go to;
> You are a saucy boy. Is't so, indeed?
> This trick may chance to scath you;—I know what.
> You must contrary me! marry, 'tis time.—
> Well said, my hearts!—You are a princox: go:
> Be quiet or—More light, more light!—For shame!
> I'll make you quiet.—What! cheerly, my hearts!'
>
> *Act I., Scene 5.*

The line

> 'This trick may chance to scath you;—I know what,'

was an allusion to the legacy Tybalt might expect; and then, seeing the lights burn dimly, Capulet turns his anger against the servants. Thus we see that no one passion is so predominant, but that it includes all the parts of the character, and the reader never has a mere abstract of a passion, as of wrath or ambition, but the whole man is presented to him—the one predominant passion acting, if I may so say, as the leader of the band to the rest.

It could not be expected that the poet should introduce such a character as Hamlet into every play; but even in those personages, which are subordinate to a hero so eminently philosophical, the passion is at least rendered instructive, and induces the reader to look with a keener eye, and a finer judgment into human nature.

Shakespeare has this advantage over all other dramatists—that he has availed himself of his psychological genius to develope all the minutiæ of the human heart: shewing us the thing that, to common observers, he seems solely intent upon, he makes visible what we should not otherwise have seen: just as, after looking at distant objects through a telescope, when we behold them subsequently with the naked eye, we see them with greater distinctness, and in more detail, than we should otherwise have done.

Mercutio is one of our poet's truly Shakespearian characters; for throughout his plays, but especially in those of the highest order, it is plain that the personages were drawn rather from meditation than from observation, or to speak correctly, more from observation, the child of meditation. It is comparatively easy for a man to go about the world, as if with a pocket-book in his hand, carefully noting down what he sees and hears: by practice he acquires considerable facility in representing what he has observed, himself frequently unconscious of its worth, or its bearings. This is entirely different from the observation of a mind, which, having formed a theory and a system upon its own nature, remarks all things that are examples of its truth, confirming it in that truth, and, above all, enabling it to convey the truths of philosophy, as mere effects derived from, what we may call, the outward watchings of life.

Hence it is that Shakespeare's favourite characters are full of such lively intellect. Mercutio is a man possessing all the elements of a poet: the whole world was, as it were, subject to his law of association. Whenever he wishes to impress anything, all things become his servants for the purpose: all things tell the same tale, and sound in unison. This faculty, moreover, is combined with the manners and feelings of a perfect gentleman, himself utterly unconscious of his powers. By his loss it was contrived that the whole catastrophe of the tragedy should be brought about: it endears him to Romeo, and gives to the death of Mercutio an importance which it could not otherwise have acquired.

I say this in answer to an observation, I think by Dryden,[1] (to which indeed Dr. Johnson has fully replied) that Shakespeare having carried the part of Mercutio as far as he could, till his genius was exhausted, had killed him in the third Act, to get him out of the way. What shallow nonsense! As I have remarked, upon the death of Mercutio the whole catastrophe depends; it is produced by it. The scene in which it occurs serves to show how indifference to any subject but one, and aversion to activity on the part of Romeo, may be overcome and roused to the most resolute and determined conduct. Had not Mercutio been rendered so amiable and so interesting, we could not have felt so strongly the necessity for Romeo's interference, connecting it immediately, and passionately, with the future fortunes of the lover and his mistress.

But what am I to say of the Nurse? We have been told that her character is the mere fruit of observation—that it is like Swift's 'Polite Conversation,' certainly the most stupendous work of human memory, and of unceasingly active attention to what passes around us, upon record. The Nurse in 'Romeo and Juliet' has sometimes been compared to a portrait by Gerard Dow, in which every hair was so exquisitely painted, that it would bear the test of the microscope. Now, I appeal confidently to my hearers whether the closest observation of the manners of one or two old nurses would have enabled Shakespeare to draw this character of admirable generalisation? Surely not. Let any man conjure up in his mind all the qualities and peculiarities that can possibly belong to a nurse, and he will find them in Shakespeare's picture of the old woman: nothing is omitted. This effect is not produced by mere observation. The great prerogative of genius (and Shakespeare felt and availed himself of it) is now to swell itself to the dignity of a god, and now to subdue and keep dormant some part of that lofty nature, and to descend even to the lowest character—to become everything, in fact, but the vicious.

Thus, in the Nurse you have all the garrulity of old age, and all its fondness; for the affection of old-age is one of the greatest consolations of humanity. I have often thought what a melancholy world this would be without children, and what an inhuman world without the aged.

---

[1] This is an alleged remark of Shakespeare, which Dryden quotes in order to differ with it. *The Conquest of Granada, Second Part, Defence of the Epilogue.* For Dr Johnson's comment, which is similar to Coleridge's, see his general note on *Romeo and Juliet.*

You have also in the Nurse the arrogance of ignorance, with the pride of meanness at being connected with a great family. You have the grossness, too, which that situation never removes, though it sometimes suspends it; and, arising from that grossness, the little low vices attendant upon it, which, indeed, in such minds are scarcely vices.—Romeo at one time was the most delightful and excellent young man, and the Nurse all willingness to assist him; but her disposition soon turns in favour of Paris, for whom she professes precisely the same admiration.   How wonderfully are these low peculiarities contrasted with a young and pure mind, educated under different circumstances!

Another point ought to be mentioned as characteristic of the ignorance of the Nurse:—it is, that in all her recollections, she assists herself by the remembrance of visual circumstances. The great difference, in this respect, between the cultivated and the uncultivated mind is this—that the cultivated mind will be found to recal the past by certain regular trains of cause and effect; whereas, with the uncultivated mind, the past is recalled wholly by coincident images, or facts which happened at the same time.[1]   This position is fully exemplified in the following passages put into the mouth of the Nurse:—

> 'Even or odd, of all days in the year,
>   Come Lammas eve at night shall she be fourteen.
>   Susan and she—God rest all Christian souls!—
>   Were of an age.—Well, Susan is with God;
>   She was too good for me.   But, as I said,
>   On Lammas eve at night shall she be fourteen;
>   That shall she, marry: I remember it well.
>   'Tis since the earthquake now eleven years;
>   And she was wean'd,—I never shall forget it,—
>   Of all the days of the year, upon that day;
>   For I had then laid wormwood to my dug,
>   Sitting in the sun under the dove-house wall:
>   My lord and you were then at Mantua.—
>   Nay, I do bear a brain:—but, as I said,
>   When it did taste the wormwood on the nipple
>   Of my dug, and felt it bitter, pretty fool,
>   To see it tetchy, and fall out with the dug!
>   Shake, quoth the dove-house: 'twas no need, I trow,
>   To bid me trudge.
>   And since that time it is eleven years;
>   For then she could stand alone.'

Act I., Scene 3.

[1] Cf. *The Friend, Works* (Shedd ed.), ii. 410.

She afterwards goes on with similar visual impressions, so true to the character.—More is here brought into one portrait than could have been ascertained by one man's mere observation, and without the introduction of a single incongruous point.

I honour, I love, the works of Fielding as much, or perhaps more, than those of any other writer of fiction of that kind: take Fielding in his characters of postillions, landlords, and land-ladies, waiters, or indeed, of any-body who had come before his eye, and nothing can be more true, more happy, or more humorous; but in all his chief personages, Tom Jones for instance, where Fielding was not directed by observation, where he could not assist himself by the close copying [1] of what he saw, where it is necessary that something should take place, some words be spoken, or some object described, which he could not have witnessed, (his soliloquies for example, or the interview between the hero and Sophia Western before the reconciliation) and I will venture to say, loving and honouring the man and his productions as I do, that nothing can be more forced and unnatural: the language is without vivacity or spirit, the whole matter is incongruous, and totally destitute of psychological truth.

On the other hand, look at Shakespeare: where can any character be produced that does not speak the language of nature? where does he not put into the mouths of his *dramatis personæ*, be they high or low, Kings or Constables, precisely what they must have said? Where, from observation, could he learn the language proper to Sovereigns, Queens, Noblemen or Generals? yet he invariably uses it.—Where, from observation, could he have learned such lines as these, which are put into the mouth of Othello, when he is talking to Iago of Brabantio?

> 'Let him do his spite:
> My services, which I have done the signiory,
> Shall out-tongue his complaints.   'Tis yet to know,
> Which, when I know that boasting is an honour,
> I shall promulgate, I fetch my life and being
> From men of royal siege; and my demerits
> May speak, unbonneted, to as proud a fortune
> As this that I have reach'd: for know, Iago,
> But that I love the gentle Desdemona,
> I would not my unhoused free condition
> Put into circumscription and confine
> For the sea's worth.'

Act I., Scene 2.

[1] Cf. ii. 85, note.

I ask where was Shakespeare to observe such language as this? If he did observe it, it was with the inward eye of meditation upon his own nature: for the time, he became Othello, and spoke as Othello, in such circumstances, must have spoken.

Another remark I may make upon 'Romeo and Juliet' is, that in this tragedy the poet is not, as I have hinted, entirely blended with the dramatist,—at least, not in the degree to be afterwards noticed in 'Lear,' 'Hamlet,' 'Othello,' or 'Macbeth.' Capulet and Montague not unfrequently talk a language only belonging to the poet, and not so characteristic of, and peculiar to, the passions of persons in the situations in which they are placed—a mistake, or rather an indistinctness, which many of our later dramatists have carried through the whole of their productions.

When I read the song of Deborah, I never think that she is a poet, although I think the song itself a sublime poem: [1] it is as simple a dithyrambic production as exists in any language; but it is the proper and characteristic effusion of a woman highly elevated by triumph, by the natural hatred of oppressors, and resulting from a bitter sense of wrong: it is a song of exultation on deliverance from these evils, a deliverance accomplished by herself. When she exclaims, 'The inhabitants of the villages ceased, they ceased in Israel, until that I, Deborah, arose, that I arose a mother in Israel,' it is poetry in the highest sense: we have no reason, however, to suppose that if she had not been agitated by passion, and animated by victory, she would have been able so to express herself; or that if she had been placed in different circumstances, she would have used such language of truth and passion. We are to remember that Shakespeare, not placed under circumstances of excitement, and only wrought upon by his own vivid and vigorous imagination, writes a language that invariably, and intuitively becomes the condition and position of each character.

On the other hand, there is a language not descriptive of passion, not uttered under the influence of it, which is at the same time poetic, and shows a high and active fancy, as when Capulet says to Paris,—

> 'Such comfort as do lusty young men feel,
> When well-apparell'd April on the heel
> Of limping winter treads, even such delight
> Among fresh female buds, shall you this night
> Inherit at my house.'

Act I., Scene 2.

[1] Cf. i. 86, 193, *B.L.* ii. 43.

Here the poet may be said to speak, rather than the dramatist; and it would be easy to adduce other passages from this play, where Shakespeare, for a moment forgetting the character, utters his own words in his own person.

In my mind, what have often been censured as Shakespeare's conceits are completely justifiable, as belonging to the state, age, or feeling of the individual.   Sometimes, when they cannot be vindicated on these grounds, they may well be excused by the taste of his own and of the preceding age; as for instance, in Romeo's speech,

> 'Here's much to do with hate, but more with love:—
> Why then, O brawling love!   O loving hate!
> O anything, of nothing first created!
> O heavy lightness! serious vanity!
> Misshapen chaos of well-seeming forms!
> Feather of lead, bright smoke, cold fire, sick health!
> Still-waking sleep, that is not what it is!'
>
> *Act I., Scene 1.*

I dare not pronounce such passages as these to be absolutely unnatural, not merely because I consider the author a much better judge than I can be, but because I can understand and allow for an effort of the mind, when it would describe what it cannot satisfy itself with the description of, to reconcile opposites and qualify contradictions, leaving a middle state of mind more strictly appropriate to the imagination than any other, when it is, as it were, hovering between images.   As soon as it is fixed on one image, it becomes understanding; but while it is unfixed and wavering between them, attaching itself permanently to none, it is imagination.   Such is the fine description of Death in Milton:—

> 'The other shape,
> If shape it might be call'd, that shape had none
> Distinguishable in member, joint, or limb,
> Or substance might be call'd, that shadow seem'd,
> For each seem'd either: black it stood as night;
> Fierce as ten furies, terrible as hell,
> And shook a dreadful dart: what seem'd his head
> The likeness of a kingly crown had on.'
>
> *Paradise Lost*, Book II.

The grandest efforts of poetry are where the imagination is called forth, not to produce a distinct form, but a strong working of the mind, still offering what is still repelled, and again creating what is again rejected; the result being what the poet wishes to impress, namely, the substitution of a sublime feeling of the unimaginable for a mere image.[1]   I have sometimes thought that the passage just read might be quoted as exhibiting the narrow limit of painting, as compared with the boundless power of poetry: painting cannot go beyond a certain point; poetry rejects all control, all confinement.   Yet we know that sundry painters have attempted pictures of the meeting between Satan and Death at the gates of Hell; and how was Death represented? Not as Milton has described him, but by the most defined thing that can be imagined—a skeleton, the dryest and hardest image that it is possible to discover; which, instead of keeping the mind in a state of activity, reduces it to the merest passivity,—an image, compared with which a square, a triangle, or any other mathematical figure, is a luxuriant fancy.

It is a general but mistaken notion that, because some forms of writing, and some combinations of thought, are not usual, they are not natural; but we are to recollect that the dramatist represents his characters in every situation of life and in every state of mind, and there is no form of language that may not be introduced with effect by a great and judicious poet, and yet be most strictly according to nature.   Take punning, for instance, which may be the lowest, but at all events is the most harmless, kind of wit, because it never excites envy.   A pun may be a necessary consequence of association: one man, attempting to prove something that was resisted by another, might, when agitated by strong feeling, employ a term used by his adversary with a directly contrary meaning to that for which that adversary had resorted to it: it might come into his mind as one way, and sometimes the best, of replying to that adversary.   This form of

---

[1] As Brandl points out (*Life of Coleridge*, Eng. trans., p. 320), Richter makes a very similar remark: 'The true poet . . . will surround limited Nature with the infinity of the idea' (*Vorschule der Aesthetik*, Section 4). But compare also Schiller's essays 'On the Sublime' and 'On Naïve and Sentimental Poetry' (which is partly based on Kant's distinction of the beautiful and the sublime.   The truth of the matter is obviously that Coleridge, Schiller, and Richter were all indebted to Kant's definition of the sublime.   When we know that Coleridge had read the *Critique of the Judgment*, we need not speculate whether he had also read Richter's *Vorschule der Aesthetik*.   Both writers were simply rephrasing Kant in a more popular manner.   Cf. Kant's *Critique of Aesthetic Judgement* (ed. Meredith, Oxford, 1911), p. 90.   'The beautiful in nature is a question of the form of the object, and this consists in limitation, whereas the sublime is to be found in an object even devoid of form, so far as it immediately involves, or else by its presence provokes, a representation of *limitlessness*, yet with a super-added thought of its totality.'   Cf. also p. 94, etc. (on the necessity of 'mental movement' in the sublime), with Coleridge's demand for 'a strong working of the mind' in 'the grandest efforts of poetry.'

speech is generally produced by a mixture of anger and contempt, and punning is a natural mode of expressing them.

It is my intention to pass over none of the important so-called conceits of Shakespeare, not a few of which are introduced into his later productions, with great propriety and effect. We are not to forget, that at the time he lived there was an attempt at, and an affectation of, quaintness and adornment, which emanated from the Court, and against which satire was directed by Shakespeare in the character of Osrick in Hamlet. Among the schoolmen of that age, and earlier, nothing was more common than the use of conceits: it began with the revival of letters, and the bias thus given was very generally felt and acknowledged.

I have in my possession a dictionary of phrases, in which the epithets applied to love, hate, jealousy, and such abstract terms, are arranged; and they consist almost entirely of words taken from Seneca and his imitators, or from the schoolmen, showing perpetual antithesis, and describing the passions by the conjunction and combination of things absolutely irreconcileable. In treating the matter thus, I am aware that I am only palliating the practice in Shakespeare: he ought to have had nothing to do with merely temporary peculiarities: he wrote not for his own only, but for all ages, and so far I admit the use of some of his conceits to be a defect. They detract sometimes from his universality as to time, person, and situation.

If we were able to discover, and to point out the peculiar faults, as well as the peculiar beauties of Shakespeare, it would materially assist us in deciding what authority ought to be attached to certain portions of what are generally called his works. If we met with a play, or certain scenes of a play, in which we could trace neither his defects nor his excellences, we should have the strongest reason for believing that he had had no hand in it. In the case of scenes so circumstanced we might come to the conclusion that they were taken from the older plays, which, in some instances, he reformed or altered, or that they were inserted afterwards by some underhand, in order to please the mob. If a drama by Shakespeare turned out to be too heavy for popular audiences, the clown might be called in to lighten the representation; and if it appeared that what was added was not in Shakespeare's manner, the conclusion would be inevitable, that it was not from Shakespeare's pen.

It remains for me to speak of the hero and heroine, of Romeo and Juliet themselves; and I shall do so with unaffected diffidence, not merely on account of the delicacy, but of the great importance of the subject.   I feel that it is impossible to defend Shakespeare from the most cruel of all charges,—that he is an immoral writer—without entering fully into his mode of pourtraying female characters, and of displaying the passion of love. It seems to me, that he has done both with greater perfection than any other writer of the known world, perhaps with the single exception of Milton in his delineation of Eve.

When I have heard it said, or seen it stated, that Shakespeare wrote for man, but the gentle Fletcher for woman,[1] it has always ‘n me something like acute pain, because to me it seems to do ‘st injustice to Shakespeare: when, too, I remember ‘ch character is formed by what we read, I cannot look ‘ as a light question, to be passed over as a mere amuse-like a game of cards or chess.   I never have been able to down my mind to think poetry a sport, or an occupation for hours.

Perhaps there is no more sure criterion of refinement in moral character, of the purity of intellectual intention, and of the deep conviction and perfect sense of what our own nature really is in all its combinations, than the different definitions different men would give of love.   I will not detain you by stating the various known definitions, some of which it may be better not to repeat: I will rather give you one of my own, which, I apprehend, is equally free from the extravagance of pretended Platonism (which, like other things which super-moralize, is sure to demoralize) and from its grosser opposite.

Consider myself and my fellow-men as a sort of link between heaven and earth, being composed of body and soul, with power to reason and to will, and with that perpetual aspiration which tells us that this is ours for a while, but it is not ourselves; considering man, I say, in this two-fold character, yet united in one person, I conceive that there can be no correct definition of love which does not correspond with our being, and with that subordination of one part to another which constitutes our perfection. I would say therefore that—

‘ Love is a desire of the whole being to be united to some thing, or some being, felt necessary to its completeness, by the most perfect means that nature permits, and reason dictates.’ [2]

It is inevitable to every noble mind, whether man or woman, to feel itself, of itself, imperfect and insufficient, not as an animal only, but as a moral being.   How wonderfully, then, has

---

[1] Cf. i. 119; ii. 93–4.
[2] This Platonic definition of love derives directly from the *Symposium*.

Providence contrived for us, by making that which is necessary to us a step in our exaltation to a higher and nobler state! The Creator has ordained that one should possess qualities which the other has not, and the union of both is the most complete ideal of human character. In everything the blending of the similar with the dissimilar is the secret of all pure delight. Who shall dare to stand alone, and vaunt himself, in himself, sufficient? In poetry it is the blending of passion with order that constitutes perfection: this is still more the case in morals, and more than all in the exclusive attachment of the sexes.

True it is, that the world and its business may be carried on without marriage; but it is so evident that Providence intended man (the only animal of all climates, and whose reason is pre-eminent over instinct) to be the master of the world, that marriage, or the knitting together of society by the tenderest, yet firmest ties, seems ordained to render him capable of maintaining his superiority over the brute creation. Man alone has been privileged to clothe himself, and to do all things so as to make him, as it were, a secondary creator of himself, and of his own happiness or misery: in this, as in all, the image of the Deity is impressed upon him.

Providence, then, has not left us to prudence only; for the power of calculation, which prudence implies, cannot have existed, but in a state which pre-supposes marriage. If God has done this, shall we suppose that he has given us no moral sense, no yearning, which is something more than animal, to secure that, without which man might form a herd, but could not be a society? The very idea seems to breathe absurdity.

From this union arise the paternal, filial, brotherly and sisterly relations of life; and every state is but a family magnified. All the operations of mind, in short, all that distinguishes us from brutes, originate in the more perfect state of domestic life.— One infallible criterion in forming an opinion of a man is the reverence in which he holds women. Plato has said, that in this way we rise from sensuality to affection, from affection to love, and from love to the pure intellectual delight by which we become worthy to conceive that infinite in ourselves, without which it is impossible for man to believe in a God. In a word, the grandest and most delightful of all promises has been expressed to us by this practical state—our marriage with the Redeemer of mankind.

I might safely appeal to every man who hears me, who in youth has been accustomed to abandon himself to his animal passions, whether when he first really fell in love, the earliest symptom was not a complete change in his manners, a contempt and a hatred of himself for having excused his conduct by asserting, that he acted according to the dictates of nature, that his vices were the inevitable consequences of youth, and that his passions at that period of life could not be conquered?   The surest friend of chastity is love: it leads us, not to sink the mind in the body, but to draw up the body to the mind—the immortal part of our nature.   See how contrasted in this respect are some portions of the works of writers, whom I need not name, with other portions of the same works: the ebullitions of comic humour have at times, by a lamentable confusion, been made the means of debasing our nature, while at other times, even in the same volume, we are happy to notice the utmost purity, such as the purity of love, which above all other qualities renders us most pure and lovely.

Love is not, like hunger, a mere selfish appetite: it is an associative quality.   The hungry savage is nothing but an animal, thinking only of the satisfaction of his stomach: what is the first effect of love, but to associate the feeling with every object in nature? the trees whisper, the roses exhale their per-fumes, the nightingales sing, nay the very skies smile in unison with the feeling of true and pure love.   It gives to every object in nature a power of the heart, without which it would indeed be spiritless.

Shakespeare has described this passion in various states and stages, beginning, as was most natural, with love in the young. Does he open his play by making Romeo and Juliet in love at first sight—at the first glimpse, as any ordinary thinker would do?   Certainly not: he knew what he was about, and how he was to accomplish what he was about: he was to develope the whole passion, and he commences with the first elements—that sense of imperfection, that yearning to combine itself with something lovely.   Romeo became enamoured of the idea he had formed in his own mind, and then, as it were, christened the first real being of the contrary sex as endowed with the perfections he desired. He appears to be in love with Rosaline; but, in truth, he is in love only with his own idea.   He felt that necessity of being beloved which no noble mind can be without.   Then our poet, our poet who so well knew human nature, introduces Romeo to Juliet, and makes it not only a violent, but a permanent love—a point for which Shakespeare has been ridiculed by the ignorant and unthinking.   Romeo is first represented in a state most susceptible of love, and then, seeing Juliet, he took and retained the infection.[1]

This brings me to observe upon a characteristic of Shakespeare, which belongs to a man of profound thought and high genius. It has been too much the custom, when anything that happened in his dramas could not easily be explained by the few words the poet has employed, to pass it idly over, and to say that it is beyond our reach, and beyond the power of philosophy—a sort of terra incognita for discoverers—a great ocean to be hereafter explored. Others have treated such passages as hints and glimpses of something now non-existent, as the sacred fragments of an ancient and ruined temple, all the portions of which are beautiful, although their particular relation to each other is unknown. Shakespeare knew the human mind, and its most minute and intimate workings, and he never introduces a word, or a thought, in vain or out of place: if we do not understand him, it is our own fault or the fault of copyists and typographers; but study, and the possession of some small stock of the knowledge by which he worked, will enable us often to detect and explain his meaning. He never wrote at random, or hit upon points of character and conduct by chance; and the smallest fragment of his mind not unfrequently gives a clue to a most perfect, regular, and consistent whole.

As I may not have another opportunity, the introduction of Friar Laurence into this tragedy enables me to remark upon the different manner in which Shakespeare has treated the priestly character, as compared with other writers. In Beaumont and Fletcher priests are represented as a vulgar mockery; and, as in others of their dramatic personages, the errors of a few are mistaken for the demeanour of the many: but in Shakespeare they always carry with them our love and respect. He made no injurious abstracts: he took no copies from the worst parts of our nature; and, like the rest, his characters of priests are truly drawn from the general body.[2]

It may strike some as singular, that throughout all his productions he has never introduced the passion of avarice. The truth is, that it belongs only to particular parts of our nature, and is prevalent only in particular states of society; hence it could not, and cannot, be permanent. The Miser of Molière and Plautus

---

[1] Cf. i. 6; ii. 118–19, for the same idea, differently developed. The note on i. 6 discusses the possibility of indebtedness to Schlegel, who makes the same comment (*Werke*, vii. 77–8).

[2] Cf. i. 8, 122, 203, 205, 206.

is now looked upon as a species of madman, and avarice as a species of madness. Elwes, of whom everybody has heard, was an individual influenced by an insane condition of mind; but, as a passion, avarice has disappeared. How admirably, then, did Shakespeare foresee, that if he drew such a character it could not be permanent! he drew characters which would always be natural, and therefore permanent, inasmuch as they were not dependent upon accidental circumstances.

There is not one of the plays of Shakespeare that is built upon anything but the best and surest foundation; the characters must be permanent—permanent while men continue men,—because they stand upon what is absolutely necessary to our existence. This cannot be said even of some of the most famous authors of antiquity. Take the capital tragedies of Orestes, or of the husband of Jocasta: great as was the genius of the writers, these dramas have an obvious fault, and the fault lies at the very root of the action. In Œdipus a man is represented oppressed by fate for a crime of which he was not morally guilty; and while we read we are obliged to say to ourselves, that in those days they considered actions without reference to the real guilt of the persons.

There is no character in Shakespeare in which envy is pourtrayed, with one solitary exception—Cassius, in 'Julius Cæsar'; yet even there the vice is not hateful, inasmuch as it is counterbalanced by a number of excellent qualities and virtues. The poet leads the reader to suppose that it is rather something constitutional, something derived from his parents, something that he cannot avoid, and not something that he has himself acquired; thus throwing the blame from the will of man to some inevitable circumstance, and leading us to suppose that it is hardly to be looked upon as one of those passions that actually debase the mind.

Whenever love is described as of a serious nature, and much more when it is to lead to a tragical result, it depends upon a law of the mind, which, I believe, I shall hereafter be able to make intelligible, and which would not only justify Shakespeare, but show an analogy to all his other characters.

THE EIGHTH LECTURE

[*Collier Report.*]

IT is impossible to pay a higher compliment to poetry, than to consider the effects it produces in common with religion, yet distinct (as far as distinction can be, where there is no division) in those qualities which religion exercises and diffuses over all mankind, as far as they are subject to its influence.

I have often thought that religion (speaking of it only as it accords with poetry, without reference to its more serious impressions) is the poetry of mankind, both having for their objects:—

1. To generalise our notions; to prevent men from confining their attention solely, or chiefly, to their own narrow sphere of action, and to their own individual circumstances. By placing them in certain awful relations it merges the individual man in the whole species, and makes it impossible for any one man to think of his future lot, or indeed of his present condition, without at the same time comprising in his view his fellow-creatures.

2. That both poetry and religion throw the object of deepest interest to a distance from us, and thereby not only aid our imagination, but in a most important manner subserve the interest of our virtues; for that man is indeed a slave, who is a slave to his own senses, and whose mind and imagination cannot carry him beyond the distance which his hand can touch, or even his eye can reach.[1]

3. The grandest point of resemblance between them is, that both have for their object (I hardly know whether the English language supplies an appropriate word) the perfecting, and the pointing out to us the indefinite improvement of our nature, and fixing our attention upon that. They bid us, while we are sitting in the dark at our little fire, look at the mountain-tops, struggling with darkness, and announcing that light which shall be common to all, in which individual interests shall resolve into one common good, and every man shall find in his fellow man more than a brother.

Such being the case, we need not wonder that it has pleased Providence, that the divine truths of religion should have been

---

[1] Cf. Schiller's essay on 'The Moral Utility of Aesthetic Manners' for an interesting parallel, which is not close enough to suggest an influence.

revealed to us in the form of poetry; and that at all times poets, not the slaves of any particular sectarian opinions, should have joined to support all those delicate sentiments of the heart (often when they were most opposed to the reigning philosophy of the day) which may be called the feeding streams of religion.

I have heard it said that an undevout astronomer is mad. In the strict sense of the word, every being capable of understanding must be mad, who remains, as it were, fixed in the ground on which he treads—who, gifted with the divine faculties of indefinite hope and fear, born with them, yet settles his faith upon that, in which neither hope nor fear has any proper field for display. Much more truly, however, might it be said that, an undevout poet is mad: in the strict sense of the word, an undevout poet is an impossibility. I have heard of verse-makers (poets they are not, and never can be) who introduced into their works such questions as these:—Whether the world was made of atoms?—Whether there is a universe?—Whether there is a governing mind that supports it? As I have said, verse-makers are not poets: the poet is one who carries the simplicity of childhood into the powers of manhood; who, with a soul unsubdued by habit, unshackled by custom, contemplates all things with the freshness and the wonder of a child; and, connecting with it the inquisitive powers of riper years, adds, as far as he can find knowledge, admiration; and, where knowledge no longer permits admiration, gladly sinks back again into the childlike feeling of devout wonder.[1]

The poet is not only the man made to solve the riddle of the universe, but he is also the man who feels where it is not solved. What is old and worn-out, not in itself, but from the dimness of the intellectual eye, produced by worldly passions and pursuits, he makes new: he pours upon it the dew that glistens, and blows round it the breeze that cooled us in our infancy. I hope, therefore, that if in this single lecture I make some demand on the attention of my hearers to a most important subject, upon which depends all sense of the worthiness or unworthiness of our nature, I shall obtain their pardon. If I afford them less amusement, I trust that their own reflections upon a few thoughts will be found to repay them.

I have been led to these observations by the tragedy of 'Romeo

---

[1] I am inclined to believe that Coleridge is echoing Schiller in this passage on the childlike simplicity of genius ('Naïve and Sentimental Poetry,' Schiller's *Essays* (Bohn), p. 272). The development of the idea is, however entirely Coleridge's own.

and Juliet,' and by some, perhaps, indiscreet expressions, certainly not well chosen, concerning falling in love at first sight. I have taken one of Shakespeare's earliest works, as I consider it, in order to show that he, of all his contemporaries (Sir Philip Sidney alone excepted), entertained a just conception of the female character. Unquestionably, that gentleman of Europe— that all-accomplished man, and our beloved Shakespeare, we the only writers of that age, who pitched their ideas of fe perfection according to the best researches of philosophy pared with all who followed them, they stand as mighty tains, the islands of a deluge, which has swallowed all the the flood of oblivion.[1]

I certainly do not mean, as a general maxim, to ju: foolish a thing as what goes by the name of love at firs but, to express myself more accurately, I should say tha. .here is, and has always existed, a deep emotion of the mind, which might be called love momentaneous—not love at first sight, nor known by the subject of it to be or to have been such, but after many years of experience.[2]

I have to defend the existence of love, as a passion in itself fit and appropriate to human nature;—I say fit for human nature, and not only so, but peculiar to it, unshared either in degree or kind by any of our fellow creatures: it is a passion which it is impossible for any creature to feel, but a being endowed with reason, with the moral sense, and with the strong yearnings, which, like all other powerful effects in nature, prophesy some future effect.

If I were to address myself to the materialist, with reference to the human kind, and (admitting the three great laws common to all beings,—1, the law of self-preservation; 2, that of continuing the race; and 3, the care of the offspring till protection is no longer needed),—were to ask him, whether he thought any motives of prudence or duty enforced the simple necessity of

---

[1] I remember, in conversing on this very point at a subsequent period,— I cannot fix the date,—Coleridge made a willing exception in favour of Spenser; but he added that the notions of the author of the 'Faery Queen' were often so romantic and heightened by fancy, that he could not look upon Spenser's females as creatures of our world; whereas the ladies of Shakespeare and Sidney were flesh and blood, with their very defects and qualifications giving evidence of their humanity: hence the lively interest taken regarding them.—J. P. C.

[2] Coleridge here made a reference to, and cited a passage from, Hooker's 'Ecclesiastical Polity'; but my note contains only a hint regarding it; and the probability is, that I did not insert more of it, because I thought I should be able, at some future time, to procure the exact words, or a reference to them, from the Lecturer. Whether I did so or not I cannot remember, but I find no trace of anything of the kind.—J. P. C.

preserving the race? or whether, after a course of serious reflection, he came to the conclusion, that it would be better to have a
posterity, from a sense of duty impelling us to seek that as our
object?—if, I say, I were to ask a materialist, whether such was
the real cause of the preservation of the species, he would laugh
me to scorn; he would say that nature was too wise to trust any
of her great designs to the mere cold calculations of fallible
mortality.

Then the question comes to a short crisis:—Is, or is not, our
moral nature a part of the end of Providence? or are we, or are
we not, beings meant for society?   Is that society, or is it not,
meant to be progressive?   I trust that none of my auditors
would endure the putting of the question—Whether, independently of the progression of the race, every individual has it not
in his power to be indefinitely progressive?—for, without
marriage, without exclusive attachment, there could be no
human society; herds, as I said, there might be, but society
there could not be: there could be none of that delightful inter-
course between father and child; none of the sacred affections;
none of the charities of humanity; none of all those many and
complex causes, which have raised us to the state we have already
reached, could possibly have existence.   All these effects are not
found among the brutes; neither are they found among savages,
whom strange accidents have sunk below the class of human
beings, insomuch that a stop seems actually to have been put to
their progressiveness.

We may, therefore, safely conclude that there is placed within
us some element, if I may so say, of our nature—something
which is as peculiar to our moral nature, as any other part can be
conceived to be, name it what you will,—name it, I will say for
illustration, devotion,—name it friendship, or a sense of duty;
but something there is, peculiar to our nature, which answers the
moral end; as we find everywhere in the ends of the moral world,
that there are proportionate material and bodily means of accom-
plishing them.

We are born, and it is our nature and lot to be composed of
body and mind; but when our heart leaps up on hearing of the
victories of our country, or of the rescue of the virtuous, but
unhappy, from the hands of an oppressor; when a parent is
transported at the restoration of a beloved child from deadly
sickness; when the pulse is quickened, from any of these or other
causes, do we therefore say, because the body interprets the
emotions of the mind and sympathises with them, asserting its

claim to participation, that joy is not mental, or that it is not moral? Do we assert, that it was owing merely to fulness of blood that the heart throbbed, and the pulse played? Do we not rather say, that the regent, the mind, being glad, its slave, its willing slave, the body, responded to it, and obeyed the impulse? If we are possessed with a feeling of having done a wrong, or of having had a wrong done to us, and it excites the blush of shame or the glow of anger, do we pretend to say that, by some accident, the blood suffused itself into veins unusually small, and therefore that the guilty seemed to evince shame, or the injured indignation? In these things we scorn such instruction; and shall it be deemed a sufficient excuse for the materialist to degrade that passion, on which not only many of our virtues depend, but upon which the whole frame, the whole structure of human society rests? Shall we pardon him this debasement of love, because our body has been united to mind by Providence, in order, not to reduce the high to the level of the low, but to elevate the low to the level of the high? We should be guilty of nothing less than an act of moral suicide, if we consented to degrade that which on every account is most noble, by merging it in what is most derogatory: as if an angel were to hold out to us the welcoming hand of brotherhood, and we turned away from it, to wallow, as it were, with the hog in the mire.

One of the most lofty and intellectual of the poets of the time of Shakespeare has described this degradation most wonderfully, where he speaks of a man, who, having been converted by the witchery of worldly pleasure and passion, into a hog, on being restored to his human shape still preferred his bestial condition:—

> 'But one, above the rest in special,
>   That had a hog been late, hight Grill by name,
>   Repined greatly, and did him miscall,
> That from *a* a hoggish form him brought to natural.

> ' Said Guyon, See the mind of beastly man!
>   That hath so soon forgot the excellence
>   Of his creation, when he life began,
>   That now he chooseth, with vile difference,
>   To be a beast and lack intelligence.
>   To whom the Palmer thus:—The dunghill kind
>   Delights in filth and foul incontinence:
>   Let Grill be Grill, and have his hoggish mind;
> But let us hence depart, whilst weather serves and wind.'

Fairy Queen, Book II., c. 12.

a Read 'that had from.'

The first feeling that would strike a reflecting mind, wishing to see mankind not only in an amiable but in a just light, would be that beautiful feeling in the moral world, the brotherly and sisterly affections,—the existence of strong affection greatly modified by the difference of sex; made more tender, more graceful, more soothing and conciliatory by the circumstance of difference, yet still remaining perfectly pure, perfectly spiritual. How glorious, we may say, would be the effect, if the instances were rare; but how much more glorious, when they are so frequent as to be only not universal.   This species of affection is the object of religious veneration with all those who love their fellow men, or who know themselves.

The power of education over the human mind is herein exemplified, and data for hope are afforded of yet unrealized excellences, perhaps dormant in our nature.   When we see so divine a moral effect spread through all classes, what may we not hope of other excellences, of unknown quality, still to be developed?

By dividing the sisterly and fraternal affections from the conjugal, we have, in truth, two loves, each of them as strong as any affection can be, or ought to be, consistently with the performance of our duty, and the love we should bear to our neighbour.   Then, by the former preceding the latter, the latter is rendered more pure, more even, and more constant: the wife has already learned the discipline of pure love in the character of a sister.   By the discipline of private life she has already learned how to yield, how to influence, how to command.   To all this are to be added the beautiful gradations of attachment which distinguish human nature;—from sister to wife, from wife to child, to uncle, to cousin, to one of our kin, to one of our blood, to our near neighbour, to our county-man, and to our country-man.

The bad results of a want of this variety of orders, of this graceful subordination in the character of attachment, I have often observed in Italy in particular, as well as in other countries, where the young are kept secluded, not only from their neighbours, but from their own families—all closely imprisoned, until the hour when they are necessarily let out of their cages, without having had the opportunity of learning to fly—without experience, restrained by no kindly feeling, and detesting the control which so long kept them from enjoying the full hubbub of licence.

The question is, How have nature and Providence secured

these blessings to us?   In this way:—that in general the affections become those which urge us to leave the paternal nest.
We arrive at a definite time of life, and feel passions that invite us
to enter into the world; and this new feeling assuredly coalesces
with a new object.   Suppose we are under the influence of a
vivid feeling that is new to us: that feeling will more firmly combine with an external object, which is likewise vivid from
novelty, than with one that is familiar.

To this may be added the aversion, which seems to have acted
very strongly in rude ages, concerning anything common to us
and to the animal creation.   That which is done by beasts man
feels a natural repugnance to imitate.   The desire to extend the
bond of relationship, in families which had emigrated from the
patriarchial seed, would likewise have its influence.

All these circumstances would render the marriage of brother
and sister unfrequent, and in simple ages an ominous feeling to
the contrary might easily prevail.   Some tradition might aid the
objections to such a union; and, for aught we know, some law
might be preserved in the Temple of Isis, and from thence
obtained by the patriarchs, which would augment the horror
attached to such connexions.   This horror once felt, and soon
propagated, the present state of feeling on the subject can easily
be explained.

Children begin as early to talk of marriage as of death, from
attending a wedding, or following a funeral: a new young visitor
is introduced into the family, and from association they soon
think of the conjugal bond.   If a boy tell his parent that he
wishes to marry his sister, he is instantly checked by a stern look,
and he is shewn the impossibility of such a union.   The con-
trolling glance of the parental eye is often more effectual, than
any form of words that could be employed; and in mature years
a mere look often prevails where exhortation would have failed.
As to infants, they are told, without any reason assigned, that it
could not be so; and perhaps the best security for moral rectitude
arises from a supposed necessity.   Ignorant persons recoil from
the thought of doing anything that has not been done, and
because they have always been informed that it must not be done.

The individual has by this time learned the greatest and best
lesson of the human mind—that in ourselves we are imperfect;
and another truth, of the next, if not of equal, importance—that
there exists a possibility of uniting two beings, each identified in
their nature, but distinguished in their separate qualities, so that
each should retain what distinguishes them, and at the same time

each acquire the qualities of that being which is contradistinguished.   This is perhaps the most beautiful part of our nature:
the man loses not his manly character: he does not become less
brave or less resolved to go through fire and water, if necessary,
for the object of his affections: rather say, that he becomes far
more brave and resolute.   He then feels the beginnings of his
moral nature: he then is sensible of its imperfection, and of its
perfectibility.   All the grand and sublime thoughts of an
improved state of being then dawn upon him: he can acquire the
patience of woman, which in him is fortitude: the beauty and
susceptibility of the female character in him becomes a desire to
display all that is noble and dignified.   In short, the only true
resemblance to a couple thus united is the pure blue sky of
heaven: the female unites the beautiful with the sublime, and the
male the sublime with the beautiful.

Throughout the whole of his plays Shakespeare has evidently
looked at the subject of love in this dignified light: he has conceived it not only with moral grandeur, but with philosophical
penetration.   The mind of man searches for something which
shall add to his perfection—which shall assist him; and he also
yearns to lend his aid in completing the moral nature of another.
Thoughts like these will occupy many of his serious moments:
imagination will accumulate on imagination, until at last some
object attracts his attention, and to this object the whole weight
and impulse of his feelings will be directed.

Who shall say this is not love?   Here is system, but it is
founded upon nature: here are associations; here are strong
feelings, natural to us as men, and they are directed and finally
attached to one object:—who shall say this is not love?   Assuredly not the being who is the subject of these sensations.—If
it be not love, it is only known that it is not by Him who knows
all things.   Shakespeare has therefore described Romeo as in
love in the first instance with Rosaline, and so completely does
he fancy himself in love that he declares, before he has seen
Juliet,

> 'When the devout religion of mine eye
>   Maintains such falsehood, then turn tears to fires;
> And these, who, often drown'd, could never die,
>   Transparent heretics, be burnt for liars.
> One fairer than my love? the all-seeing sun
> Ne'er saw her match since first the world begun.'
>   *Act I., Scene ii.*[a]

[a] Collier, 'Scene i.'

This is in answer to Benvolio, who has asked Romeo to compare the supposed beauty of Rosaline with the actual beauty of other ladies; and in this full feeling of confidence Romeo is brought to Capulet's, as it were by accident: he sees Juliet, instantly becomes the heretic he has just before declared impossible, and then commences that completeness of attachment which forms the whole subject of the tragedy.[1]

Surely Shakespeare, the poet, the philosopher, who combined truth with beauty and beauty with truth, never dreamed that he could interest his auditory in favour of Romeo, by representing him as a mere weathercock, blown round by every woman's breath; who, having seen one, became the victim of melancholy, eating his own heart, concentrating all his hopes and fears in her, and yet, in an instant, changing, and falling madly in love with another. Shakespeare must have meant something more than this, for this was the way to make people despise, instead of admiring his hero. Romeo tells us what was Shakespeare's purpose: he shows us that he had looked at Rosaline with a different feeling from that with which he had looked at Juliet. Rosaline was the object to which his over-full heart had attached itself in the first instance: our imperfect nature, in proportion as our ideas are vivid, seeks after something in which those ideas may be realised.

So with the indiscreet friendships sometimes formed by men of genius: they are conscious of their own weakness, and are ready to believe others stronger than themselves, when, in truth, they are weaker: they have formed an ideal in their own minds, and they want to see it realised; they require more than shadowy thought. Their own sense of imperfection makes it impossible for them to fasten their attachment upon themselves, and hence the humility of men of true genius: in, perhaps, the first man they meet, they only see what is good; they have no sense of his deficiencies, and their friendship becomes so strong, that they almost fall down and worship one in every respect greatly their inferior.

What is true of friendship is true of love, with a person of ardent feelings and warm imagination. What took place in the mind of Romeo was merely natural; it is accordant with every day's experience. Amid such various events, such shifting scenes, such changing personages, we are often mistaken, and discover that he or she was not what we hoped and expected;

[1] For similar remarks cf. i. 6; ii. 108.

we find that the individual first chosen will not complete our imperfection; we may have suffered unnecessary pangs, and have indulged idly-directed hopes, and then a being may arise before us, who has more resemblance to the ideal we have formed.   We know that we loved the earlier object with ardour and purity, but it was not what we feel for the later object. Our own mind tells us, that in the first instance we merely yearned after an object, but in the last instance we know that we have found that object, and that it corresponds with the idea we had previously formed.[1]

[1] Here my original notes abruptly break off: the brochure in which I had inserted them was full, and I took another for the conclusion of the Lecture, which is unfortunately lost.—[J. P .C.]

THE NINTH LECTURE [1]

[Collier Report.]

It is a known but unexplained phenomenon, that among the ancients statuary rose to such a degree of perfection, as almost to baffle the hope of imitating it, and to render the chance of excelling it absolutely impossible; yet painting, at the same period, notwithstanding the admiration bestowed upon it by Pliny and others, has been proved to be an art of much later growth, as it was also of far inferior quality. I remember a man of high rank, equally admirable for his talents and his taste, pointing to a common sign-post, and saying that had Titian never lived, the richness of representation by colour, even there, would never have been attained. In that mechanical branch of painting, perspective, it has been shown that the Romans were very deficient. The excavations and consequent discoveries, at Herculaneum and elsewhere, prove the Roman artists to have been guilty of such blunders, as to give plausibility to the assertions of those, who maintain that the ancients were wholly ignorant of perspective. However, that they knew something of it is established by Vitruvius in the introduction to his second book.

Something of the same kind, as I endeavoured to explain in a previous lecture, was the case with the drama of the ancients, which has been imitated by the French, Italians, and by various writers in England since the Restoration. All that is there represented seems to be, as it were, upon one flat surface: the theme,[2] if we may so call it in reference to music, admits of nothing more than the change of a single note, and excludes that which is the true principle of life—the attaining of the same result by an infinite variety of means.

The plays of Shakespeare are in no respect imitations of the

---

[1] By the time of this lecture, 16 December, Coleridge seems to have built up a considerable reputation for his lectures, if one can rely upon Byron's testimony: 'To-morrow I dine with Rogers, and am to hear Coleridge, who is a kind of rage at present.' (Byron's *Letters and Journals*, ii. 90.)

[2] Here occurs another evident mistake of mine, in my original shorthand note, in consequence of mishearing: I hastily wrote *scheme*, instead of 'theme,' which last must have been the word of the Lecturer.—[J. P. C.]

Greeks: they may be called analogies, because by very different means they arrive at the same end; whereas the French and Italian tragedies I have read, and the English ones on the same model, are mere copies, though they cannot be called likenesses, seeking the same effect by adopting the same means, but under most inappropriate and adverse circumstances.

I have thus been led to consider, that the ancient drama (meaning the works of Æschylus, Euripides, and Sophocles, for the rhetorical productions of the same class by the Romans are scarcely to be treated as original theatrical poems) might be contrasted with the Shakespearian drama.—I call it the Shakespearian drama to distinguish it, because I know of no other writer who has realized the same idea, although I am told by some,[1] that the Spanish poets, Lopez de Vega and Calderon, have been equally successful. The Shakespearean drama and the Greek drama may be compared to statuary and painting. In statuary, as in the Greek drama, the characters must be few, because the very essence of statuary is a high degree of abstraction, which prevents a great many figures being combined in the same effect. In a grand group of Niobe, or in any other ancient heroic subject, how disgusting even it would appear, if an old nurse were introduced. Not only the number of figures must be circumscribed, but nothing undignified must be placed in company with what is dignified: no one personage must be brought in that is not an abstraction: all the actors in the scene must not be presented at once to the eye; and the effect of multitude, if required, must be produced without the intermingling of anything discordant.

Compare this small group with a picture by Raphael or Titian, in which an immense number of figures may be introduced, a beggar, a cripple, a dog, or a cat; and by a less degree of labour, and a less degree of abstraction, an effect is produced equally harmonious to the mind, more true to nature with its varied colours, and, in all respects but one, superior to statuary. The man of taste feels satisfied, and to that which the reason conceives possible, a momentary reality is given by the aid of imagination.[2]

[1] Schlegel, *Werke*, vi. 158–60.

[2] In this comparison of ancient drama with sculpture and romantic drama with painting, Coleridge is developing in his own words ideas from Schlegel (*Werke*, v. 9–10, vi. 32–3, 161–3). There can be little doubt of his immediate source, but Coleridge probably knew of these ideas before, so far as they appear in Schiller's essay 'On Naïve and Sentimental Poetry.' See Schiller's *Essays* (Bohn ed., 1875), p. 288, and the Introduction to the present edition of Coleridge's criticism, vol. i, pp. xxiii–xxiv. (Cf. also i. 196.)

I need not here repeat what I have said before, regarding the circumstances which permitted Shakespeare to make an alteration, not merely so suitable to the age in which he lived, but, in fact, so necessitated by the condition of that age. I need not again remind you of the difference I pointed out between imitation and likeness, in reference to the attempt to give reality to representations on the stage. The distinction between imitation and likeness depends upon the admixture of circumstances of dissimilarity; an imitation is not a copy, precisely as likeness is not sameness, in that sense of the word 'likeness' which implies difference conjoined with sameness. Shakespeare reflected manners in his plays, not by a cold formal copy, but by an imitation; that is to say, by an admixture of circumstances, not absolutely true in themselves, but true to the character and to the time represented.[1]

It is fair to own that he had many advantages. The great of that day, instead of surrounding themselves by the *chevaux de frise* of what is now called high breeding, endeavoured to distinguish themselves by attainments, by energy of thought, and consequent powers of mind. The stage, indeed, had nothing but curtains for its scenes, but this fact compelled the actor, as well as the author, to appeal to the imaginations, and not to the senses of the audience: thus was obtained a power over space and time, which in an ancient theatre would have been absurd, because it would have been contradictory. The advantage is vastly in favour of our own early stage: the dramatic poet there relies upon the imagination, upon the reason, and upon the noblest powers of the human heart; he shakes off the iron bondage of space and time; he appeals to that which we most wish to be, when we are most worthy of being, while the ancient dramatist binds us down to the meanest part of our nature, and the chief compensation is a simple acquiescence of the mind in the position, that what is represented might possibly have occurred in the time and place required by the unities. It is a poor compliment to a poet to tell him, that he has only the qualifications of a historian.[2]

In dramatic composition the observation of the unities of

---

[1] Cf. i. 177, note.
[2] In the latter half of this paragraph Coleridge is again developing in his own words ideas borrowed from Schlegel and Schiller. The unfortunate condescension toward Greek drama is evidence that Coleridge is borrowing directly from Schlegel, not from Schiller, even if we did not know that Coleridge had recently read Schlegel's lectures. Schlegel, *Werke*, v. 9–17; Schiller, *Essays* (Bohn), pp. 284–9.

time and place so narrows the period of action, so impoverishes
the sources of pleasure, that of all the Athenian dramas there is
scarcely one in which the absurdity is not glaring, of aiming at an
object, and utterly failing in the attainment of it: events are sometimes brought into a space in which it is impossible for them to
have occurred, and in this way the grandest effort of the dramatist,
that of making his play the mirror of life, is entirely defeated.[1]

The limit allowed by the rules of the Greek stage was twenty-
four hours; but, inasmuch as, even in this case, time must have
become a subject of imagination, it was just as reasonable to
allow twenty-four months, or even years.   The mind is acted
upon by such strong stimulants, that the period is indifferent;
and when once the boundary of possibility is passed, no restric-
tion can be assigned.[2]   In reading Shakespeare, we should first
consider in which of his plays he means to appeal to the reason,
and in which to the imagination, faculties which have no relation
to time and place, excepting as in the one case they imply a
succession of cause and effect, and in the other form a harmonious picture, so that the impulse given by the reason is
carried on by the imagination.

We have often heard Shakespeare spoken of as a child of
nature, and some of his modern imitators, without the genius
to copy nature, by resorting to real incidents, and treating them
in a certain way, have produced that stage-phenomenon which is
neither tragic nor comic, nor tragi-comic, nor comi-tragic, but
sentimental.   This sort of writing depends upon some very
affecting circumstances, and in its greatest excellence aspires no
higher than the genius of an onion,—the power of drawing tears;
while the author, acting the part of a ventriloquist, distributes
his own insipidity among the characters, if characters they can
be called, which have no marked and distinguishing features.   I
have seen dramas of this sort, some translated and some the
growth of our own soil, so well acted, and so ill written, that if I
could have been made for the time artificially deaf, I should have

---

[1] This new aggressiveness of tone is perhaps an instance of the general
encouraging and confirmatory influence of Schlegel's criticism upon Coleridge's.   But if external evidence proved that Coleridge had any acquaintance
with the English critics, Webb and Kames, this passage might well be taken
as an echo of their attacks upon the unities.   See Introduction, i. xvi–xviii.
[2] This argument appears in Schlegel's lectures (*Werke*, vi. 24), but also in
Howard's Preface to *The Duke of Lerma*, Farquhar's *Discourse upon Comedy*,
the anonymous essay called *Some Remarks on the Tragedy of Hamlet*, Dr
Johnson's essay in *The Rambler* (No. 156), Dr Johnson's Preface to Shakespeare, etc.   Even though Coleridge had just been reading Schlegel, there is
no necessity to speak of influences in regard to so old a theme.

been pleased with that performance as a pantomime, which was intolerable as a play.

Shakespeare's characters, from Othello and Macbeth down to Dogberry and the Grave-digger, may be termed ideal realities. They are not the things themselves, so much as abstracts of the things, which a great mind takes into itself, and there naturalizes them to its own conception. Take Dogberry: are no important truths there conveyed, no admirable lessons taught, and no valuable allusions made to reigning follies, which the poet saw must for ever reign? He is not the creature of the day, to disappear with the day, but the representative and abstract of truth which must ever be true, and of humour which must ever be humorous.

The readers of Shakespeare may be divided into two classes:—

1. Those who read his works with feeling and understanding;

2. Those who, without affecting to criticise, merely feel, and may be said to be the recipients of the poet's power.

Between the two no medium can be endured. The ordinary reader, who does not pretend to bring his understanding to bear upon the subject, often feels that some real trait of his own has been caught, that some nerve has been touched; and he knows that it has been touched by the vibration he experiences—a thrill, which tells us that, by becoming better acquainted with the poet, we have become better acquainted with ourselves.

In the plays of Shakespeare every man sees himself, without knowing that he does so: as in some of the phenomena of nature, in the mist of the mountain, the traveller beholds his own figure, but the glory round the head distinguishes it from a mere vulgar copy. In traversing the Brocken, in the north of Germany, at sunrise, the brilliant beams are shot askance, and you see before you a being of gigantic proportions, and of such elevated dignity, that you only know it to be yourself by similarity of action. In the same way, near Messina, natural forms, at determined distances, are represented on an invisible mist, not as they really exist, but dressed in all the prismatic colours of the imagination. So in Shakespeare: every form is true, everything has reality for its foundation; we can all recognize the truth, but we see it decorated with such hues of beauty, and magnified to such proportions of grandeur, that, while we know the figure, we know also how much it has been refined and exalted by the poet.

It is humiliating to reflect that, as it were, because heaven has given us the greatest poet, it has inflicted upon that poet the most incompetent critics: none of them seem to understand even his language, much less the principles upon which he wrote, and the peculiarities which distinguish him from all rivals. I will not now dwell upon this point, because it is my intention to devote a lecture more immediately to the prefaces of Pope and Johnson. Some of Shakespeare's contemporaries appear to have understood him, and imitated him in a way that does the original no small honour; but modern preface-writers and commentators, while they praise him as a great genius, when they come to publish notes upon his plays, treat him like a schoolboy; as if this great genius did not understand himself, was not aware of his own powers, and wrote without design or purpose. Nearly all they can do is to express the most vulgar of all feelings, wonderment—wondering at what they term the irregularity of his genius, sometimes above all praise, and at other times, if they are to be trusted, below all contempt. They endeavour to reconcile the two opinions by asserting that he wrote for the mob; as if a man of real genius ever wrote for the mob. Shakespeare never consciously wrote what was below himself: careless he might be, and his better genius may not always have attended him; but I fearlessly say, that he never penned a line that he knew would degrade him. No man does anything equally well at all times; but because Shakespeare could not always be the greatest of poets, was he therefore to condescend to make himself the least? [1]

Yesterday afternoon a friend left a book for me by a German critic, of which I have only had time to read a small part; but what I did read I approved, and I should be disposed to applaud the work much more highly, were it not that in so doing I should, in a manner, applaud myself. The sentiments and opinions are coincident with those to which I gave utterance in my lectures at the Royal Institution. It is not a little wonderful, that so many ages have elapsed since the time of Shakespeare, and that it should remain for foreigners first to feel truly, and to appreciate justly, his mighty genius. The solution of this circumstance must be sought in the history of our nation: the English have become a busy commercial people, and they have unquestionably derived from this propensity many social and physical advantages: they have grown to be a mighty empire—one of the great nations of the world, whose moral superiority enables it to

---

[1] It is certain that my shorthand note in this place affords another instance of mishearing: it runs literally thus—'but because Shakespeare could not always be the greatest of poets, was he therefore to condescend to make himself a beast?' For 'a beast,' we must read *the least*, the antithesis being between 'greatest' and 'least,' and not between 'poet' and 'beast.' Yet 'beast' may be reconciled with sense. . . .—[J. P. C.]

struggle successfully against him, who may be deemed the evil genius of our planet.[1]

On the other hand, the Germans, unable to distinguish themselves in action, have been driven to speculation: all their feelings have been forced back into the thinking and reasoning mind. To do, with them is impossible, but in determining what ought to be done, they perhaps exceed every people of the globe. Incapable of acting outwardly, they have acted internally: they first rationally recalled the ancient philosophy, and set their spirits to work with an energy of which England produces no parallel, since those truly heroic times, heroic in body and soul, the days of Elizabeth.

If all that has been written upon Shakespeare by Englishmen were burned, in the want of candles, merely to enable us to read one half of what our dramatist produced, we should be great gainers.[2] Providence has given England the greatest man that ever put on and put off mortality, and has thrown a sop to the envy of other nations, by inflicting upon his native country the most incompetent critics. I say nothing here of the state in which his text has come down to us, farther than that it is evidently very imperfect: in many places his sense has been perverted, in others, if not entirely obscured, so blunderingly represented, as to afford us only a glimpse of what he meant, without the power of restoring his own expressions. But whether his dramas have been perfectly or imperfectly printed, it is quite clear that modern inquiry and speculative ingenuity in this kingdom have done nothing; or I might say, without a solecism, less than nothing (for some editors have multiplied corruptions) to retrieve the genuine language of the poet. His critics among us, during the whole of the last century, have neither understood nor appreciated him; for how could they appreciate what they could not understand?

---

[1] Napoleon, of course.

[2] 'I can testify to his saying on one occasion, but which I do not know, "If all the comments that have ever been written on S. by his editors could have been collected into a pile and set on fire that by the blaze Sch[legel] might have written his lectures, the world would have been equally a gainer by the books destroyed and the book written." This I say confidently, and a better proof could not be afforded that he did not mean to gain credit by pilfering thoughts out of a magazine which he invited his hearers to explore.' H. C. Robinson to Mrs H. N. Coleridge (Sara Coleridge), 30 October 1848.— Quoted by Mrs Coleridge (with a slight alteration) in her notes. See *Coleridge's Works* (Shedd), iv. 479. I quote from the original letter in the possession of the Rev. G. H. B. Coleridge.

Could it be that Robinson had a confused recollection of the remarks recorded above by Collier?

His contemporaries, and those who immediately followed him, were not so insensible of his merits, or so incapable of explaining them; and one of them, who might be Milton when a young man of four and twenty, printed, in the second folio of Shakespeare's works, a laudatory poem, which, in its kind, has no equal for justness and distinctness of description, in reference to the powers and qualities of lofty genius.   It runs thus, and I hope that, when I have finished, I shall stand in need of no excuse for reading the whole of it.

> 'A mind reflecting ages past, whose clear
> And equal surface can make things appear,
> Distant a thousand years, and represent
> Them in their lively colours, just extent:
> To outrun hasty time, retrieve the fates,
> Roll back the heavens, blow ope the iron gates
> Of death and Lethe, where confused lie
> Great heaps of ruinous mortality:
> In that deep dusky dungeon to discern
> A royal ghost from churls; by art to learn
> The physiognomy of shades, and give
> Them sudden birth, wondering how oft they live;
> What story coldly tells, what poets feign
> At second hand, and picture without brain,
> Senseless and soul-less shows: to give a stage
> (Ample and true with life) voice, action, age,
> As Plato's year, and new scene of the world,
> Them unto us, or us to them had hurl'd:
> To raise our ancient sovereigns from their herse,
> Make kings his subjects; by exchanging verse,
> Enlive their pale trunks; that the present age
> Joys at their joy, and trembles at their rage:
> Yet so to temper passion, that our ears
> Take pleasure in their pain, and eyes in tears
> Both weep and smile; fearful at plots so sad,
> Then laughing at our fear; abus'd, and glad
> To be abus'd; affected with that truth
> Which we perceive is false, pleas'd in that ruth
> At which we start, and, by elaborate play,
> Tortur'd and tickl'd; by a crab-like way
> Time past made pastime, and in ugly sort
> Disgorging up his ravin for our sport:—
> —While the plebeian imp, from lofty throne,
> Creates and rules a world, and works upon
> Mankind by secret engines; now to move
> A chilling pity, then a rigorous love;
> To strike up and stroke down, both joy and ire
> To steer th' affections; and by heavenly fire
> Mold us anew, stol'n from ourselves:—
>   This, and much more, which cannot be express'd

But by himself, his tongue, and his own breast,
Was Shakespeare's freehold; which his cunning brain
Improv'd by favour of the nine-fold train;
The buskin'd muse, the comick queen, the grand
And louder tone of Clio, nimble hand
And nimbler foot of the melodious pair,
The silver-voiced lady, the most fair
Calliope, whose speaking silence daunts,
And she whose praise the heavenly body chants;
These jointly woo'd him, envying one another;
(Obey'd by all as spouse, but lov'd as brother)
And wrought a curious robe, of sable grave,
Fresh green, and pleasant yellow, red most brave,
And constant blue, rich purple, guiltless white,
The lowly russet, and the scarlet bright;
Branch'd and embroider'd like the painted spring;
Each leaf match'd with a flower, and each string
Of golden wire, each line of silk: there run
Italian works, whose thread the sisters spun;
And these did sing, or seem to sing, the choice
Birds of a foreign note and various voice:
Here hangs a mossy rock; there plays a fair
But chiding fountain, purled: not the air,
Nor clouds, nor thunder, but were living drawn;
Not out of common tiffany or lawn,
But fine materials, which the Muses know,
And only know the countries where they grow.
    Now, when they could no longer him enjoy,
In mortal garments pent,—death may destroy,
They say, his body; but his verse shall live,
And more than nature takes our hands shall give:
In a less volume, but more strongly bound,
Shakespeare shall breathe and speak; with laurel crown'd,
Which never fades; fed with ambrosian meat,
In a well-lined vesture, rich, and neat.
So with this robe they clothe him, bid him wear it;
For time shall never stain, nor envy tear it.'

This poem is subscribed J. M. S., meaning, as some have explained the initials, 'John Milton, Student': the internal evidence seems to me decisive, for there was, I think, no other man, of that particular day, capable of writing anything so characteristic of Shakespeare, so justly thought, and so happily expressed.[1]

It is a mistake to say that any of Shakespeare's characters

---

[1] Coleridge's opinion on this point is not likely to be generally acceptable; but no alternative which carries conviction has been suggested. For a brief discussion of various conjectures, with references, see *The Shakespeare Allusion Book*, i. 366–8.

Schlegel also praises the poem (*Werke*, vi. 166), but the coincidence or influence is beneath notice.

strike us as portraits: they have the union of reason perceiving, of judgment recording, and of imagination diffusing over all a magic glory. While the poet registers what is past, he projects the future in a wonderful degree, and makes us feel, however slightly, and see, however dimly, that state of being in which there is neither past nor future, but all is permanent in the very energy of nature.

Although I have affirmed that all Shakespeare's characters are ideal, and the result of his own meditation, yet a just separation may be made of those in which the ideal is most prominent— where it is put forward more intensely—where we are made more conscious of the ideal, though in truth they possess no more nor less ideality; and of those which, though equally idealized, the delusion upon the mind is of their being real. The characters in the various plays may be separated into those where the real is disguised in the ideal, and those where the ideal is concealed from us by the real. The difference is made by the different powers of mind employed by the poet in the representation.

At present I shall only speak of dramas where the ideal is predominant; and chiefly for this reason—that those plays have been attacked with the greatest violence. The objections to them are not the growth of our own country, but of France—the judgment of monkeys, by some wonderful phenomenon, put into the mouths of people shaped like men. These creatures have informed us that Shakespeare is a miraculous monster, in whom many heterogeneous components were thrown together, producing a discordant mass of genius—an irregular and ill-assorted structure of gigantic proportions.

Among the ideal plays, I will take 'The Tempest,' by way of example. Various others might be mentioned, but it is impossible to go through every drama, and what I remark on 'The Tempest' will apply to all Shakespeare's productions of the same class.

In this play Shakespeare has especially appealed to the imagination, and he has constructed a plot well adapted to the purpose. According to his scheme, he did not appeal to any sensuous impression (the word 'sensuous' is authorized by Milton) of time and place, but to the imagination, and it is to be borne in mind, that of old, and as regards mere scenery, his works may be said to have been recited rather than acted—that is to say, description and narration supplied the place of visual exhibition: the audience was told to fancy that they saw what they only heard described; the painting was not in colours, but in words.

This is particularly to be noted in the first scene—a storm and its confusion on board the king's ship. The highest and the lowest characters are brought together, and with what excellence! Much of the genius of Shakespeare is displayed in these happy combinations—the highest and the lowest, the gayest and the saddest; he is not droll in one scene and melancholy in another, but often both the one and the other in the same scene. Laughter is made to swell the tear of sorrow, and to throw, as it were, a poetic light upon it, while the tear mingles tenderness with the laughter. Shakespeare has evinced the power, which above all other men he possessed, that of introducing the profoundest sentiments of wisdom, where they would be least expected, yet where they are most truly natural. One admirable secret of his art is, that separate speeches frequently do not appear to have been occasioned by those which preceded, and which are consequent upon each other, but to have arisen out of the peculiar character of the speaker.

Before I go further, I may take the opportunity of explaining what is meant by mechanic and organic regularity. In the former the copy must appear as if it had come out of the same mould with the original; in the latter there is a law which all the parts obey, conforming themselves to the outward symbols and manifestations of the essential principle. If we look to the growth of trees, for instance, we shall observe that trees of the same kind vary considerably, according to the circumstances of soil, air, or position; yet we are able to decide at once whether they are oaks, elms, or poplars.[1]

So with Shakespeare's characters: he shows us the life and principle of each being with organic regularity. The Boatswain, in the first scene of 'The Tempest,' when the bonds of reverence are thrown off as a sense of danger impresses all, gives a loose to his feelings, and thus pours forth his vulgar mind to the old Counsellor:—

'Hence! What care these roarers for the name of King? To cabin: silence! trouble us not.'

Gonzalo replies—'Good; yet remember whom thou hast aboard.' To which the Boatswain answers—'None that I more love than myself. You are a counsellor: if you can command these elements to silence, and work the peace of the present, we will not hand a rope more; use your authority: if you cannot,

---

[1] (Cf. i. 198.) In making this important distinction between mechanic and organic regularity, Coleridge acknowledged his indebtedness to Schlegel (*Werke*, vi. 157–8).

give thanks that you have lived so long, and make yourself ready in your cabin for the mischance of the hour, if it so hap.—Cheerly, good hearts!—Out of our way, I say.'

An ordinary dramatist would, after this speech, have represented Gonzalo as moralizing, or saying something connected with the Boatswain's language; for ordinary dramatists are not men of genius: they combine their ideas by association, or by logical affinity; but the vital writer, who makes men on the stage what they are in nature, in a moment transports himself into the very being of each personage, and, instead of cutting out artificial puppets, he brings before us the men themselves.   Therefore, Gonzalo soliloquizes,—'I have great comfort from this fellow: methinks, he hath no drowning mark upon him; his complexion is perfect gallows.   Stand fast, good fate, to his hanging! make the rope of his destiny our cable, for our own doth little advantage.   If he be not born to be hanged, our case is miserable.'

In this part of the scene we see the true sailor with his contempt of danger, and the old counsellor with his high feeling, who, instead of condescending to notice the words just addressed to him, turns off, meditating with himself, and drawing some comfort to his own mind, by trifling with the ill expression of the boatswain's face, founding upon it a hope of safety.

Shakespeare had pre-determined to make the plot of this play such as to involve a certain number of low characters, and at the beginning he pitched the note of the whole.   The first scene was meant as a lively commencement of the story; the reader is prepared for something that is to be developed, and in the next scene he brings forward Prospero and Miranda.   How is this done?   By giving to his favourite character, Miranda, a sentence which at once expresses the violence and fury of the storm, such as it might appear to a witness on the land, and at the same time displays the tenderness of her feelings—the exquisite feelings of a female brought up in a desert, but with all the advantages of education, all that could be communicated by a wise and affectionate father.   She possesses all the delicacy of innocence, yet with all the powers of her mind unweakened by the combats of life.   Miranda exclaims:—

> 'O! I have suffered
> With those that I saw suffer: a brave vessel,
> Who had, no doubt, some noble creatures [a] in her,
> Dash'd all to pieces.'

[a] Read 'creature.'   'Creatures' is Theobald's reading.

The doubt here intimated could have occurred to no mind but to that of Miranda, who had been bred up in the island with her father and a monster only: she did not know, as others do, what sort of creatures were in a ship; others never would have introduced it as a conjecture.   This shows, that while Shakespeare is displaying his vast excellence, he never fails to insert some touch or other, which is not merely characteristic of the particular person, but combines two things—the person, and the circumstances acting upon the person.   She proceeds:—

> 'O! the cry did knock
> Against my very heart.   Poor souls! they perish'd.
> Had I been any god of power, I would
> Have sunk the sea within the earth, or e'er [a]
> It should the good ship so have swallow'd, and
> The fraughting souls within her.'

She still dwells upon that which was most wanting to the completeness of her nature—these fellow creatures from whom she appeared banished, with only one relict to keep them alive, now in her memory, but in her imagination.

Another proof of excellent judgment in the poet, for I am now principally adverting to that point, is to be found in the preparation of the reader for what is to follow.   Prospero is introduced, first in his magic robe, which, with the assistance of his daughter, he lays aside, and we then know him to be a being possessed of supernatural powers.   He then instructs Miranda in the story of their arrival in the island, and this is conducted in such a manner, that the reader never conjectures the technical use the poet has made of the relation, by informing the auditor of what it is necessary for him to know.

The next step is the warning by Prospero, that he means, for particular purposes, to lull his daughter to sleep; and here he exhibits the earliest and mildest proof of magical power.   In ordinary and vulgar plays we should have had some person brought upon the stage, whom nobody knows or cares anything about, to let the audience into the secret.   Prospero having cast a sleep upon his daughter, by that sleep stops the narrative at the very moment when it was necessary to break it off, in order to excite curiosity, and yet to give the memory and understanding sufficient to carry on the progress of the history uninterruptedly.

Here I cannot help noticing a fine touch of Shakespeare's knowledge of human nature, and generally of the great laws of

[a] Read 'ere.'

the human mind: I mean Miranda's infant remembrance.
Prospero asks her—

> 'Canst thou remember
> A time before we came unto this cell?
> I do not think thou canst, for then thou wast not
> Out three years old.'

Miranda answers,

> 'Certainly, sir, I can.'

Prospero inquires,

> 'By what? by any other house or person?
> Of any thing the image tell me, that
> Hath kept with thy remembrance.'

To which Miranda returns,

> ''Tis far off;
> And rather like a dream than an assurance
> That my remembrance warrants.   Had I not
> Four or five women once, that tended me?'
>
> *Act I., Scene 2.*

This is exquisite!   In general, our remembrances of early life
arise from vivid colours, especially if we have seen them in
motion: for instance, persons when grown up will remember a
bright green door, seen when they were quite young; but
Miranda, who was somewhat older, recollected four or five
women who tended her.   She might know men from her
father, and her remembrance of the past might be worn out by
the present object, but women she only knew by herself, by the
contemplation of her own figure in the fountain, and she recalled
to her mind what had been.   It was not, that she had seen such
and such grandees, or such and such peeresses, but she remembered to have seen something like the reflection of herself: it
was not herself, and it brought back to her mind what she had
seen most like herself.

In my opinion the picturesque power displayed by Shakespeare, of all the poets that ever lived, is only equalled, if
equalled, by Milton and Dante.   The presence of genius is not
shown in elaborating a picture: we have had many specimens of
this sort of work in modern poems, where all is so dutchified, if I
may use the word, by the most minute touches, that the reader
naturally asks why words, and not painting, are used?   I know
a young lady of much taste, who observed, that in reading recent

versified accounts of voyages and travels, she, by a sort of instinct, cast her eyes on the opposite page, for coloured prints of what was so patiently and punctually described.

The power of poetry is, by a single word perhaps, to instil that energy into the mind, which compels the imagination to produce the picture.   Prospero tells Miranda,

> 'One midnight,
> Fated to the purpose, did Antonio open
> The gates of Milan; and i' the dead of darkness,
> The ministers for the purpose hurried thence
> Me, and thy crying self.'

Here, by introducing a single happy epithet, 'crying,' in the last line, a complete picture is presented to the mind, and in the production of such pictures the power of genius consists.

In reference to preparation, it will be observed that the storm, and all that precedes the tale, as well as the tale itself, serve to develope completely the main character of the drama, as well as the design of Prospero.   The manner in which the heroine is charmed asleep fits us for what follows, goes beyond our ordinary belief, and gradually leads us to the appearance and disclosure of a being of the most fanciful and delicate texture, like Prospero, preternaturally gifted.

In this way the entrance of Aricl, if not absolutely forethought by the reader, was foreshewn by the writer: in addition, we may remark, that the moral feeling called forth by the sweet words of Miranda,

> 'Alack, what trouble
> Was I then to you!'

in which she considered only the sufferings and sorrows of her father, puts the reader in a frame of mind to exert his imagination in favour of an object so innocent and interesting.   The poet makes him wish that, if supernatural agency were to be employed, it should be used for a being so young and lovely.   'The wish is father to the thought,' and Ariel is introduced.   Here, what is called poetic faith is required and created, and our common notions of philosophy give way before it: this feeling may be said to be much stronger than historic faith, since for the exercise of poetic faith the mind is previously prepared.   I make this remark, though somewhat digressive, in order to lead to a future subject of these lectures—the poems of Milton.   When adverting to those, I shall have to explain farther the distinction between the two.

Many Scriptural poems have been written with so much of Scripture in them, that what is not Scripture appears to be not true, and like mingling lies with the most sacred revelations. Now Milton, on the other hand, has taken for his subject that one point of Scripture of which we have the mere fact recorded, and upon this he has most judiciously constructed his whole fable. So of Shakespeare's 'King Lear': we have little historic evidence to guide or confine us, and the few facts handed down to us, and admirably employed by the poet, are sufficient, while we read, to put an end to all doubt as to the credibility of the story. It is idle to say that this or that incident is improbable, because history, as far as it goes, tells us that the fact was so and so. Four or five lines in the Bible include the whole that is said of Milton's story, and the Poet has called up that poetic faith, that conviction of the mind, which is necessary to make that seem true, which otherwise might have been deemed almost fabulous.

But to return to 'The Tempest,' and to the wondrous creation of Ariel. If a doubt could ever be entertained whether Shakespeare was a great poet, acting upon laws arising out of his own nature, and not without law, as has sometimes been idly asserted, that doubt must be removed by the character of Ariel. The very first words uttered by this being introduce the spirit, not as an angel, above man; not a gnome, or a fiend, below man; but while the poet gives him the faculties and the advantages of reason, he divests him of all mortal character, not positively, it is true, but negatively. In air he lives, from air he derives his being, in air he acts; and all his colours and properties seem to have been obtained from the rainbow and the skies. There is nothing about Ariel that cannot be conceived to exist either at sun-rise or at sun-set: hence all that belongs to Ariel belongs to the delight the mind is capable of receiving from the most lovely external appearances. His answers to Prospero are directly to the question, and nothing beyond; or where he expatiates, which is not unfrequently, it is to himself and upon his own delights, or upon the unnatural situation in which he is placed, though under a kindly power and to good ends.

Shakespeare has properly made Ariel's very first speech characteristic of him. After he has described the manner in which he had raised the storm and produced its harmless consequences, we find that Ariel is discontented—that he has been freed, it is true, from a cruel confinement, but still that he is bound to obey Prospero, and to execute any commands imposed upon him. We feel that such a state of bondage is almost unnatural to him, yet we see that it is delightful for him to be so employed.—It is as if we were to command one of the winds in a different direction to that which nature dictates, or one of the waves, now rising and now sinking, to recede before it bursts upon the shore: such is the feeling we experience, when we learn that a being like Ariel is commanded to fulfil any mortal behest.

When, however, Shakespeare contrasts the treatment of Ariel by Prospero with that of Sycorax, we are sensible that the liberated spirit ought to be grateful, and Ariel does feel and acknowledge the obligation; he immediately assumes the airy being, with a mind so elastically correspondent, that when once a feeling has passed from it, not a trace is left behind.

Is there anything in nature from which Shakespeare caught the idea of this delicate and delightful being, with such child-like simplicity, yet with such preternatural powers? He is neither born of heaven, nor of earth; but, as it were, between both, like a May-blossom kept suspended in air by the fanning breeze, which prevents it from falling to the ground, and only finally, and by compulsion, touching earth. This reluctance of the Sylph to be under the command even of Prospero is kept up through the whole play, and in the exercise of his admirable judgment Shakespeare has availed himself of it, in order to give Ariel an interest in the event, looking forward to that moment when he was to gain his last and only reward—simple and eternal liberty.

Another instance of admirable judgment and excellent preparation is to be found in the creature contrasted with Ariel—Caliban; who is described in such a manner by Prospero, as to lead us to expect the appearance of a foul, unnatural monster. He is not seen at once: his voice is heard; this is the preparation; he was too offensive to be seen first in all his deformity, and in nature we do not receive so much disgust from sound as from sight. After we have heard Caliban's voice he does not enter, until Ariel has entered like a water-nymph. All the strength of contrast is thus acquired without any of the shock of abruptness, or of that unpleasant sensation, which we experience when the object presented is in any way hateful to our vision.

The character of Caliban is wonderfully conceived: he is a sort of creature of the earth, as Ariel is a sort of creature of the air.[1] He partakes of the qualities of the brute, but is distinguished from brutes in two ways:—by having mere understanding without moral reason; and by not possessing the instincts

---

[1] Schlegel (vi. 236–7) makes exactly the same remark. This probably indicates an influence, though coincidence is possible. (Cf. i. 120.)

which pertain to absolute animals.   Still, Caliban is in some respects a noble being: the poet has raised him far above contempt: he is a man in the sense of the imagination: all the images he uses are drawn from nature, and are highly poetical; they fit in with the images of Ariel.   Caliban gives us images from the earth, Ariel images from the air.   Caliban talks of the difficulty of finding fresh water, of the situation of morasses, and of other circumstances which even brute instinct, without reason, could comprehend.   No mean figure is employed, no mean passion displayed, beyond animal passion, and repugnance to command.

The manner in which the lovers are introduced is equally wonderful, and it is the last point I shall now mention in reference to this, almost miraculous, drama.   The same judgment is observable in every scene, still preparing, still inviting, and still gratifying, like a finished piece of music.   I have omitted to notice one thing, and you must give me leave to advert to it before I proceed: I mean the conspiracy against the life of Alonzo.   I want to shew you how well the poet prepares the feelings of the reader for this plot, which was to execute the most detestable of all crimes, and which, in another play, Shakespeare has called 'the murder of sleep.'

Antonio and Sebastian at first had no such intention: it was suggested by the magical sleep cast on Alonzo and Gonzalo; but they are previously introduced scoffing and scorning at what was said by others, without regard to age or situation—without any sense of admiration for the excellent truths they heard delivered, but giving themselves up entirely to the malignant and unsocial feeling, which induced them to listen to everything that was said, not for the sake of profiting by the learning and experience of others, but of hearing something that might gratify vanity and self-love, by making them believe that the person speaking was inferior to themselves.

This, let me remark, is one of the grand characteristics of a villain; and it would not be so much a presentiment, as an anticipation of hell, for men to suppose that all mankind were as wicked as themselves, or might be so, if they were not too great fools.   Pope, you are perhaps aware, objected to this conspiracy; but in my mind, if it could be omitted, the play would lose a charm which nothing could supply.

Many, indeed innumerable, beautiful passages might be quoted from this play, independently of the astonishing scheme of its construction.   Every body will call to mind the grandeur

of the language of Prospero in that divine speech, where he takes
leave of his magic art; and were I to indulge myself by repetitions
of the kind, I should descend from the character of a lecturer to
that of a mere reciter.   Before I terminate, I may particularly
recal one short passage, which has fallen under the very severe,
but inconsiderate, censure of Pope and Arbuthnot,[1] who pronounce it a piece of the grossest bombast.   Prospero thus
addresses his daughter, directing her attention to Ferdinand:

> 'The fringed curtains of thine eye advance,
> And say what thou seest yond.'
>
> *Act I., Scene 2.*

Taking these words as a periphrase of—'Look what is coming
yonder,' it certainly may to some appear to border on the ridiculous, and to fall under the rule I formerly laid down,—that whatever, without injury, can be translated into a foreign language in
simple terms, ought to be in simple terms in the original language; but it is to be borne in mind, that different modes of
expression frequently arise from difference of situation and
education: a blackguard would use very different words, to
express the same thing, to those a gentleman would employ, yet
both would be natural and proper; difference of feeling gives rise
to difference of language: a gentleman speaks in polished terms,
with due regard to his own rank and position, while a blackguard,
a person little better than half a brute, speaks like half a brute,
showing no respect for himself, nor for others.

But I am content to try the lines I have just quoted by the
introduction to them; and then, I think, you will admit, that
nothing could be more fit and appropriate than such language.
How does Prospero introduce them?   He has just told Miranda
a wonderful story, which deeply affected her, and filled her with
surprise and astonishment, and for his own purposes he afterwards lulls her to sleep.   When she awakes, Shakespeare has
made her wholly inattentive to the present, but wrapped up in
the past.   An actress, who understands the character of Miranda,
would have her eyes cast down, and her eyelids almost covering
them, while she was, as it were, living in her dream.   At this
moment Prospero sees Ferdinand, and wishes to point him out to
his daughter, not only with great, but with scenic solemnity,
he standing before her, and before the spectator, in the dignified

---

[1] *Memoirs of Martinus Scriblerus*, Bk II ('The Art of Sinking in Poetry')
ch. xii.

character of a great magician. Something was to appear to Miranda on the sudden, and as unexpectedly as if the hero of a drama were to be on the stage at the instant when the curtain is elevated. It is under such circumstances that Prospero says, in a tone calculated at once to arouse his daughter's attention,

> 'The fringed curtains of thine eye advance,
> And say what thou seest yond.'

Turning from the sight of Ferdinand to his thoughtful daughter, his attention was first struck by the downcast appearance of her eyes and eyelids; and, in my humble opinion, the solemnity of the phraseology assigned to Prospero is completely in character, recollecting his preternatural capacity, in which the most familiar objects in nature present themselves in a mysterious point of view. It is much easier to find fault with a writer by reference to former notions and experience, than to sit down and read him, recollecting his purpose, connecting one feeling with another, and judging of his words and phrases, in proportion as they convey the sentiments of the persons represented.

Of Miranda we may say, that she possesses in herself all the ideal beauties that could be imagined by the greatest poet of any age or country; but it is not my purpose now, so much to point out the high poetic powers of Shakespeare, as to illustrate his exquisite judgment, and it is solely with this design that I have noticed a passage with which, it seems to me, some critics, and those among the best, have been unreasonably dissatisfied. If Shakespeare be the wonder of the ignorant, he is, and ought to be, much more the wonder of the learned: not only from profundity of thought, but from his astonishing and intuitive knowledge of what man must be at all times, and under all circumstances, he is rather to be looked upon as a prophet than as a poet. Yet, with all these unbounded powers, with all this might and majesty of genius, he makes us feel as if he were unconscious of himself, and of his high destiny, disguising the half god in the simplicity of a child.

THE TWELFTH LECTURE

[*Collier Report.*]

IN the last lecture I endeavoured to point out in Shakespeare those characters in which pride of intellect, without moral feeling, is supposed to be the ruling impulse, such as Iago, Richard III., and even Falstaff.[1] In Richard III., ambition is, as it were, the channel in which this impulse directs itself; the character is drawn with the greatest fulness and perfection; and the poet has not only given us that character, grown up and completed, but he has shown us its very source and generation. The inferiority of his person made the hero seek consolation and compensation in the superiority of his intellect; he thus endeavoured to counterbalance his deficiency. This striking feature is pourtrayed most admirably by Shakespeare, who represents Richard bringing forward his very defects and deformities as matters of boast. It was the same pride of intellect, or the assumption of it, that made John Wilkes vaunt that, although he was so ugly, he only wanted, with any lady, ten minutes' start of the handsomest man in England. This certainly was a high compliment to himself; but a higher to the female sex, on the supposition that Wilkes possessed this superiority of intellect, and relied upon it for making a favourable impression, because ladies would know how to estimate his advantages.

I will now proceed to offer some remarks upon the tragedy of 'Richard II.,' on account of its not very apparent, but still intimate, connection with 'Richard III.' As, in the last, Shakespeare has painted a man where ambition is the channel in which the ruling impulse runs, so, in the first, he has given us a character, under the name of Bolingbroke, or Henry IV., where ambition itself, conjoined unquestionably with great talents, is the ruling impulse. In Richard III. the pride of intellect makes use of ambition as its means; in Bolingbroke the gratification of ambition is the end, and talents are the means.

One main object of these lectures is to point out the superiority of Shakespeare to other dramatists, and no superiority can be more striking, than that this wonderful poet could take two

Cf. i. 206; ii. 26, etc.

characters, which at first sight seem so much alike, and yet, when carefully and minutely examined, are so totally distinct.

The popularity of 'Richard II.' is owing, in a great measure, to the masterly delineation of the principal character; but were there no other ground for admiring it, it would deserve the highest applause, from the fact that it contains the most magnificent, and, at the same time, the truest eulogium of our native country that the English language can boast, or which can be produced from any other tongue, not excepting the proud claims of Greece and Rome.   When I feel, that upon the morality of Britain depends the safety of Britain, and that her morality is supported and illustrated by our national feeling, I cannot read these grand lines without joy and triumph.   Let it be remembered, that while this country is proudly pre-eminent in morals, her enemy has only maintained his station by superiority in mechanical appliances.   Many of those who hear me will, no doubt, anticipate the passage I refer to, and it runs as follows [1]:—

> 'This royal throne of kings, this scepterd isle,
> This earth of majesty, this seat of Mars,
> This other Eden, demi-paradise;
> This fortress, built by nature for herself
> Against infection and the hand of war;
> This happy breed of men, this little world,
> This precious stone set in the silver sea,
> Which serves it in the office of a wall,
> Or as a moat defensive to a house,
> Against the envy of less happier lands;
> This blessed plot, this earth, this realm, this England,
> This nurse, this teeming womb of royal kings,
> Feared by their breed, and famous by their birth,
> Renowned for their deeds as far from home,
> For Christian service and true chivalry,
> As is the Sepulchre in stubborn Jewry
> Of the world's ransom, blessed Mary's son:
> This land of such dear souls, this dear, dear land,
> Dear for her reputation through the world,
> Is now leas'd out, I die pronouncing it,
> Like to a tenement, or pelting farm.
> England, bound in with the triumphant sea,
> Whose rocky shore beats back the envious siege
> Of watery Neptune, is now bound in with shame,
> With inky blots, and rotten parchment bonds.'
>
> *Act II., Scene 1.*

Every motive to patriotism, every cause producing it, is here collected, without one of those cold abstractions so frequently

---

[1] For other uses of this favourite passage cf. i. 129–30, 138; ii. 230.

substituted by modern poets.   If this passage were recited in a theatre with due energy and understanding, with a proper knowledge of the words, and a fit expression of their meaning, every man would retire from it secure in his country's freedom, if secure in his own constant virtue.

The principal personages in this tragedy are Richard II., Bolingbroke, and York.   I will speak of the last first, although it is the least important; but the keeping of all is most admirable. York is a man of no strong powers of mind, but of earnest wishes to do right, contented in himself alone, if he have acted well: he points out to Richard the effects of his thoughtless extravagance, and the dangers by which he is encompassed, but having done so, he is satisfied; there is no after action on his part; he does nothing; he remains passive.   When old Gaunt is dying, York takes care to give his own opinion to the King, and that done he retires, as it were, into himself.

It has been stated, from the first, that one of my purposes in these lectures is, to meet and refute popular objections to particular points in the works of our great dramatic poet; and I cannot help observing here upon the beauty, and true force of nature, with which conceits, as they are called, and sometimes even puns, are introduced.   What has been the reigning fault of an age must, at one time or another, have referred to something beautiful in the human mind; and, however conceits may have been misapplied, however they may have been disadvantageously multiplied, we should recollect that there never was an abuse of anything, but it previously has had its use.   Gaunt, on his death-bed, sends for the young King, and Richard, entering, insolently and unfeelingly says to him:

'What, comfort, man! how is't with aged Gaunt?'

Act II., Scene 1.

and Gaunt replies:

'O, how that name befits my composition!
Old Gaunt, indeed; and gaunt in being old:
Within me grief hath kept a tedious fast,
And who abstains from meat, that is not gaunt?
For sleeping England long time have I watched;
Watching breeds leanness, leanness is all gaunt:
The pleasure that some fathers feed upon
Is my strict fast, I mean my children's looks;
And therein fasting, thou hast *a* made me gaunt.
Gaunt am I for the grave, gaunt as a grave,
Whose hollow womb inherits nought but bones.'

a Theobald's reading.   Read 'hast thou.'

Richard inquires,

> 'Can sick men play so nicely with their names?'

To which Gaunt answers, giving the true justification of conceits [1]:

> 'No; misery makes sport to mock itself:
> Since thou dost seek to kill my name in me,
> I mock my name, great king, to flatter thee.'

He that knows the state of the human mind in deep passion must know, that it approaches to that condition of madness, which is not absolute frenzy or delirium, but which models all things to one reigning idea; still it strays from the main subject of complaint, and still it returns to it, by a sort of irresistible impulse. Abruptness of thought, under such circumstances, is true to nature, and no man was more sensible of it than Shakespeare. In a modern poem a mad mother thus complains:

> 'The breeze I see is in yon [a] tree:
> It comes to cool my babe and me.' [2]

This is an instance of the abruptness of thought, so natural to the excitement and agony of grief; and if it be admired in images, can we say that it is unnatural in words, which are, as it were, a part of our life, of our very existence? In the Scriptures themselves these plays upon words are to be found, as well as in the best works of the ancients, and in the most delightful parts of Shakespeare; and because this additional grace, not well understood, has in some instances been converted into a deformity—because it has been forced into places, where it is evidently improper and unnatural, are we therefore to include the whole application of it in one general condemnation? When it seems objectionable, when it excites a feeling contrary to the situation, when it perhaps disgusts, it is our business to enquire whether the conceit has been rightly or wrongly used—whether it is in a right or in a wrong place?

In order to decide this point, it is obviously necessary to consider the state of mind, and the degree of passion, of the person using this play upon words. Resort to this grace may, in some cases, deserve censure, not because it is a play upon

---

[a] Read 'the.'

[1] Cf. i. 135, 138; ii. 231 for similar references to Gaunt's puns.

[2] Wordsworth's poem, 'Her Eyes are Wild.'

words, but because it is a play upon words in a wrong place, and at a wrong time. What is right in one state of mind is wrong in another, and much more depends upon that, than upon the conceit (so to call it) itself. I feel the importance of these remarks strongly, because the greater part of the abuse, I might say filth, thrown out and heaped upon Shakespeare, has originated in want of consideration. Dr. Johnson asserts that Shakespeare loses the world for a toy, and can no more withstand a pun, or a play upon words, than his Antony could resist Cleopatra.[1] Certain it is, that Shakespeare gained more admiration in his day, and long afterwards, by the use of speech in this way, than modern writers have acquired by the abandonment of the practice: the latter, in adhering to, what they have been pleased to call, the rules of art, have sacrificed nature.

Having said thus much on the, often falsely supposed, blemishes of our poet—blemishes which are said to prevail in 'Richard II.' especially,—I will now advert to the character of the King. He is represented as a man not deficient in immediate courage, which displays itself at his assassination; or in powers of mind, as appears by the foresight he exhibits throughout the play: still, he is weak, variable, and womanish, and possesses feelings, which, amiable in a female, are misplaced in a man, and altogether unfit for a king. In prosperity he is insolent and presumptuous, and in adversity, if we are to believe Dr. Johnson, he is humane and pious.[2] I cannot admit the latter epithet, because I perceive the utmost consistency of character in Richard: what he was at first, he is at last, excepting as far as he yields to circumstances: what he shewed himself at the commencement of the play, he shews himself at the end of it. Dr. Johnson assigns to him rather the virtue of a confessor than that of a king.[3]

True it is, that he may be said to be overwhelmed by the earliest misfortune that befalls him; but, so far from his feelings or disposition being changed or subdued, the very first glimpse of the returning sunshine of hope reanimates his spirits, and exalts him to as strange and unbecoming a degree of elevation, as he was before sunk in mental depression: the mention of those in his misfortunes, who had contributed to his downfall,

---

[1] Preface to Shakespeare. Cf. also the final note on *R. and J.*
[2] *Richard II.*, III. iv., note (Cambridge ed., III. ii. 93).
[3] Though this sounds like an adverse criticism and is doubtless meant to be such, Coleridge is merely quoting from Dr Johnson, who describes Richard's 'passive fortitude,' as 'the virtue of a confessor rather than of a king.'

but who had before been his nearest friends and favourites, calls forth from him expressions of the bitterest hatred and revenge. Thus, where Richard asks:

> 'Where is the Earl of Wiltshire?   Where is Bagot?
> What is become of Bushy?   Where is Green?
> That they have let the dangerous enemy
> Measure our confines with such peaceful steps?
> If we prevail, their heads shall pay for it.
> I warrant they have made peace with Bolingbroke.'
>
> *Act III., Scene 2.*

Scroop answers:

> 'Peace have they made with him, indeed, my lord.'

Upon which Richard, without hearing more, breaks out:

> 'O villains! vipers, damn'd without redemption!
> Dogs, easily won to fawn on any man!
> Snakes, in my heart-blood warm'd, that sting my heart!
> Three Judases, each one thrice worse than Judas!
> Would they make peace? terrible hell make war
> Upon their spotted souls for this offence!'

Scroop observes upon this change, and tells the King how they had made their peace:

> 'Sweet love, I see, changing his property
> Turns to the sourest and most deadly hate.
> Again uncurse their souls: their peace is made
> With heads and not with hands: those whom you curse
> Have felt the worst of death's destroying wound,
> And lie full low, grav'd in the hollow ground.'

Richard receiving at first an equivocal answer,—'Peace have they made with him, indeed, my lord,'—takes it in the worst sense: his promptness to suspect those who had been his friends turns his love to hate, and calls forth the most tremendous execrations.

From the beginning to the end of the play he pours out all the peculiarities and powers of his mind: he catches at new hope, and seeks new friends, is disappointed, despairs, and at length makes a merit of his resignation.   He scatters himself into a multitude of images, and in conclusion endeavours to shelter himself from that which is around him by a cloud of his own thoughts.   Throughout his whole career may be noticed the most rapid transitions—from the highest insolence to the lowest humility—from hope to despair, from the extravagance of love to the agonies of resentment, and from pretended resignation to the bitterest reproaches. The whole is joined with the utmost richness and copiousness of thought, and were there an actor capable of representing Richard, the part would delight us more than any other of Shakespeare's master-pieces,—with, perhaps, the single exception of King Lear. I know of no character drawn by our great poet with such unequalled skill as that of Richard II.

Next we come to Henry Bolingbroke, the rival of Richard II. He appears as a man of dauntless courage, and of ambition equal to that of Richard III.; but, as I have stated, the difference between the two is most admirably conceived and preserved. In Richard III. all that surrounds him is only dear as it feeds his inward sense of superiority: he is no vulgar tyrant—no Nero or Caligula: he has always an end in view, and vast fertility of means to accomplish that end. On the other hand, in Bolingbroke we find a man who in the outset has been sorely injured: then, we see him encouraged by the grievances of his country, and by the strange mismanagement of the government, yet at the same time scarcely daring to look at his own views, or to acknowledge them as designs. He comes home under the pretence of claiming his dukedom, and he professes that to be his object almost to the last; but, at the last, he avows his purpose to its full extent, of which he was himself unconscious in the earlier stages.

This is proved by so many passages, that I will only select one of them; and I take it the rather, because out of the many octavo volumes of text and notes, the page on which it occurs is, I believe, the only one left naked by the commentators. It is where Bolingbroke approaches the castle in which the unfortunate King has taken shelter: York is in Bolingbroke's company—the same York who is still contented with speaking the truth, but doing nothing for the sake of the truth,—drawing back after he has spoken, and becoming merely passive when he ought to display activity. Northumberland says,

> 'The news is very fair and good, my lord:
> Richard not far from hence hath hid his head.'
>
> *Act III., Scene 2.*

York rebukes him thus:

> 'It would beseem the Lord Northumberland
> To say King Richard:—Alack, the heavy day,
> When such a sacred king should hide his head!'

Northumberland replies:

> 'Your grace mistakes me [a]: only to be brief
> Left I his title out.'

To which York rejoins:

> 'The time hath been,
> Would you have been so brief with him, he would
> Have been so brief with you, to shorten you,
> For taking so the head, your whole head's length.'

Bolingbroke observes,

> 'Mistake not, uncle, farther than you should;'

And York answers, with a play upon the words 'take' and 'mistake':

> 'Take not, good cousin, farther than you should,
> Lest you mistake. [b]   The heavens are o'er our heads.'

Here, give me leave to remark in passing, that the play upon words is perfectly natural, and quite in character: the answer is in unison with the tone of passion, and seems connected with some phrase then in popular use.   Bolingbroke tells York:

> 'I know it, uncle, and oppose not myself
> Against their will.'

Just afterwards, Bolingbroke thus addresses himself to Northumberland:

> 'Noble lord,[c]
> Go to the rude ribs of that ancient castle;
> Through brazen trumpet send the breath of parle [c]
> Into his ruin'd ears, and thus deliver.'

Here, in the phrase 'into his ruin'd ears,' I have no doubt that Shakespeare purposely used the personal pronoun, 'his,' to shew, that although Bolingbroke was only speaking of the castle, his thoughts dwelt on the king.   In Milton the pronoun, 'her' is employed, in relation to 'form,' in a manner somewhat similar. Bolingbroke had an equivocation in his mind, and was thinking of the king, while speaking of the castle.   He goes on to tell Northumberland what to say, beginning,

> 'Henry Bolingbroke,'

---

[a] *Omit 'me.'*   [b] *Read 'Lest you mistake the.*
[c] *Ff Q5 'lord,' 'parle'; Q1Q2Q3Q4 and Cambridge editors, 'lords,' 'parlee.'*

which is almost the only instance in which a name forms the whole line; Shakespeare meant it to convey Bolingbroke's opinion of his own importance:—

> 'Henry Bolingbroke
> On both his knees doth kiss King Richard's hand,
> And sends allegiance and true faith of heart
> To his most royal person; hither come
> Even at his feet to lay my arms and power,
> Provided that, my banishment repealed,
> And lands restor'd again, be freely granted.
> If not, I'll use th' advantage of my power,
> And lay the summer's dust with showers of blood,
> Rain'd from the wounds of slaughter'd Englishmen.'

At this point Bolingbroke seems to have been checked by the eye of York, and thus proceeds in consequence:

> 'The which, how far off from the mind of Bolingbroke
> It is, such crimson tempest should bedrench
> The fresh green lap of fair King Richard's land,
> My stooping duty tenderly shall show.'

He passes suddenly from insolence to humility, owing to the silent reproof he received from his uncle.   This change of tone would not have taken place, had Bolingbroke been allowed to proceed according to the natural bent of his own mind, and the flow of the subject.   Let me direct attention to the subsequent lines, for the same reason; they are part of the same speech:

> 'Let's march without the noise of threat'ning drum,
> That from the ª castle's tatter'd battlements
> Our fair appointments may be well perused.
> Methinks, King Richard and myself should meet
> With no less terror than the elements
> Of fire and water, when their thundering shock
> At meeting tears the cloudy cheeks of heaven.'

Having proceeded thus far with the exaggeration of his own importance, York again checks him, and Bolingbroke adds, in a very different strain,

> 'He be ᵇ the fire, I'll be the yielding water:
> The rage be his, while ᶜ on the earth I rain
> My waters; on the earth, and not on him.'

I have thus adverted to the three great personages in this drama, Richard, Bolingbroke, and York; and of the whole play

ª Read 'this.'   ᵇ Read 'be he.'
ᶜ Ff Q₅ 'while'; Q₁Q₂Q₃Q₄ and Cambridge editors 'whilst.'

it may be asserted, that with the exception of some of the last scenes (though they have exquisite beauty) Shakespeare seems to have risen to the summit of excellence in the delineation and preservation of character.

We will now pass to 'Hamlet,' in order to obviate some of the general prejudices against the author, in reference to the character of the hero. Much has been objected to, which ought to have been praised, and many beauties of the highest kind have been neglected, because they are somewhat hidden.

The first question we should ask ourselves is—What did Shakespeare mean when he drew the character of Hamlet? He never wrote any thing without design, and what was his design when he sat down to produce this tragedy? My belief is, that he always regarded his story, before he began to write, much in the same light as a painter regards his canvas, before he begins to paint—as a mere vehicle for his thoughts—as the ground upon which he was to work. What then was the point to which Shakespeare directed himself in Hamlet? He intended to pourtray a person, in whose view the external world, and all its incidents and objects, were comparatively dim, and of no interest in themselves, and which began to interest only, when they were reflected in the mirror of his mind. Hamlet beheld external things in the same way that a man of vivid imagination, who shuts his eyes, sees what has previously made an impression on his organs.

The poet places him in the most stimulating circumstances that a human being can be placed in. He is the heir apparent of a throne; his father dies suspiciously; his mother excludes her son from his throne by marrying his uncle. This is not enough; but the Ghost of the murdered father is introduced, to assure the son that he was put to death by his own brother. What is the effect upon the son?—instant action and pursuit of revenge? No: endless reasoning and hesitating—constant urging and solicitation of the mind to act, and as constant an escape from action; ceaseless reproaches of himself for sloth and negligence, while the whole energy of his resolution evaporates in these reproaches. This, too, not from cowardice, for he is drawn as one of the bravest of his time—not from want of forethought or slowness of apprehension, for he sees through the very souls of all who surround him, but merely from that aversion to action, which prevails among such as have a world in themselves.

How admirable, too, is the judgment of the poet! Hamlet's own disordered fancy has not conjured up the spirit of his father; it has been seen by others: he is prepared by them to witness its re-appearance, and when he does see it, Hamlet is not brought forward as having long brooded on the subject. The moment before the Ghost enters, Hamlet speaks of other matters: he mentions the coldness of the night, and observes that he has not heard the clock strike, adding, in reference to the custom of drinking, that it is

> 'More honour'd in the breach than the observance.'
>> *Act I., Scene 4.*

Owing to the tranquil state of his mind, he indulges in some moral reflections.   Afterwards, the Ghost suddenly enters.

> '*Hor.*   Look, my lord! it comes.
> *Ham.*   Angels and ministers of grace defend us!'

The same thing occurs in 'Macbeth': in the dagger-scene, the moment before the hero sees it, he has his mind applied to some indifferent matters; 'Go, tell thy mistress,' &c.   Thus, in both cases, the preternatural appearance has all the effect of abruptness, and the reader is totally divested of the notion, that the figure is a vision of a highly wrought imagination.

Here Shakespeare adapts himself so admirably to the situation —in other words, so puts himself into it—that, though poetry, his language is the very language of nature.   No terms, associated with such feelings, can occur to us so proper as those which he has employed, especially on the highest, the most august, and the most awful subjects that can interest a human being in this sentient world.   That this is no mere fancy, I can undertake to establish from hundreds, I might say thousands, of passages. No character has been drawn, in the whole list of his plays, could so well and fitly express himself, as in the language Shakespeare has put into his mouth.

There is no indecision about Hamlet, as far as his own sense of duty is concerned; he knows well what he ought to do, and over and over again he makes up his mind to do it.   The moment the players, and the two spies set upon him, have withdrawn, of whom he takes leave with a line so expressive of his contempt,

> 'Ay so; good bye you.[a]—Now I am alone,'

he breaks out into a delirium of rage against himself for neglecting to perform the solemn duty he had undertaken, and contrasts

---

[a] *Cambridge editors, 'God be wi' ye' (Capell); $F_1F_2F_3$ 'God buy ye.'*

the factitious and artificial display of feeling by the player with his own apparent indifference;

> 'What's Hecuba to him, or he to Hecuba,
> That he should weep for her?'

Yet the player did weep for her, and was in an agony of grief at her sufferings, while Hamlet is unable to rouse himself to action, in order that he may perform the command of his father, who had come from the grave to incite him to revenge:—

> 'This is most brave!
> That I, the son of a dear father murder'd,
> Prompted to my revenge by heaven and hell,
> Must, like a whore, unpack my heart with words,
> And fall a cursing like a very drab,
> A scullion.'
>
> *Act II., Scene 2.*

It is the same feeling, the same conviction of what is his duty, that makes Hamlet exclaim in a subsequent part of the tragedy:

> 'How all occasions do inform against me,
> And spur my dull revenge!   What is a man,
> If his chief good, and market of his time,
> Be but to sleep and feed?   A beast, no more. . . .
>   . . . . I do not know
> Why yet I live to say—'this thing's to do,'
> Sith I have cause and will and strength and means
> To do't.'
>
> *Act IV., Scene 4.*

Yet with all this strong conviction of duty, and with all this resolution arising out of strong conviction, nothing is done. This admirable and consistent character, deeply acquainted with his own feelings, painting them with such wonderful power and accuracy, and firmly persuaded that a moment ought not to be lost in executing the solemn charge committed to him, still yields to the same retiring from reality, which is the result of having, what we express by the terms, a world within himself.

Such a mind as Hamlet's is near akin to madness.   Dryden has somewhere said,[1]

> 'Great wit to madness nearly is allied,'

and he was right; for he means by 'wit' that greatness of genius, which led Hamlet to a perfect knowledge of his own character,

---

[1] 'Great wits are sure to madness near allied.'
Absolom and Achitophel, 163.

which, with all strength of motive, was so weak as to be unable to carry into act his own most obvious duty.

With all this he has a sense of imperfectness, which becomes apparent when he is moralizing on the skull in the churchyard. Something is wanting to his completeness—something is deficient which remains to be supplied, and he is therefore described as attached to Ophelia. His madness is assumed, when he finds that witnesses have been placed behind the arras to listen to what passes, and when the heroine has been thrown in his way as a decoy.

Another objection has been taken by Dr. Johnson, and Shakespeare has been taxed very severely. I refer to the scene where Hamlet enters and finds his uncle praying, and refuses to take his life, excepting when he is in the height of his iniquity. To assail him at such a moment of confession and repentance, Hamlet declares,

> 'Why,^a this is hire and salary, not revenge.'
>
> Act III., Scene 3.^b

He therefore forbears, and postpones his uncle's death, until he can catch him in some act

> 'That has no relish of salvation in't.'

This conduct, and this sentiment, Dr. Johnson has pronounced to be so atrocious and horrible, as to be unfit to be put into the mouth of a human being.[1] The fact, however, is that Dr. Johnson did not understand the character of Hamlet, and censured accordingly: the determination to allow the guilty King to escape at such a moment is only part of the indecision and irresoluteness of the hero. Hamlet seizes hold of a pretext for not acting, when he might have acted so instantly and effectually: therefore, he again defers the revenge he was bound to seek, and declares his determination to accomplish it at some time,

> 'When he is drunk, asleep,^c or in his rage,
> Or in th' incestuous pleasures ^d of his bed.'

This, allow me to impress upon you most emphatically, was

---

^a *Ff and Cambridge editors, 'O'; Qq 'Why.'*
^b *Collier, 'Act III. Scene iv.'*
^c *Ff and Cambridge editors, 'drunk asleep.'   Qq 'drunk, asleep.'*
^d *Read 'pleasure.'*
[1] Cf. i. 30 and note.

merely the excuse Hamlet made to himself for not taking advantage of this particular and favourable moment for doing justice upon his guilty uncle, at the urgent instance of the spirit of his father.[1]

Dr. Johnson farther states, that in the voyage to England, Shakespeare merely follows the novel as he found it, as if the poet had no other reason for adhering to his original;[2] but Shakespeare never followed a novel, because he found such and such an incident in it, but because he saw that the story, as he read it, contributed to enforce, or to explain some great truth inherent in human nature. He never could lack invention to alter or improve a popular narrative; but he did not wantonly vary from it, when he knew that, as it was related, it would so well apply to his own great purpose. He saw at once how consistent it was with the character of Hamlet, that after still resolving, and still deferring, still determining to execute, and still postponing execution, he should finally, in the infirmity of his disposition, give himself up to his destiny, and hopelessly place himself in the power, and at the mercy of his enemies.

Even after the scene with Osrick, we see Hamlet still indulging in reflection, and hardly thinking of the task he has just undertaken: he is all dispatch and resolution, as far as words and present intentions are concerned, but all hesitation and irresolution, when called upon to carry his words and intentions into effect; so that, resolving to do everything, he does nothing. He is full of purpose, but void of that quality of mind which accomplishes purpose.

Anything finer than this conception, and working out of a great character, is merely impossible. Shakespeare wished to impress upon us the truth, that action is the chief end of existence —that no faculties of intellect, however brilliant, can be considered valuable, or indeed otherwise than as misfortunes, if they withdraw us from, or render us repugnant to action, and lead us

---

[1] Both Richardson and Robertson anticipated Coleridge in his interpretation of this passage. William Richardson, 'Additional Observations on Hamlet,' *Essays on Shakespeare's Dramatic Characters* (1784); Thomas Robertson, 'An Essay on the Character of Hamlet,' *Transactions of the Royal Society of Edinburgh*, vol. ii. (1790). Robertson's note (p. 261) indicates that his criticism is independent of Richardson's.

[2] This is an error, I believe. It scarcely seems worth while to speculate regarding the actual source of Coleridge's recollection. But it may be said in passing that Malone quotes at the end of his notes on *Hamlet* the anonymous pamphlet, *Some Remarks on the Tragedy of Hamlet* (1736). In this pamphlet (p. 33) there is a criticism of Shakespeare for Hamlet's feigned madness, which the critic explains as due only to Shakespeare's desire to keep to his source. The madness, he says, causes Hamlet's being sent to England.

to think and think of doing, until the time has elapsed when we can do anything effectually. In enforcing this moral truth, Shakespeare has shown the fulness and force of his powers: all that is amiable and excellent in nature is combined in Hamlet, with the exception of one quality. He is a man living in medita-tion, called upon to act by every motive human and divine, but the great object of his life is defeated by continually resolving to do, yet doing nothing but resolve.

NEWSPAPER REPORTS

[Report of the First Lecture.[1]]

MR. COLERIDGE commenced yesterday evening his long announced lectures on the principles of poetry. To those who consider poetry in no other light than as a most *entertaining* species of composition, this gentleman's mode of inquiring into its principles may want attraction. Unlike most professional critics on works of taste, his great object appears to be to exhibit in poetry the principles of moral wisdom, and the laws of our intellectual nature, which form the basis of social existence. In the introductory lecture delivered last night, Mr. C. deduced the causes of false criticism on works of imagination from circumstances which may hitherto have been thought to stand in no very close connection with our literary habits; viz., the excessive stimulus produced by the wonderful political events of the age; the facilities afforded to general and indiscriminate reading; the rage for public speaking, and the habit consequently induced of requiring instantaneous intelligibility; periodical criticism, which teaches those to fancy they can judge who ought to be content to learn; the increase of cities, which has put an end to the old-fashioned village-gossiping, and substituted literary small talk in its place; and the improved habits of domestic life, and higher purity of moral feelings, which in relation to the drama have produced effects unfavourable to the exertion of poetic talent or of judgment. From such topics it will be seen that Mr. Coleridge is original in his views. On all occasions, indeed, he shews himself to be a man who really thinks and feels for himself; and in the development of his moral philosophy something may be expected from him very different from critics

---

[1] By H. C. Robinson, *The Times*, 19 November 1811. (Cf. ii. 168.) A briefer report of this lecture appeared in the *Dublin Correspondent* and was reprinted in *Notes and Queries*, 4 August 1855, along with another report of the seventh lecture. The latter report is identical with that in the *Morning Chronicle*. In this newspaper report, and in those which follow, the editor has silently corrected the punctuation, capitalization, and spelling. He has also omitted the heading of this article, 'From a Correspondent.' These newspaper reports were first reprinted by Thomas Ashe in the Bohn edition of Coleridge's *Lectures and Notes on Shakspere* (1883).

in general on Shakespeare, Milton, and our other national poets. However serious the design of Mr. C.'s lectures, in the execution he shews himself by no means destitute of talents of humour, irony, and satire.

[*Report of the Third Lecture.*[1]]

Last night Mr. Coleridge delivered his third lecture. He commenced by resuming his definition, or rather, as he expressed it, description of poetry. He said that the proper antithesis of poetry was not prose, but science, and that the former was distinguished from the latter by having intellectual pleasure for its object, and attaining its end by the language natural to us [in] a state of powerful excitement. It was different from other kinds of composition by producing pleasure from the whole, in consistency with the subordinate pleasure from the component parts; and the design of it was to communicate as much immediate pleasure as is consistent with the largest sum of pleasure from the whole. It is not enough that the poet renders more grateful what is already pleasing, but he must perform the more difficult duty, by the magic of his art, of extracting pleasure from pain. The lecturer having much amplified in this portion of his address, deeming it absolutely necessary that it should be correctly understood, in order that what he should in future offer might be intelligible, he next adverted to some passages in the Psalms and Isaiah, to shew the numerous hexameters with which the sacred writings abound, as the poetical form in which we express ourselves under the strong impulses of passion. Having disposed of this introductory matter, he advanced to the consideration of the wonderful powers of Shakespeare, which he prefaced with some remarks on the unities, particularly those of time and place, the neglect of which he justified in our great poet, pointing out the reasons which made it necessary that by the Greek dramatists they should be attentively regarded. Among these were the constant presence of the chorus, and the extent of their theatres adapted to receive an entire state within the enclosure. Among the objections to Shakespeare he observed that it had been said that he was not a close copyist of nature. Mr. Coleridge contended that such a transcript of nature, instead of being a beauty, would be a blemish; that his

Morning Chronicle, 26 November. Heading: 'Mr. Coleridge's Lecture.'

business was not to copy but to imitate. It was not the Nurse in *Romeo and Juliet*, not the Dogberry in another of his productions we admired, but it was the poet himself, assuming these shapes, and exhibiting under such forms all the force and magnitude of his own powers. It reminded him, said the lecturer, of the Proteus in the elegant mythology of the ancients, who became a sea or a lion, but under these and the multitudinous resemblances he assumed, retaining always the awful character of the divinity. Mr. Coleridge concluded with remarking that in his future addresses he should perhaps shock the feelings of many of his auditors by differing in sentiment from those whom they had long venerated, but he must make every other consideration yield to the paramount authority of truth, whatever might be the consequences to himself or others.

[*Report of the Fourth Lecture.*[1]]

The lecturer commenced his address with adverting to the period when Shakespeare wrote, and the discouragements of the poet, from the prejudices which prevailed against his sublime art. He conceived, with Malone, that Shakespeare began his public career about 1591, when he was 27 years of age. From the rank his father sustained, he did not credit the stories of the humble situation of the poet, whose earliest productions he considered to be the *Venus and Adonis*, and *Lucrece*, and from these it was easy to predict his future greatness. '*Poeta nascitur non fit.*' With these models we could discern that he possessed at least two indications of his character: he was not merely endowed with a thirst for the end, but he enjoyed an ample capability of the means; and in the selection of his subject he distinguished one that was far removed from his private interests, feelings, and circumstances. A third was, that the *Venus and Adonis* is immediate in its impulse on the senses; everything is seen and heard as if represented by the most consummate actors. The poet, not as Ariosto, not as Wieland, speaks to our sensual appetites, but he has by his wonderful powers raised the student to his own level, a thousand exterior images forming his rich drapery, and all tending to profound reflection, so as to overpower and extinguish everything derogatory and humiliating.

---

[1] *Morning Chronicle*, 29 November. An identical report appeared in the *Courier*, 30 November. I have omitted the heading: 'Mr. Coleridge's Fourth Lecture.'

As little can the mind, thus agitated, yield to low desire, as the mist can sleep on the surface of our northern Windermere, when the strong wind is driving the lake onward with foam and billows before it.   There are three requisites to form the poet: 1. sensibility; 2. imagination; 3. powers of association.   The last and least is principally conspicuous in this production; but, although the least, it is yet a characteristic and great excellence of his art. The lecturer having read the description of the horse and the hare in the same piece, next proceeded to discuss the merits of the *Lucrece*, in which he said we observe impetuous vigour and activity, with a much larger display of profound reflection, and a perfect dominion over the whole of our language, but nothing deeply pathetic.

Shakespeare was no child of nature, he was not possessed, but he was in possession of all.   He was under no exterior control, but early comprehending every part and incident of human being, his knowledge became habitual, and at length he acquired that superiority, by which obtaining the two golden pillars of our English Parnassus, he gave the second to Milton, reserving for himself the first.

In examining the dramatic works of Shakespeare, Mr. Coleridge said he should rather pursue the psychological than the chronological order which had been so warmly disputed.   To the first stage he should refer *Love's Labour['s] Lost*, *All's Well that Ends Well*, *Romeo and Juliet*, the *Midsummer Night's Dream*, *As You Like It*, *Twelfth Night*—which were produced when the genius of the poet was ripening.   Then he should follow him through *Troilus and Cressida*, *Cymbeline*, *The Merchant of Venice*, and *Much Ado About Nothing*.   Last, to the grandest efforts of his pen, *Macbeth*, *Lear*, *Hamlet*, and *Othello*.   These interesting subjects were reserved for the next and the ensuing lectures. After some short comparative observations, principally in vindication of the great dramatist,[a] Mr. Coleridge concluded with a single passage from Burns, to shew the capacity of the poet to give novelty and freshness, profundity and wisdom, entertainment and instruction, to the most familiar objects. This is eminently conspicuous, when the transient character of his subject is thus beautifully expressed by the Scottish bard:—

> 'Like snow that falls upon a river,
> A moment white, then gone for ever.'

[a] *Morning Chronicle*, 'Dramatists,'

[*Report of the Seventh Lecture.*[1]]

Mr. Coleridge, having concluded the preliminary discussions on the nature of the Shakespearean drama, and the genius of the poet, and briefly noticed *Love's Labour['s] Lost*, as the link which connected together the poet and the dramatist, proceeded in his seventh lecture to an elaborate review of *Romeo and Juliet*, a play in which are to be found all the individual excellences of the author, but less happily combined than in his riper productions. This he observed to be the characteristic of genius, that its earliest works are never inferior in beauties, while the merits which taste and judgment can confer are of slow growth. Tybalt and Capulet he shewed to be representatives of classes which he had observed in society, while in Mercutio he exhibited the first character of his own conception; a being formed of poetic elements, which meditation rather than observation had revealed to him; a being full of high fancy and rapid thought, conscious of his own powers, careless of life, generous, noble, a perfect gentleman. On his fate hangs the catastrophe of the tragedy. In commenting on the character of the Nurse, Mr. C. strenuously resisted the suggestion that this is a mere piece of Dutch painting, a portrait in the style of Gerard Dow. On the contrary, her character is exquisitely generalized, and is subservient to the display of fine moral contrasts. Her fondness for Juliet is delightfully pathetic. 'What a melancholy world would this be without children, how inhuman without old age.' Her loquacity is characteristic of a vulgar mind which recollects merely by coincidence of time and place, while cultivated minds connect their ideas by cause and effect. Having admitted that these lower persons might be suggested to Shakespeare by observation, Mr. C. reverted to his ideal characters, and said, 'I ask, where Shakespeare observed this?' (some heroic sentiments by Othello); 'it was with his inward eye of meditation on his own nature. He became Othello, and therefore spoke like him. Shakespeare became, in fact, all beings but the vicious; but in drawing his characters he regarded essential, not accidental relations. Avarice he never portrayed, for avarice is a

---

[1] *Morning Chronicle*, 10 December. The heading is 'Mr. Coleridge's Lectures.' This report is by H. C. Robinson. (Cf. ii. 171.) All of the reports in the newspapers were written either by Robinson, by J. P. Collier, or by the older Mr. Collier. (Cf. ii. 181.) This report was copied by the *Dublin Correspondent*, 17 December. See *Notes and Queries*, 4 August 1855, and ii. 156, note.

factitious passion. The Miser of Plautus and Molière is already obsolete.' Mr. C. entered into a discussion of the nature of fancy; [1] shewed how Shakespeare, composing under a feeling of the unimaginable, endeavouring to reconcile opposites by producing a strong working of the mind, was led to those earnest *conceits* which are consistent with passion, though frigidly imitated by writers without any. He illustrated this part of his subject by a reference to Milton's conception of Death, which the painters absurdly endeavour to strip of its fanciful nature, and render definite by the figure of a skeleton, the dryest of all images, compared with which a square or a triangle is a luxuriant fancy.

Mr. C. postponed the examination of the hero and heroine of the piece, but prefaced his inquiry by remarks on the nature of love, which he defined to be 'a perfect desire of the whole being to be united to some thing or being which is felt necessary to its perfection, by the most perfect means that nature permits, and reason dictates'; and took occasion, with great delicacy, to contrast this link of our higher and lower nature, this noblest energy of our humane and social being, with what, by a gross misnomer, usurps its name; and asserted that the criterion of honour and worth among men is their habit of sentiment on the subject of love.

We are compelled to omit the partial illustration of this in the characters of *Romeo and Juliet*, the continuation of which we are promised in the succeeding lecture.

[*Report of the Eighth Lecture.*[2]]

Mr. Coleridge commenced his eighth lecture by pointing out the great similarity in the effects produced by poetry and religion, the latter of which he had ever deemed the poetry of all mankind, in which the divinest truths were revealed. He had heard it said that 'an undevout astronomer is mad'; much more truly might it be stated than an undevout poet is insane; in fact, it was an impossibility. After impressing upon his audience what a poet was, viz., that he combined all the feelings of the child with the powers of the man, he proceeded to trace the

[1] Coleridge certainly said 'imagination' and would have been shocked to see the word 'fancy' substituted for it.

[2] *Morning Chronicle*, 13 December 1811. An identical report was published in the *Courier*, 14 December. Heading in the *Morning Chronicle*: 'Mr. Coleridge's Lectures.'

passion of love from its earliest origin, asserting by the way that Shakespeare and Sir Philip Sydney only, of all their contemporaries, entertained a fit notion of the female character. They rose like the heads of two mighty mountains in a deluge, remaining islands, while all around them was swallowed up by the oblivious flood. He next entered at length into a defence of the existence of love as a passion fitted only for, and appropriate only to, human nature, during which he with much force combated the doctrines of the materialists, maintaining that man was formed of body and of mind, and that in the heights of joy or the depths of sorrow, although the former was the willing and sympathizing servant, the latter was mainly acted upon by the delight or by the sorrow. He asserted that without marriage, the result of exclusive attachment, which was dictated by Heaven, men might be herds, but could not form society: without it all the sacred affections and charities of our nature could never have existence.[1]

The origin and cause of love was a consciousness of imperfection, and an unceasing desire to remedy it; it was a yearning after an ideal image necessary to complete the happiness of man, by supplying what in him was deficient, and Shakespeare throughout his works had viewed the passion in this dignified light; he had conceived it not only with moral grandeur, but with philosophical penetration. Romeo had formed his ideal; he imagined that Rosaline supplied the deficiency; but the moment he beheld Juliet he discovered his mistake. He felt a nearer affinity to her, he became perfectly enamoured, and the love he felt formed the foundation of the tragedy. The feeling of Romeo towards Juliet was wholly different, as he himself expressed it, from that he had experienced towards Rosaline.

The lecturer went on to notice the analogy between the operations of the mind with regard to taste and love, as with the former an ideal had been created which the reason was anxious to realize. Other passions distort whatever object is presented to them. Lear accused the elements of ingratitude, and the madman imagined the straws on which he trampled the golden pavement of a palace; but, with love, everything was in harmony, and all produced natural and delightful associations. In Mr. Coleridge's opinion, the conceits put into the mouths of Romeo and Juliet were perfectly natural to their age and inexperience. It

---

[1] In the Bohn edition of Coleridge's *Lectures and Notes on Shakspere*, this first paragraph was omitted, as an unnecessary duplication of Collier's report.

was Shakespeare's intention in this play to represent love as existing rather in the imagination than in the feelings, as was shewn by the imaginative dialogue between the hero and heroine, in the parting scene in the third act. The passion of the youthful Romeo was wholly different from that of the deliberate Othello, who entered the marriage state with deep moral reflections on its objects and consequences. The lecturer insisted that love was an act of the will, and ridiculed the sickly nonsense of Sterne and his imitators, French and English, who maintained that it was an involuntary emotion. Having adverted to the trueness to nature of the tragic parts of *Romeo and Juliet*, Mr. Coleridge concluded by referring to Shakespeare's description of the Apothecary, too often quoted against those of unfortunate physiognomy, or those depressed by poverty. Shakespeare meant much more; he intended to convey that in every man's face there was either to be found a history or a prophecy; a history of struggles past or a prophecy of events to come. In contemplating the face of the most abandoned of mankind, many lineaments of villainy would be seen, yet in the under features (if he might so express himself) would be traced the lines that former sufferings and struggles had impressed, which would always sadden, and frequently soften the observer, and raise a determination in him not to despair, but to regard the unfortunate object with the feelings of a brother.

RECORDS BY H. C. ROBINSON OF
THE LECTURES OF 1811–12, Etc.

In 1811 Henry Crabb Robinson began keeping his Diary, which gives henceforth an invaluable comment upon Coleridge's lectures. Robinson's records are painfully brief, but they have the advantage of representing the contemporary criticism of a man who admired Coleridge heartily and yet with a detachment of mind which permitted adverse criticism. His judgments are sometimes limited, but they are nearly always full of a good sense which demands the respect of all students of Coleridge.

Before he began his Diary he made a few memoranda of Coleridge's conversations, which are preserved among his miscellaneous papers at Dr Williams's Library.[1] Though these belong to the year preceding the lectures of 1811–12, they may be printed here more appropriately than at any other place.

A few of these records come from another source, Robinson's *Reminiscences*.[2] These manuscripts are based chiefly upon the notes in the Diary, which are much fuller. In consequence, the present editor has republished only those parts of the reminiscences of Coleridge which add to the Diary.

The last, but the most valuable of the materials from Robinson, are the letters to his brother and to his old friend, Mrs Clarkson, who was also a friend of Coleridge's. With these is printed a letter from Coleridge to Robinson which gives some interesting details in regard to the lectures.

Detached Memoranda of 1810.

Dec[r]. 20th. Met Coleridge by accident with C. and Miss Lamb. . . . We talked of Shakespeare. He did not agree with C. Lamb in his admiration of those playful and delightful pieces *Love's Labour['s] Lost* and *Midsummer Night's Dream*; but both affirmed that not a line of *Titus Andronicus* could have been written by Shakespeare. C. L. ascribed it to Marlowe, it bearing so close a resemblance to the *Jew of Malta*. L. observed that Marlowe's works are all of a different kind.

---

[1] 'Bundle II. vii. 24.'
[2] The excerpts in question come from 'Reminiscences—Coleridge—Wordsworth—Lamb,' which are to be found in the back of the bound volume of the 'Reminiscences' which covers 1834–43. All that is there recorded was written by Robinson in 1849.

Dec.[r] 23[d]. C. dined with us. . . . His remarks on Shakespeare were singularly ingenious. S., he said, delighted in portraying characters in which the intellectual powers were found in a preëminent degree, while the moral faculties were wanting, at the same time that he taught the superiority of moral greatness.[1] Such is the contrast exhibited in Iago and Othello. Iago's most marked feature is his delight in governing by fraud and superior understanding the noble minded and generous Moor. In Richard the 3[d]. cruelty is less the prominent trait than pride, to which a sense of personal deformity gave a deadly venom. C., however, asserted his belief that S. wrote hardly anything of this play besides the character of Richard. He found the piece a stock play and rewrote the parts which developed the hero's character. He certainly did not write the scenes in which Lady Anne yielded to the usurper's solicitations. —He considered *Pericles* as illustrating the way in which S. handled a piece he had to refit for representation. At first he proceeded with indifference, now and then only troubling himself to put in a thought or an image,[a] but as he advanced he interested himself in his employment, and the last two acts are almost altogether by him.

Hamlet he considered in a point of view which seems to agree very well with the representation given in *Wilhelm Meister*.[2] H. is a man whose *ideal* and internal images are so vivid that all real objects are faint and dead to him. This we see in his soliloquies on the nature of man and his disregard of life. Hence also his vacillation and the purely convulsive energies he displayed. He acts only by fits and snatches. He manifests a strong inclination to suicide. On my observing that it appeared strange S. did not give *this*, the natural termination to his piece, C. replied that S. wished to shew how even such a character is at last obliged to be the sport of chance, a salutary moral doctrine. But I thought this the suggestion of the moment only and not a happy one to obviate a seeming objection.—Hamlet remains at last the helpless *un*practical being, tho' every inducement to

---

[a] *MS. 'imagine.'*

[1] Cf. i. 206; ii. 26, 141, 237, and *B.L.* ii. 189.

[2] *Wilhelm Meister's Apprenticeship*, Bk IV, ch. xiii. On this point cf. Introduction, vol. i, p. xx. Mackenzie, Richardson, and Robertson anticipated Goethe, but neither these nor Goethe anticipated Coleridge in his interpretation of Hamlet's supposed weakness. Robinson's note is extremely important because it shows that Coleridge was interpreting Hamlet in this manner before Schlegel's discussion of Hamlet's character was published (1811).

activity is given which the very appearance of the spirit of his murdered father could bring with it.

Falstaff C. also considered as an instance of the predominance of intellectual power. He is content to be thought both a liar and a coward in order to obtain influence over the minds of his associates. His aggravated lies about the robbery are conscious and purposed, not inadvertent untruths. On my observing that this account seemed to justify Cooke's [1] representation, according to which a foreigner imperfectly understanding the character would fancy F. to be the designing knave who actually does outwit the Prince, C. answered that in his *own* estimation F. is the superior who cannot easily be convinced that the prince has escaped him; but that as in other instances S. has shewn us the defeat of mere intellect by a noble feeling, the Prince being the superior moral character who rises above his insidious companion.

On my noticing Hume's obvious preference of the French tragedians to Shakespeare, C. exclaimed Hume comprehended as much of S. as an apothecary's phial would placed under the falls of the Niagara [2]. . . .

Reminiscences. 1811.

. . . Coleridge this winter delivered a course of fifteen lectures on Milton and Shakespeare in Fleet Street, which I attended. To me they were less interesting than they would otherwise have been, because having lately been much in his company, the leading ideas were familiar to me. The difference was not great between his conversation, which was a sort of lecturing and soliloquizing, and his lectures, which were colloquial, and in which, as he was himself aware, it was impossible for him to be methodical. And those hearers who enjoyed him most, probably enjoyed most his digressions. The same subjects haunted his mind for many years, so that I do not doubt that on comparing my scanty notes with those on Shakespeare published lately by Mrs. H. Coleridge I should find a great resemblance. A report of these lectures appeared occasionally in the *Morning Chronicle* from J. P. Collier.[3] With difficulty I obtained permission from

---

[1] This seems to be a reference to the performance of Falstaff by George Frederick Cooke (1756–1811), the greatest actor of his time in the role of Falstaff, whom he resembled in character only too much.
[2] Cf. i. 195.   [3] Cf. ii. 171, 181.

Walter to insert a paragraph in the *Times*.[1] The only condition of its appearance was that it should be cold and dry. . . .

The concluding lectures were of the same kind [2] and produced the same comment. They were but indifferently attended, and scoffers were not unfrequently among the number, among my personal acquaintances not a few. I always took a lady with me, and among the ladies he had many admirers. . . . One evening I saw *Rogers* there, and with him was Lord Byron. He was wrapped up, but I recognized his club foot and his countenance and general appearance [3]. . . .

Diary, 1811–12.

[January] 29. Dined at Rickman's. . . . C. as we walked talked on Shakespeare, particularly his Fools. These he considered as supplying the place of the ancient chorus.[4] The ancient drama, he observed, is distinguished from the Shakespearian in this, that it exhibits a sort of abstraction, not of character, but of idea. A certain sentiment or passion was exhibited in all its purity, unmixed with any thing that could interfere with its effect. Shakespeare imitates life, mingled as we find it with joy and sorrow. We meet with characters who are, as it were, unfeeling spectators of the most passionate situations, constantly in life. The Fool serves to supply the place of some such uninterested person where all the characters besides have interest. The most genuine and real of S.'s Fools is in *Lear*. In *Hamlet* the Fool is, as it were, divided into several parts, dispersed thro' the piece.

C. seemed willing to censure Schiller's and Schlegel's ideas concerning the German idea of the Greek chorus, but he did not fix any reproach upon them that I could comprehend. Neither did he shew the analogy between the chorus and Fool. In both

[1] Cf. ii. 168.
[2] H. C. R. has just copied out his letter of 13 December to Mrs Clarkson. In this (cf. ii. 178–9) he has censured Coleridge's digressions.
[3] Cf. ii. 174.
[4] Jean Paul Richter calls the fool the 'chorus of the comedy,' and in a later footnote says, 'In Shakespeare the fools or clowns have more wit than humour in the real comedies, but in the serious pieces the whimsicalities of tragi-comic actors becomes humour' (*Vorschule der Aesthetik*, Section 40). This looks like an instance of indebtedness, but it is scarcely unreasonable to suppose that it is rather a striking coincidence, in the face of Coleridge's statement that he read Richter's book for the first time in 1817 (*Letters*, p. 683). (Cf. Introduction, vol. i, p. xxv.) The reader's judgment will depend entirely on his attitude toward the possibility of such coincidences.

the poet took what he found, could not dispense with, and dared not abruptly dismiss.[1] . . .

Monday, [November] 18. . . . With Walter to request he would put in a paragraph for Coleridge this evening.[2] He hesitated, and I was hurt. He consented, not with a good grace; and after the lecture, I sent an article which I affix on the other side. In the meanwhile, Walter had become more civil and left a note saying any article I might send should appear. . . .

Of Coleridge's lecture itself I fear the general opinion is not very favourable. It wanted popularity. And the moral remarks he made were not shewn to have an immediate bearing upon the subject. I can not myself well judge of the effect such remarks might have on strangers, for to me almost every individual observation was familiar. I had heard the same things from C. in private conversation, and frequently in a better style than in the lecture itself. There was throughout too much apology, too much reference to what he had before written, too much promise of what was to come. This is his great fault. In the *Friend* he was guilty of it. He will commit it in his lectures. The observations he made were in the main just and often striking. But the lecture hardly equalled his conversation. Meggison very loudly and before the lecturer had left his rostrum began to abuse him, and alarmed me as to the general impression C. might have produced.

Wed., 20 . . . Evening at Captain Burney's. A card party. Coleridge there. I just found opportunity to intimate to him the necessity of abstaining from apologies, prefaces, etc. . . .

---

[1] This paragraph is a very curious and interesting record which has never before been published. The reference to Schiller's discussion of the chorus in the Preface to *The Bride of Messina* is of no especial importance; but the reference to Schlegel is extremely interesting and mystifying. Could Robinson have quoted Schlegel? Coleridge has told us, of course, that he did not see Schlegel's lectures until late in this year (cf. ii. 126, 188–9), and he could not, indeed, have at this time seen the lectures on Shakespeare which were published in 1811. But the first volume and the first part of the second were published in 1809, and these contain Schlegel's pronouncements on the chorus, part of which Coleridge later borrowed. (Cf. i. 155–7, and Schlegel, *Werke*, v. 60, 77–8. Cf. ii. 55, note 1, and ii. 203, note 2.)

[2] Robinson was acting at the suggestion of Coleridge. (Cf. Coleridge's letter of 6 November, ii. 175.) In the stirring years of the Napoleonic wars, the small newspapers of the day found little space for literary news, and Coleridge had good reason for asking Robinson to exert his personal influence. Robinson had been connected with *The Times* as a special correspondent in Germany (1807) and in Spain (1808), being the first representative of that profession. He was also foreign editor of *The Times* in the first half of 1808 and during part of 1809. John Walter, the second of *The Times* dynasty, was chief proprietor, sole manager, and, at that time, editor of *The Times*.

Thursday [1] . . . Evening at Coleridge's second lecture, which was a vast improvement on the first. It was delivered with ease, was popular, and contained interesting matter on that which the auditors wished to hear about. I had prepared short notes, but J. Collier having made an elaborate report which I can hereafter refer to I shall reserve a connected account of the whole series of lectures for a future page.

24th, Sunday. Rose late. Breakfasted with Serjt. Rough, and then walked with him to see Coleridge at Hammersmith. We found him not quite well, but very eloquent. He soon mounted his hobby, and I was not a little surprised to find him very much of a Schellingianer, of which I had no idea. At least his mode of comparing the fine arts and of antithetically considering all their elements appeared to me very similar. [2] He observed of poetry that it united passion with order, [3] and he very beautifully illustrated the nature of the human mind which requires and seeks to gratify contrary propensities (as sloth and the horror of vacancy) at the same time; [4] and from this he deduced many of our likings and dislikings. He spoke of Calderon, defining him to be a Shakespeare, but without his philosophy—having all his imagination and fancy. His usual distinction between these last mentioned qualities he repeated on this occasion, assigning great fancy but no imagination to Southey, and much imagination but a sterile fancy to Wordsworth.—Our visit was short . . .

25th, Monday. . . . In the evening Coleridge delivered his third lecture. Excepting too much repetition in the definition, etc., of poetry, in which he was not at last very successful, and in the account of the Greek theatre, which might have been spared, at first he was successful till the close, when he absurdly and almost whiningly apologized for the freedoms he intended to use towards certain names of authority (Johnson, Addison, etc.) . . .

28, Thursday . . . Coleridge's 4th lecture. He proceeded

---

[1] 21 November.

[2] Robinson is referring to the treatment of art in Schelling's *Transcendental Idealism*, Part VI. He is probably right in regard to the influence upon Coleridge of Schelling's discussion of art as a reconciliation of opposites. But the influence is not a significant one, for Coleridge would have been previously familiar with the point of view from Kant's Introduction to the *Critique of Aesthetic Judgement*, however different the ultimate conclusions of Kant and Schelling. And the logical analysis of the reconciliation of opposites was familiar in various Platonic sources.

[3] This idea is found in Schelling, but it is too commonplace to attribute to any specific source. See the *Transcendental Idealism, Werke* (Stuttgart, Augsburg, 1856–61, Abth. I), iii. 620.

[4] Cf. i. 218, ii. 33, and *B.L.* i. 34, Coleridge's note.

to the discussion of the merits of Shakespeare and noticed his
Venus and Adonis, on which he made some striking observations
(*Vide* [1] next book, p.   ), passed over to his *Tarquin and
Lucrece* [2] on which he had nothing to say, and then classified the
dramas. Finding his time not yet elapsed, he again reverted to
the general topics of poetry, its essential nature, etc., and tho'
some of these things were good, yet the habit of thus chewing
the cud of his past lectures will be offensive. Hearers require to
have the sense of getting on. And I begin to fear that C.'s
laziness will lead him to be content with dreaming on, playing
over certain favorite ideas which he delights in but which some
of his hearers will be tired of. He certainly might with a little
exertion have collected matter enough for *one* lecture at least out
of the poems of Shakespeare. But he utterly passed over the
Sonnets and made no remark on the reception the poems have
met with from modern critics. . . .

[December] 2[d]. Coleridge's 5th lecture. An amusing
declamation against reviewers, French philosophy, precocity,
etc. in the education of children, but unluckily scarcely one
observation on Shakespeare, Milton, or even on poetry. However, his manner was animated, and he was apparently in good
spirits.

5th Thursday. . . . Accompanied Mrs. Rutt to Coleridge's
lecture. In this he surpassed himself in the art of talking very
amusingly without speaking at all on the subject to which the
audience were especially invited. According to advertisement
C. was to lecture on *Romeo and Juliet* and Shakespeare's female
characters. Instead, he began with a defence of school-flogging,
at least in preference to Lancaster's mode of punishing, without
pretending to find the least connection between that topic and
poetry. Afterwards he remarked on the character of the age of
Elizabeth and James 1st at the commencement, in which intellect
predominated, over that of Charles 1st, in which moral feeling
prevailed. He distinguished between wit and fancy, not very
clearly; he discoursed on the character of the different languages
of Europe, attacked the fashionable notion concerning poetic
diction, and abused Johnson's lines

'If observation with extensive view,' etc.

ridiculing the tautology.[3] And he commented on the alleged

---

[1] Robinson never amplified these notes, as this parenthesis seems to
promise.
[2] *The Rape of Lucrece.*   [3] Cf. ii. 89.

impurity of Shakespeare and vindicated him against the charge with warmth! ! ! ! !   The man is absolutely incorrigible.   But his *vitia* are indeed *splendida*.   I would have reported for the *Morning Chronicle*, but it was too late.

While Coleridge was so irrelevantly commenting on Lancaster's mode of punishing boys, C. Lamb [a] whispered 'It is a pity he did not leave this till he got to Henry 6th, and then he might say, he could not help taking part against the Lancastrians.' And afterwards, when C. was so extravagantly running from topic to topic without any guide whatever, C. L. said: 'This is not so much amiss.   C. said in his advertisement he would speak about the Nurse in *Romeo and Juliet*; and so he is delivering the lecture in the character of the Nurse.'. . .

Monday, 9th. . . .   Tea with Rough.   Accompanied Mrs. R. to Coleridge's 7th and incomparably best lecture.   C. declaimed with great eloquence on *Love* without wandering from his subject, *Romeo and Juliet*.   He was spirited; for the greater part intelligible, tho' profound; and he was methodical (*v.* page [1]   ).   Drew up a hasty report of the lecture for the *Morning Chronicle*, which was inserted.[2]

10 . . . C. L. spoke well about Shakespeare.   I had objected to Coleridge's assertion in his lecture, that Shakespeare became every thing *except the vicious*, observing that if Shakespeare becoming a character is to be determined by the truth and vivacity with which he describes them and enters into their feelings, [Shakespeare becomes vicious characters also].   C. L. justified Coleridge's remark by saying (what by the bye was inclusive [conclusive?]) that Shakespeare never gives truly odious and detestable characters.   He always mingles strokes of nature and humanity in his pictures.   I adduced the King in *Hamlet* as altogether mean.   He allowed this to be the worst of Shakespeare's characters.   He has not another like it.   I cited Lady Macbeth.   I think this one of Shakespeare's worst characters, said Lamb.   It is at the same time inconsistent with itself.   Her sleep-walking does not suit such a hardened being.—(It however occurs to me that this sleep-walking is perhaps the vindication of Shakespeare in his portraiture of the character, as it certainly is his excellence that he does not create monsters, but always saves the honour of human nature, if I may use such an expression.   So in this, while the voluntary actions and sentiments of Lady M. are all inhuman, her involuntary nature rises against her

[a] *MS. 'C. Lamb's.'*
[1] Cf. ii. 170, note 1.   [2] Cf. ii. 160.

habitual feelings springing out of depraved passions, and in her sleep she shews to be a woman, while waking she is a monster.) I then referred to the Bastard in *Lear*, but Lamb considers his character as vindicated by the provocation arising out of his illegitimacy. And L. mentioned as admirable illustrations of the skill with which Shakespeare could make his worst characters interesting, Iago and Richard III. I noticed King John and Lewis, as if Shakespeare meant like a Jacobin to shew how base and vile kings are; L. did not remark on this, but said *King John* is one of the plays he likes the least. He praised on the contrary *Richard II*. . . .

Thursday, 12th. . . . Evening tea with Mrs. Flaxman, who accompanied me to Coleridge's lecture. C. unhappily relapsed into his desultory habit and delivered, I think, his *worst* lecture. He began with identifying religion and love, delivered a rhapsody on brotherly and sisterly love, which seduced him into a dissertation on incest. I at last lost all power of attending to him any longer . . .

Sunday, 15. . . . Called on Godwin. He spoke with great severity of Coleridge's lectures, which he thinks infinitely below his conversation in private company. That always impresses you with the vast extent of his knowledge. In his lectures he appears grossly ignorant. G. noticed C.'s remark that Shakespeare's plays are only to be read, not acted, as absolutely false. No plays but Shakespeare's deserve to be represented, so well are they fitted for performance.[1] . . .

Monday, 16. . . . Afternoon a letter to brother, giving him an account of Coleridge's lectures,[2] etc., and in the evening took Miss Flaxman to the lecture. C. was again very desultory during half the lecture; repeating old remarks on the analogy between the antient and modern drama, etc. But at length he bethought himself of Shakespeare, and tho' he forgot at last what we had been four times successively to hear, viz., Romeo and Juliet as lovers, yet he began a new subject and treated beautifully of the *Tempest* and especially Prospero, Miranda, Ariel and Caliban.—This part most excellent. Manning at the lecture; but moderately pleased.

Thursday, 19. . . . Evening at Coleridge's lecture, which was on *Midsummer Night's Dream* and much less digressive than usual.[3] . . .

---

[1] Cf. ii. 57, 68, etc.   [2] Cf. ii. 180–1.
[3] This lecture is one of our great losses, for we have practically nothing from Coleridge on this subject.

Monday, 30. . . . A dinner party at Dr. Adam's. . . . Allowed to make my retreat to Coleridge's lectures; went with Miss Burger, who called for me. I had drunk too much to be quite clear-headed; however I was pleased to find C. very methodical. He kept to his subject and, in conformity with an opinion I gave him, intimated his intention to deliver two lectures on Milton. He had written to me stating his dilemma, having so much to do in so little time; and I wrote to him an answer in which I gently hinted at his digressions—those *splendida peccata* which his friends best apologized for by laying the emphasis on the adjective. . . .

1812.

Thursday, [January 2] . . . Coleridge's lecture, perhaps his very best. On *Richard II* and *Hamlet*, etc., etc. In the latter, striking observations on the virtue of action and the futility of talents that divert from rather than lead to action. I doubt whether he did not design that an application should be made to himself, and whether he is not well content to meet the censure his own remarks convey, for the sake of the reputation of those talents apparently depreciated. . . .

9th [1]. . . Evening, Coleridge's lecture on Johnson's Preface. C. succeeded admirably in the exposure of Johnson, and tho' he was sometimes obscure, the many palpable and intelligible *hits* must have given general satisfaction. . . .

Monday, 13 . . . Evening, accompanied Mrs. C. Aikin to Coleridge's lecture—his continuation of remarks on Johnson's Preface. Very feeble and unmeaning compared with his last. He had no answer to the general faults ascribed but the complaint of the generality of the imputation. His subsequent remarks on *Lear*, and a vindication of the melancholy catastrophe. On Othello, opinion that he is not a jealous character very excellent. Mrs. C. A. enjoyed the lecture . . .

16th . . . In the evening at Coleridge's lecture. C. to-night began on Milton. He reviewed Johnson's Preface and vindicated Milton's moral and political character with warmth, but I

---

[1] According to schedule, Coleridge should have delivered his thirteenth lecture on Monday, 6 January, and it was announced in *The Times* for that date. The lecture which Robinson attended on 9 January was also announced in *The Times* as the thirteenth lecture, and we may assume, I think, that the lecture of 6 January was postponed. Robinson's *Diary* has no reference to a lecture on that date. Thomas Ashe suggests that the thirteenth lecture covered two evenings (Coleridge's *Lectures on Shakspere*, Bohn ed., p. 165), but this seems to be a rather strained interpretation of the facts.

think with less than his usual ability.   He excited a hiss once by calling *Johnson* a fellow, for which he happily apologised by observing that it was in the nature of evil to beget evil, and that he had, therefore, in censuring Johnson, fallen into the same fault.   He remarked on Milton's minor poems and the nature of blank verse, and the latter half of his lecture was very good. . . .

20, Monday . . . Evening, Coleridge's lecture, conclusion of Milton.[1]   Not one of his happiest lectures.   Among the audience, Lord Byron and Rogers, the banker. . . .

27, Monday . . . Coleridge's concluding lecture. . . .

The lecture was exceedingly well attended; and Coleridge was very animated in parts.   His development of the character of Satan, his apology for Milton's mode of treating the character of the Supreme Being, etc., etc., were excellent.   There were some excrescences in the lecture; and he offended me by an unhandsome and unmanly attack upon Mrs. Barbauld.   He ridiculed some expressions [a] in her 'Ode to Content': 'The hamlet's brown primrose and violet,' etc.   Criticisms he added which Wordsworth made to me at Charles Lamb's two [2] years ago.[3]   That he should select among the living authors a woman and that woman a lady who has been among his admirers formerly, and I believe always shewed him civilities, is ungenerous and unworthy his better feelings.   He analysed a passage in Pope's Homer (a description of moonlight) and shewed its want of propriety and taste with great spirit.   At the same time he introduced this censure with a very insincere eulogium.

Mr. and Mrs. Becker at the lecture.   I joined them at Aders's. They had been much gratified by the lecture.[4]

[a] *MS.* '*expresses.*'
[1] This lecture and that immediately preceding were the only lectures announced on Milton.   There is no foundation for the remark of Thomas Ashe that 'promise and performance varied and . . . Milton was all but passed over.'   Bohn edition of Coleridge's *Lectures on Shakspere*, p. 165.
[2] Read 'four.'   See note 3, below.
[3] Cf. ii. 183, and H. C. R.'s *Diary* (1872), i. 139.   This was Robinson's first meeting with Wordsworth, 15 March 1808.   The incident is retailed at greater length in *The Correspondence of H. C. Robinson with the Wordsworth Circle* (Oxford, 1927), i. 53–4.
It is worth pointing out that Wordsworth's expression of this criticism nearly four years before we hear of it in the mouth of Coleridge does not afford certain evidence that it is originally his, rather than Coleridge's, any more than the appearance of an observation in Dorothy Wordsworth's Diary before its publication in a poem by Wordsworth or Coleridge assures us that it comes originally from her.
[4] Robinson attended every lecture of this series, for which he furnishes a complete calendar, confirmed by the announcements in the newspapers. Through the care of the Morgans, Coleridge was systematic in his adherence to his schedule, with two exceptions only.   The thirteenth lecture should

[February] 10th, Monday . . . Read evening at home Schlegel's lectures on Shakespeare. Coleridge, I find, did not disdain to borrow observations from Schlegel, tho' the coincidences between the two lecturers are for the greater part coincidences merely and not the one caused by the other.

LETTERS

I. *Coleridge to Robinson.*

6 November, 1811.

MY DEAR ROBINSON,

The Coachmakers' Hall having no literary or philosophical redolence, or rather smelling somewhat unsavory to the *nares intellectuales* of all my wealthy acquaintance, partly from past political spouting clubs, and partly from its present assignment to hops and the instruction of grown gentlemen in dancing, I have at length procured another room every way answering my purposes—a spacious handsome room with an academical stair-case and the lecture room itself fitted up in a very grave authentic poetico-phi[losophic [a]] style with the busts of Newton, Milton, Sha[kespeare [a]], Pope, and Locke, behind the lecturer's *cathedra.* I have, likewise, lowered the prices from three and four to two and three guineas. I am sure you will say what you can for me among your friends; but what I more particularly wish you to do is to see it advertised in the *Times* if by *favor* it can be done so as to *advertise* only as many lines as will not exceed the price of an ordinary advertisement, and to let the rest appear as a part of the paper itself. I certainly should do my best to repay it by sending occasional articles to the *Times*, prose or verse. Perhaps you may have it in your power

---

have been delivered on 6 January and was apparently postponed until 9 January (cf. ii. 173 and note); the concluding lecture (the seventeenth) should have been delivered on 23 January instead of 27 January. On 23 January the hall was engaged for another purpose. Between 19 December and 30 December was an intermission for the Christmas holidays.

So far as I have been able to discover, none of the advertisements give information about the subjects of the lectures which we do not already possess from Robinson's memoranda, except *The Times* advertisement of the last lecture, which announced that the lecture would consist of ' Strictures on the Modern Poets.'

[a] *The MS. is torn here.*

to conciliate Mr. Walter's good will towards me in this business. Likewise, do you know any member of the Russell Institution to whom you could entrust a few prospectuses to be placed in their library or chatting room?   I have left two or three at the Westminster Library.   At present my dormitory at least is at Mr. Morgan's, Portland Place, Hammersmith.

I am very anxious to see Schlegel's *Werke* before the Lectures commence.[1]   May God bless you, my dear Sir, and

> Your sincere friend,
> S. T. COLERIDGE.

II. *Robinson to Mrs. Clarkson.*[2]

29 Novr., 1811.

Of course you have already heard of the lectures on poetry which Coleridge is now delivering and, I fear, have begun to think me inattentive in not sending you some account of them, or rather, I should say, of his success in the undertaking. Yesterday he delivered the fourth; and I could not before form anything like an opinion of the probable result.   Indeed it is hardly otherwise now with me; but were I to wait till I could form a judgement, the very subject itself might escape from observation.   Coleridge has about 150 hearers on an average, and I fear the number is rather likely to diminish than increase. A large proportion of these have been accidental droppers in (at a dollar a head).   On the second night £12. were received at the door; and there may be, I should suppose, about 40 who come in with orders.   You may, therefore, calculate in a great measure what the produce may be.   The ladies, I should add, do not form above a third.   Their subscription coming with a gent is only one guinea: he pays two guineas for his ticket.

A scruple just now flew in my face at having filled a whole side with such *low* concerns, but it subsided on the reflection that interested as I know you to be in the comfort and well being of your friend, you will read with interest anything that affects it materially.   And certainly C. would never have roused himself to this effort, if he had not felt an immediate want that impelled

---

[1] If we may rely on Coleridge's own testimony, this wish to see Schlegel's *Werke* was not gratified until after the eighth lecture.   (Cf. ii. 126, 188–9.)

[2] In this letter, and in those succeeding, the place '56, Hatton Garden,' the complimentary address, 'My dear friend,' and the signature, etc., are omitted.

him to make it. He has left the *Courier* some weeks and I saw a letter he had written to an old acquaintance (Serjt. Rough), in which he frankly assigned as his inducement, the necessity of discharging an old debt incurred by the publication of the *Friend*, in order to finish the volume in numbers and afterwards publish quarterly volumes. This intention may perhaps be new to you, as I believe he has not yet written. He begged me the other day to remember him most affectionately to you; he has been about writing to you these several months. And he added he wanted to see me before my journey, that I might have delivered a verbal explanation concerning his affair with Wordsworth. This was the sole allusion he ever made to the affair. Of course I did not question him further. But to return to the lectures. They have been brilliant; that is, in passages. But I doubt much his capacity to render them popular, or rather, I should say, I doubt any man's power to render a system of philosophy popular which supposes so much unusual attention and rare faculties of thinking, even in the hearer. The majority of what are called sensible and thinking men have, to borrow a phrase from C., 'the passion of clear ideas.' And as all poets have a very opposite passion, that of warm feelings, and a delight in musing over conceptions and imaginings beyond the reach of the analytic faculty, no wonder there is a sort of natural hostility between these classes of minds. This will ever be a bar to C.'s extensive popularity; besides which he has certain unfortunate habits, which he *will* not (perhaps *can* not) correct, very detrimental to his interests. I mean the vice of apologising, anticipating, and repeating. We have had four lectures, and are still in the prolegomena to the Shakespearean drama. When we are to begin Milton I have no idea. With all these defects, there will always be a small circle who will listen with delight to his eloquent effusions (for that is the appropriate expression). I have not missed a lecture and have always left the room with satisfaction, which the hearkening to the display of truth in a beautiful form always gives. I have a German friend who attends also, and who is delighted to find the logic and the rhetoric of his country delivered in a foreign language. There is no doubt that Coleridge's mind is much more German than English. My friend has pointed out striking analogies between C. and German authors whom he has never seen. This is very interesting to me, tho' I now neglect everything, except the lectures, for *law*. . . .

III. *Robinson to Mrs. Clarkson.*

13th Decr., 1811.

. . . Yesterday I should have been able to send you a far more pleasant letter than I can possibly furnish you with now; for I should have then have had to speak of one of the most gratifying and delightful exertions of C.'s mind on Monday last.   And now I am both pained and provoked by as unworthy a sequel to his preceding lecture.   And you know it is a law of our nature

> 'As high as we have mounted in delight
> In our dejection do we sink as low.' [1]

You have so beautifully and exactly expressed the sentiment that every considerate and kind observer of your friend must entertain, that it is quite needless to give you any account of his lectures with a view to direct any judgement you might wish to form or any feeling you might be disposed to encourage.   You will, I am sure, anticipate the way in which he will execute his lectures.   As evidences of splendid talent, original thought, and rare powers of expression and fancy, they are all his *admirers* can wish; but as a discharge of his undertaking, a fulfilment of his promise to the public, they give his *friends* great uneasiness. As you express it, 'an enchanter's spell seems to be upon him,' which takes from him the power of treating upon the only subject his hearers are anxious he should consider, while it leaves him infinite ability to riot and run wild on a variety of moral and religious themes.   In his fifth lecture, he was by advertisement to speak of *Romeo and Juliet* and Shakespeare's females.   Unhappily some demon whispered the name of Lancaster in his ear; and we had in one evening—an attack on the poor Quaker, a defence of boarding-school flogging, a parallel between the ages of Elizabeth and Charles, a defence of what is untruly called unpoetic language, an account of the different languages of Europe, and a vindication of Shakespeare against the imputation of grossness! ! !   I suspect he did discover that offence was taken at this; for his succeeding lecture on Monday was all we could wish.   He confined himself to *Romeo and Juliet* for a time, treated of the inferior characters, and delivered a most eloquent discourse on love, with a promise to point out how Shakespeare

---

[1] Wordsworth's *Resolution and Independence.*

had shewn the same truths in the persons of the lovers. Yesterday we were to have a continuation of the theme. Alas! C. began with a parallel between religion and love, which, tho' one of his favorite themes, he did not manage successfully. He then treated of brotherly and sisterly love, and suffered himself to be seduced into a long digression on *incest*. Romeo and Juliet were forgotten. And in the next lecture we are really to hear something of these lovers. Now this will be the fourth time that his hearers will have been invited expressly to hear of this play. There are to be only fifteen lectures in the whole (half have been delivered); and the course is to include Shakespeare and Milton, the modern poets, etc. ! ! ! I fear if we look close we shall find that indolence lies at the root of this. He *will not* look into Shakespeare. The Morgans are continually laying the book in his way; but as if spell-bound, he cannot prepare himself for his lecture. The consequence is that he has recourse to his old MS. commonplace book, which I dare say you well recollect; and instead of a lecture on a definite subject, we have an immethodical rhapsody, very delightful to you and me, and only offensive from the certainty that it may and ought to offend those who come with other expectations ! ! ! Yet with all this, I cannot but be charmed with these *splendida vitia*, and my chief displeasure is occasioned by my being forced to hear the strictures of persons infinitely below C., without any power of refuting or contradicting them. Yet it is lucky that he has hitherto omitted no lecture. Living with the Morgans, they force him to come with them to the lecture room; and this is a great point gained.

I only see him the lecture evenings now; and I fear this is not the time to get him to write to you, but if I can judge from his manner whenever your name is mentioned, he would certainly read your letter. But let it not reach him on a Thursday or Monday.

In the *Morning Chronicle* appear after the lectures short reports, 'by different hands.' They serve better than an advertisement to keep up the public attention and I have no doubt draw auditors. I have written one, but if you do get the papers they will furnish you with little information. . . .

IV. *H. C. Robinson to Thomas Robinson.*

16th Decr.[1] [1811].

. . . You will I dare say be curious to know my opinion of Coleridge's lectures, and I had thought of referring you for that purpose to two letters written to Mrs. Clarkson. But as I can imagine she would have no great pleasure in reading them (your surmise being in fact well founded) I must compress in a narrow compass and say plainly what I wrote to her more at length and with that *management* which is due to a friend.

In a word, then, Coleridge's lectures do high honour to him as a man of genius, but are discreditable to him (perhaps I might use without injustice a stronger word) as a man who has a duty to discharge; for either he wants judgement to know what he ought to introduce in his lectures, or is overpowered by very culpable indolence, and will not qualify himself to do justice to his subject, his hearers, or himself. His pretended lectures are immethodical rhapsodies, moral, metaphysical, and literary, abounding in brilliant thoughts, fine flashes of rhetoric, ingenious paradoxes, occasionally profound and salutary truths, but they are not a scientific or instructive course of readings on any one subject a man can wish to fix his attention on. He is to lecture on Shakespeare, Milton, and the modern poets. We have in fact had one lecture on the minor poems of Shakespeare and have been *three nights* alone employed on *Romeo and Juliet*, which we are promised the conclusion of. The course is to consist of fifteen lectures, and eight are over ! ! !

As a specimen, I will give you a syllabus of his sixth lecture, advertised to be on *Romeo and Juliet* and Shakespeare's female characters: viz., a defence of the old singing mode of reading; an attack upon Lancaster, especially his modes of punishment; a defence of school-flogging; then by a mighty spring (tho' I could not see where he fixed his foot to leap from) a beautiful statement of the opposite character of the ages of Elizabeth and Charles I.; a commonplace dissertation on the different character of the European languages; an abuse of poetic diction *à la* Wordsworth; and a long attempt to vindicate Shakespeare from the charge of impurity. However, his following lecture was most excellent: he discussed the minor characters of *Romeo and Juliet* and

---

[1] This letter was begun on 14 December. The date of the continuation is Robinson's, not mine.

delivered an eloquent declamation on the nature of love, which he promised in the next lecture to apply to the lovers. Alas, the next and last lecture was worse, if possible, than the sixth. He began unhappily with an analogy he resolved to draw between religion and love—no very great undertaking for a man of such powers of combination; but then he proceeded to the nature of brotherly and sisterly love and gave us a dissertation on incest. I could not attend to the rest; I know only that we are for the fourth time to hear of *Romeo and Juliet* to-night.   The fact is that C. cannot be induced to read Shakespeare; and finding himself unprepared with particular and appropriate observations, he has recourse to his old commonplace books, out of which he reads whatever chances to catch his eye, in which he certainly finds very beautiful things, which only offend me from their being thus impertinently and irrelevantly brought forward. By the bye, if you have access to the *Morning Chronicle* you will find a report of the lecture.   It is written in this house; sometimes by Mr. Collier, sometimes by John C., and sometimes by myself.   We are all anxious to insert the most attractive and relevant matter, as that from the report you might infer more connection than there is in fact. . . .

V. *Robinson to Mrs. Clarkson.*

3 Jany., 1812.

I received your letter last night and will write the answer immediately, tho' I cannot forward it till I have seen your brother for your address.   I have a better, a much better account to give of Coleridge's lectures than formerly.   His last three lectures have for the greater part been all that his friends could wish, his admirers expect.   Your sister heard the two last, and from her you will learn much more than I could put into a letter, had I all the leisure I now want, or the memory I never had. His disquisitions on the characters of Richard III., Iago, Falstaff, were full of paradox, but very ingenious and in the main fine; his remarks on Richard II. and Hamlet very excellent. Last night he concluded his fine development of the Prince of Denmark by an eloquent statement of the moral of the play: 'Action,' he said, 'is the great end of all.   No intellect, however grand, is valuable if it draw us from action and lead us to think and think till the time of action is passed by and we can do nothing.'   Somebody said to me, 'This is a satire on himself.'—

'No,' said I, 'it is an elegy.'   A great many of his remarks on
Hamlet were capable of a like application.   I should add that he
means to deliver several lectures beyond the promised number.
This will gain him *credit* in the City-sense of the word; and for
the sake of his future success in lecturing, I am very glad he is
thus prudent.

You see, I am viewing the subject from a very low point of
view.   At the same time I am able to place myself on higher
ground, and then I lament equally with the Wordsworths and
yourself that such a man should be compelled to have recourse
to such means.   But after all what is there in this lamentation
more than a particular instance of the general complaint of all
ages that highmindedness should stoop to vulgarity; that the low
wants of man should drag down the elevated to low pursuits;
and that the noblest powers of intellect should not be accompanied with meaner but indispensable capacities? . . .

VI.   *Robinson to Mrs. Clarkson.*[1]

28 Jany., 1812.

You will be interested to hear how Coleridge's lectures closed.
They ended with éclat.   The room was crowded; and the
lecture had several passages more than brilliant; they were
luminous, and the light gave conscious pleasure to every person
who knew that he could both see the glory and the objects
around it at once, while (you know) mere splendour like the
patent lamps present[s] a flame that only puts out the eyes.
C.'s explanation of the character of Satan, his vindication of
Milton against the charge of falling below his subject where he
introduces the Supreme Being, and his illustration of the
difference between poetic and abstract truth, and of the *diversity
in identity* between the philosopher and the poet, were equally
wise and beautifully demonstrated.   He concluded with a few
strokes of satire.   But I cannot forgive him for selecting *alone*
(except an attack on Pope's Homer, qualified by insincere eulogy)
Mrs. Barbauld.   She is a living writer, a woman, and a person
who, however discordant from himself in character and taste,
has still always shewn him civilities and attentions.   She had
friends in the room, and the ridicule will be repeated by every
one who knew the author from whom his citations were taken.

[1] Written from Gray's Inn.

It was surely ungenerous and unmanly.   My only excuse for
him is that he wished to fix a sting on some one and had
sharpened no other.   All the remarks, namely, on the *brown
hamlet*, the 'moss rose and violet,' etc., were made by Wordsworth to me when in town.[1]   I know not who is the author of
them.   They are in themselves good, but the merit of making
them does not in my mind outweigh the demerit of so delivering them. . . .

[1] Cf. ii. 174 and note.

A LETTER BY COLERIDGE ON
PLAGIARISM

Among the Coleridge manuscripts in the British Museum, there is a long holograph letter [1] dealing with Scott's supposed plagiarism from *Christabel*, with the striking parallelisms of Schlegel's and Coleridge's own lectures, and with plagiarism in general. This magnificent unpublished letter, which was written between 15 December and 21 December 1811,[2] is indorsed as follows: 'Rough draft of a letter written to a man $(-,\delta-\gamma\kappa\ o\gamma\theta$ [3]$)$ who offered to review W. Scott's poems to his injury. To have been copied [and?] [4] sent to Lord B.[5]

SIR:

As I am bound to thank you for your good-will, and the high opinion you have been pleased to express of my genius, so I ask in return that you should give me credit for perfect sincerity in the motives and feelings which I shall assign for my inability to comply with your request.[a]

Excuse me, if I say that I have ever held parallelisms adduced in proof of plagiarism or even of intentional imitation, in the

---

[a] *After this sentence, Coleridge first wrote, 'There are two kinds of head in the world—the one I would call springs, the other tanks.' Without striking it out, he indicated a text like that above, by crosses at the beginning and end of the sentence, and by the word 'insert' at the beginning of the following sentence.*

[1] Additional MSS. 34, 225, folios 175–81. The letter is written on the back of prospectuses for the second lecture of 1811–12.

[2] Cf. ii. 188–9, note 3.

[3] Coleridge's private cipher. The editor cannot interpret this name.

[4] This word is on the extreme margin and was pasted over in binding the manuscripts into a volume. It seems to be the symbol for 'and,' the ampersand.

[5] The second sentence (which is not continuous with the first) is struck out in the manuscript; but still legible. Lord B. is, presumably, Lord Byron. If so, Coleridge's indorsement is probably later in date than the letter itself. In 1815 Coleridge began a short correspondence with Byron. During this brief correspondence Scott's indebtedness to *Christabel* was mentioned (see Byron's *Letters and Journals*, iii. 228) and Coleridge probably conceived the idea of forwarding this old letter to Byron as evidence of his unresentful attitude toward the plagiarist. But the letters of Coleridge which I have in my possession do not indicate that he acted upon this impulse.

In an extremely interesting letter on Scott written to Allsop in 1820, Coleridge makes a passing reference to this letter. Allsop, *Coleridge's Letters*, etc. (1858), p. 27. I know of no other reference to it except a quotation by E. H. Coleridge. (Cf. ii. 190, note 3.)

utmost contempt.   There are two kinds of heads in the world of
literature.   The one I would call, SPRINGS: the other, TANKS.
The latter class, habituated to receiving only, full or low,
according to the state of its feeders, attach[es] no distinct notion
to living production as contra-distinguished from mechanical
formation.   If they find a fine passage in Thomson, they refer
it to Milton; if in Milton, to Euripides or Homer; and if in
Homer, they take for granted its pre-existence in the lost works
of Linus or Musaeus.   It would seem as if it was a part of their
creed, that all thoughts are traditional, and that not only the
alphabet was revealed to Adam, but all that was ever written in
it that was worth writing.[1]   But I come to the point.   I can
scarcely call myself an acquaintance of Mr. Walter Scott's; but I
have met him twice or thrice in company.   Those who hold
that a man's nature is shewn in his countenance would not need
the confident assurance, which all his friends and acquaintances
so unanimously give, that he is of the most frank and generous
disposition, incapable of trick or concealment.   The mere
expression of his features, and the tones of his voice in conversation, independent of the matter, sufficiently attest the fervour
and activity of his mind.   The proofs must be strong indeed,
sir, which could convince me that such a man could consciously
make an unfair and selfish use of *any* manuscript that came by
accident into his possession—least of all, one of a known contemporary   What then are they, the facts that are to weaken this
presumption?

    First, that the fragment, entitled 'Christabel,' was composed
many *years*, and known and openly admired by Mr. Scott some
time, before the *publication* of the 'Lay of the Last Minstrel.'
(For be pleased to observe, it is no part of the known *fact* that
the 'Lay of the Last Minstrel' was not composed in part at least
or at least *planned*, before Mr. S. had seen the fragment in
question.[2])

---

[1] Coleridge borrowed parts of this brilliant satire for his Preface to
Christabel (1816).   Cf. also the letter of 1810 which was published by the
present editor in *Modern Language Notes*, xliii. (1928), 378.

[2] The facts are as follows: *Christabel* was composed in 1797 (Part I)
and 1800 (Part II).   Scott heard John Stoddart recite *Christabel* in 1802,
when he was beginning *The Lay of the Last Minstrel*, which he published
in 1805.   He acknowledged his obligations in conversation, he tells us; and in
his Introduction to *The Lay of the Last Minstrel* in 1830 he made a public
acknowledgment—generous, as befitted Scott's character, but undoubtedly
rather late.   The facts are fully presented in the Introduction above mentioned, but the account there given would place the recitation during Stoddart's visit of 1800.   This may be the preferable date, but I give the date
1802 on the authority of E. H. Coleridge.   (Cf. ii. 190, note 3.)

Secondly, that of those who had seen or heard the fragment a large proportion were struck with certain lines the same or nearly the same in the L. L. M., with similar movements in the manner of narration and the arrangement of the imagery, and lastly with that general resemblance which is exprest by the words—the one still reminded them of the other.   Before I proceed to the arguments on the other side, I will examine these, and if I can rely on my own feelings at the present moment, exactly as I would wish a friend of mine to do if I had been the fortunate author of the 'Lay of the Last Minstrel' and the 'Marmion,' and Mr. W. S. the earlier writer of the 'Christabel.'

Now it must be obvious on the first calm reflection, that Mr. W. S. could have had no previous intention of using the 'Christabel,' from the very fact which has furnished the main strength of the contrary presumption.   For before the appearance of the 'Lay of the L. M.' he not only mentioned the 'Christabel' repeatedly to persons who had never before heard of it, not only praised it with warmth, but *recited* it.   In order to evade or weaken this fact, we must make the arbitrary supposition, that he had not at that time planned his poem as it now appears: and that the purpose was formed in his mind afterwards, and while he was composing.   A purpose, of course, implies consciousness. Now this again is rendered in the highest degree improbable by another of the facts above stated, and by one too that has assuredly had no small share in occasioning the suspicion,— the existence, I mean, of a number of lines the same or nearly the same in both authors.   I have not the poems by me; but I distinctly remember, that the greater part consisted of phrases, such as 'Jesu Maria! shield thee well,' [1] etc., which might have occurred to a score of writers who had been previously familiar with poems and romances written before the Reformation or translated from the Spanish—and the small remainder contain nothing remarkable either in language, thought, feeling, or imagery.[2]   From long disuse, I cannot have the tenth part of the fluency in versification as Mr. Scott or Southey have: and yet I would undertake in a couple of hours to alter every one of these lines or couplets without the least injury to the context, to retain

[1] *Christabel*, 54, 582. 'Jesu, Maria, shield her well!'   69. 'Mary mother, save me now!' *Lay*, Canto I. i. 5. 'Jesu Maria, shield us well.' (Scott acknowledged this borrowing.   Introduction to the *Lay of the Last Minstrel*.) *Christabel*, 44. 'Is it the wind that moaneth bleak?' *Lay*, Canto I. xii. 11. 'Is it the wind that swings the oaks?'
[2] For other echoes, cf. the style of Canto I. xiii, Canto II. xxvi–xxvii, with the beginning of *Christabel*.

the same meaning in words equally poetical and suitable, and yet entirely remove all the *appearance* of likeness.   And this, sir, is what an intentional plagiarist would have done.   He would have *translated*, not transcribed.

If then there be any just ground for the charge of 'stolen feathers' (say rather, for an imitation of the mode of flying), it must be found in the supposed close likeness of the metre,[1] the *movements*, the way of relating an event,—in short, in the general resemblance of the great features which have given to the physiognomy of Mr. W. S.'s late poems their marked originality in the public feeling.   Now that several persons, and those too persons of education and liberal minds, at several times, and without any knowledge of each other's opinions, have been struck with this general resemblance, and have expressed themselves more or less strongly on the subject, I do not pretend to deny: for it is a fact of my own knowledge.   But it would be most dishonorable in me if I did not add, that *if* I had framed my expectations exclusively by the opinions and assertions of others, those whose expressions were most limited would have excited anticipations which my own after perusal of the 'Lay of the Last Minstrel' were far from verifying [?] to my own mind.   But I will admit that of this neither I or Mr. S. are or can be the proper judges.   A poet may be able to appreciate the merit of each particular part of his own poem as well, or (if he have a well-disciplined mind) better than any other can do: but of the *effect* of the whole as a whole, he cannot from the very nature of things (from the foreknowledge of each following part, from the parts having been written at different times, from the blending of the pleasures and disgusts of composing with the composition itself, etc.) have the same sensation as the reader or auditor to whom the whole is new and simultaneous.   The case must then be thus stated.   Put aside the fact of the previous acquaintance with the 'Christabel'; suppose that no circumstances were known that rendered it probable.   Would the resemblances in and of themselves have enforced, or at least have generally *suggested*, the suspicion that [the] later poem was an intentional imitation of the elder?   In other words, is the general likeness, or [anything] in the particular resemblances, such as a liberal and enlightened reader could not with any probability consider as the result of mere coincidence between two writers of similar

---

[1] This is, of course, the chief obligation of Scott, whose imitation of Coleridge's remarkably original metre inevitably prevented it from making upon the public the impression which it might have made.

pursuits, and (*argumenti causâ loquor*) of nearly equal talent.   Coincidence is here used as a negative, not as implying that the likeness between the works is merely accidental, the effect of chance, but as asserting that it is not the effect of imitation.

Now how far coincidence in this sense and under the supposed conditions is possible, I can myself supply an instance, which happened at my lectures in Flower de Luce Court [1] only last week, and the accuracy of which does not rely on *my* evidence only, but can be proved by the separate testimony of some hundred individuals—that is, by as many as have attended and retained any distinct recollection of my lectures at the Royal Institution or at Fetter Lane.[2]   After the close of my lecture on *Romeo and Juliet*,[3] a German gentleman, a Mr. Bernard Krusve, introduced himself to me, and after some courteous compliments said, 'Were it not almost impossible, I must have believed that you had either heard or read my countryman Schlegel's lecture on this play, given at Vienna: the principles, thought, and the very illustrations are so nearly the same.   But the lectures were but just published as I left Germany,[4] scarcely more than a week since, and the only two copies of the work in England I have reason to think that I myself have brought over.   One I retain:

[1] This is the series of 1811–12, given in the rooms of the London Philosophical Society, Scots Corporation Hall, Crane Court, Fleet Street (or Flower de Luce Court, Fetter Lane).   Crane Court and Flower de Luce Court (now Fleur de Lis Court) lead off from Fleet Street and Fetter Lane respectively and both lead, from different directions, to the building in which Coleridge's lectures were given.   The present structure separates the two courts, but the editor has been informed that the courts formerly communicated with each other.   A map of Coleridge's time seems to confirm this.   These details have been given to prevent confusion in Coleridge's references to the lectures.

[2] That is, the series of 1808 and 1811–12, the latter being still in progress.

[3] The seventh and eighth lectures both dealt with *Romeo and Juliet*—with digressions.   Coleridge refers to the eighth (12 December 1811), for in the ninth lecture (cf. ii. 126) he mentioned his recent reading of Schlegel's lectures: 'Yesterday afternoon [15 December] a friend left a book for me by a German critic,' etc.   The date inferred from the remark just quoted differs slightly from that given below in the present letter.   If, as Coleridge says, 'The next morning [after the eighth lecture] Mr Krusve called on me and made me a present of the book,' the date of receiving a copy of Schlegel's *Vorlesungen* was 13 December, not 15 December.

As the meeting with Mr Krusve occurred 'only last week,' the date of the present letter lies between Sunday, 15 December, and Saturday, 21 December 1811.

[4] The first volume and the first part of the second volume of Schlegel's *Vorlesungen* were published in 1809; the second part of the second volume in 1811.   The second part of the second volume included Schlegel's lectures on English drama, which he had rewritten and expanded after the oral delivery at Vienna in 1808.

the other is at Mr. Boosey's.'[1]   I replied that I had not even heard of these lectures, nor had indeed seen any work of Schlegel's except a volume of translations from Spanish poetry,[2] which the Baron Von Humboldt[3] had lent me when I was at Rome—one piece of which, a translation of a play of Calderon, I had compared with the original, and formed in consequence a high opinion of Schlegel's taste and genius.   A friend standing by me added, 'This cannot be a question of dates, sir; for if the gentleman whose name you have mentioned, first gave his lectures at Vienna in 1810,[4] I can myself bear witness that I heard Mr. Coleridge deliver all the *substance* of to-night's lecture at the Royal Institution some years before.'   The next morning, Mr. Krusve called on me and made me a present of the book; and as much as the resemblance of the L. of L. M. fell below the anticipations which the accounts of others were calculated to excite, so much did this book transcend [them], not in one lecture, but in all the lectures that related to Shakespeare or to poetry in general: the grounds, train of reasoning, etc., were different in language only and often not even in that.   The thoughts too were so far peculiar that to the best of my knowledge they did not exist in any prior work of criticism.   Yet I was far more flattered, or to speak more truly, I was more confirmed, than surprize[d].   For Schlegel and myself had both studied deeply and perseverantly the philosophy of Kant, the distinguishing feature of which [is] to treat every subject in reference to the operation of the mental faculties to which it specially appertains, and to commence by the cautious discrimination of what is essential, i.e. explicable by mere consideration of the faculties in themselves, from what is empirical, i.e. the modifying or disturbing forces of time, place, and circumstances. Suppose myself and Schlegel (my argument, not my vanity, leads to these seeming self-flatteries) nearly equal in natural powers, of similar pursuits and acquirements, and it is only necessary for both to have mastered the spirit of Kant's *Critique of the Judgement* to render it morally certain that, writing on the same

---

[1] Mr Boosey was the New Broad Street bookseller.

[2] *Spanisches Theater*, B. I. (1803).   It should be pointed out, however, that Coleridge had tried to get Schlegel's *Werke* from H. C. Robinson more than a month (6 November) before this date (15–21 December).   (Cf. ii. 176, and also ii. 168, and note.)

[3] This is the elder Von Humboldt, Karl Wilhelm, philologist, diplomatist, and statesman.

[4] This important date is blotted, but still decipherable. Cf. ii. 245, Coleridge's letter of 1818 to Mudford, where Coleridge says that Schlegel's lectures 'were not given orally till two years after mine.'

subject, we should draw the same conclusions, by the same brains, from the same principles, write to one purpose and with one spirit.[1]

Now, sir, apply this to Mr. W. Scott.   If his poem had been in any sense a borrowed thing, its elements likewise would surely be assumed, not nature.   But no insect was ever more like in the color of its skin and juices to the leaf it fed on,[2] than Scott's muse is to Scott himself.[3]   Habitually conversant with the antiquities of his country, and of all Europe during the ruder periods of society, living, as it were, in whatever is found in them imposing either to the fancy or interesting to the feelings, passionately fond of natural scenery, abundant in local anecdote, and besides learned in

> 'all the antique scrolls of faery land,
> Processions, tournaments, spells, chivalry.' [4]

in all languages, from Apuleius to 'Tam o' Shanter,'—how else or what else could he have been expected to write?   His poems are evidently the indigenous products of his mind and habits.

But I have wearied myself, and shall weary you.   I will only add that I have a volume of poems now before me, completely made up of gross plagiarisms from Akenside, Thomson, Bowles, Southey, and the *Lyrical Ballads*.   It is curious to observe how many artifices the poor author has used to disguise the theft,—transpositions, dilutions, substitutions of synonyms, etc. etc.,—and yet not the least resemblance to any one of the poets whom

---

[1] This of course is an exaggeration of the influence of Kant, which would be just only if the names of Lessing, Schiller, Herder, Heyne, etc., were added to explain the common background of Coleridge's and Schlegel's criticism.   The reference to Kant is, nevertheless, very important, because it indicates that the obligation is not so much in specific ideas as in method, and that the method is essentially psychological.
Coleridge's exaggeration of his obligations to Kant may be read to advantage in the light of Kant's modest and profoundly true observation that 'the formation or culture of taste . . . will pursue its course in the future, as in the past, independently of such inquiries [as studies of aesthetic]' (*Critique of Aesthetic Judgement*, Preface, p. 6, trans. Meredith, Oxford, 1911).   Literary criticism like Coleridge's is inductive, and it is concerned primarily with 'the formation or culture of taste.'

[2] It is curious to note Coleridge's recurrences to favourite images.   Cf. *The Friend, Works*, ii. 307.

[3] Ernest Hartley Coleridge quoted this line in his edition of *Christabel* (London, 1907), p. 45.   He there discusses Scott's indebtedness.   See also pp. 64, note 2, 67, note 1, for his other references to the indebtedness of Scott and Byron.

[4] The editor cannot identify these verses and is inclined to believe that they are by Coleridge himself.

he pillaged.   He who can catch the spirit of an original, has it already.   It will not [be] by dates that posterity will judge of the originality of a poem; but by the original spirit itself.   This is to be found neither in a tale, however interesting, which is but the canvas; no, nor yet in the fancy or the imagery, which are but forms and colors.   It is a subtle spirit, all in each part, reconciling and unifying all.   Passion and imagination are its most appropriate names; but even these say little—for it must be not merely passion but poetic passion, poetic imagination.

THE LECTURES OF 1812

After the successful conclusion of the lectures of 1811–12 on 27 January, Coleridge spent several months in the Lake District, tormented by his physical nearness to the Wordsworth family and his alienation from their affection. The Lakes could no longer be his home, and he returned to them no more. For the time being, he settled himself with the Morgans in London and began plans for a new series of lectures. We hear of these for the first time in a letter to Mrs Coleridge,[1] dated 21 April 1812. On 24 April he writes again to his wife and tells her that he has found a place for the lectures and settled upon the date of their commencement, the first Tuesday in May[2] (5 May). This hope was not fulfilled, but on 11 May the *Courier* contained the following advertisement, which was also printed on cards as a brief prospectus.[3]

Lectures on the Drama.

MR. COLERIDGE proposes to give a SERIES of LECTURES on the drama of the Greek, French, English, and Spanish stage, chiefly with reference to the Works of Shakespeare: at Willis's Rooms, King Street, St. James's-Square, on the Tuesdays and Fridays in May and June, at three o'clock precisely. The Course will contain Six Lectures, at One Guinea. Tickets transferable.

An account is opened at Messrs. Ransom, Morland and Co.'s Bankers, Pall-Mall, in the Names of Sir G. Beaumont, Bart. Sir T. Bernard, Bart. W. Sotheby, Esq. where Subscriptions will be received, and Tickets issued. The first Lecture on Tuesday, 12th of May.

S. T. C. 71, Berners-street.

The three aristocratic and wealthy patrons, the West End banking-house, and the more fashionable location of the lecture-hall, did not bring forth as many subscribers as Coleridge expected, and on 8 May he wrote complainingly to Stuart that 'the five hundred half-promised are likely to shrink below fifty.'[4] The failure of subscribers to appear

---

[1] *Letters*, p. 579. [2] Ibid., p. 585.
[3] Ibid., p. 595. The present editor has seen none of these cards and prints the announcement from the *Courier*.
[4] *Letters*, p. 595. Cf. also *Letters from the Lake Poets to Daniel Stuart* (1889), p. 212.

in sufficient numbers probably caused the first postponement of the lectures from 5 May to 12 May, and the assassination of the prime minister, the Right Honourable Spencer Perceval, which took place on 11 May, caused a second postponement to Tuesday, 19 May.[1]   No more delays intervened; and five, at least, of the six lectures were delivered according to the announcement, except that the second lecture was delivered on Saturday, 23 May, a day late.[2]   Robinson does not mention the lecture which should have been given on Tuesday, 2 June, and perhaps Coleridge may have failed his audience on this occasion.[3]   Robinson's brief notes make it clear, as the announcements would have led us to suspect, that Coleridge was in these lectures chiefly engaged in delivering his notes from Schlegel.   In the first four lectures Coleridge did not proceed beyond his discussion of Greek drama and the accompanying distinction of classic and romantic. A large part of this material is probably represented by the manuscript notes on Greek drama,[4] which do not seem to have been used in any other course of lectures, unless in that delivered at the Surrey Institution in 1812–13.   The last lecture on the *Winter's Tale* and *Othello*, was probably much the same as the lecture delivered at Bristol in 1813, for which Coleridge's manuscript notes survive.   Apparently the 'French, English, and Spanish stage' received very little specific attention, except as inevitable illustrations of the distinction between the classic and the romantic.

No records of this course are known to exist, except those of Robinson, which are here republished from the original manuscripts; but our loss is probably small.

A Letter from H. C. Robinson to Thomas Robinson,
25 May, 1812.

. . . Coleridge began his course of lectures at Willis's Rooms on Tuesday.   He very obligingly gave me a ticket for myself and *friends*.   Of course, I design not to abuse this good nature and mean not to take anybody with me who either would or ought to have taken tickets.   On Tuesday I took Mrs. Pattison, her mother and sister.   Mrs. P. found out Wordsworth by his

[1] This is Coleridge's own testimony (*Letters*, pp. 597–8).   There is no need for the conjecture of Campbell that the delay was due to 'agitation produced by the negotiations then being carried on by Robinson for the reconciliation with Wordsworth.'

[2] H. C. Robinson's *Diary*.   (Cf. ii. 195.)   This date is confirmed by an advertisement in the *Courier*, 22 May.

[3] In his *Reminiscences* Robinson says that there were five lectures and that he attended all.   But these *Reminiscences* were written nearly forty years afterward (1849) and are of little value when they deviate from the *Diary* on which they are founded.   Perhaps Robinson merely failed to attend on 2 June.   I have sought, but have not found, additional evidence on this point.

[4] Cf. i. 150–7.

face.   The lecture we lost, not entering the room till about a quarter of an hour before the lecture closed.   I fear it was not a successful beginning.   I heard not a word about poetry, but a great deal about chivalry and the Gothic gallantry, Christianity and paganism, etc., etc., etc. . . .

Robinson's Diary.

[May] 19. . . .   Wordsworth called on me about 12 o'clock. . . .   At two, I went to Howel's, where I was joined by Mesdames Pattison, Thornthwaite, and Blood.   After a cold luncheon, we proceeded to Coleridge's first lecture in Willis's Rooms.   We heard C. about a quarter of an hour.   Of course we could not enter into it.   I perceived only that he was in a digressing vein.   He spoke of religion, the spirit of chivalry, the Gothic reverence for the female sex, and a classification of poetry into the ancient and romantic.[1]—Mrs. P. was, however, sufficiently delighted by the sight of eminent persons. . . .   W. came and chatted with us a few moments. . . .

23d . . . Coleridge's lecture was a beautiful dissertation on the Greek drama.   His analysis of the trilogy of Aeschylus, the *Agamemnon, Orestes,* and *Eumenides* of Euripides [2] was interesting, as well as his account of the *Prometheus*; [3] and his remarks on the antique tragedy were more connected, better and more closely than when delivered in Fetter Lane. . . .

26 . . . Heard Coleridge's third lecture.   It was wholly on the Greek drama, and, as he promised to proceed this day to the modern drama, this want of progress, I dare say, will do him harm with the public.   His lecture was in itself excellent and very German.   He adopted the Teutonic analogies and compared Aeschylus, Sophocles, and Euripides to Phidias, Polyclitus, and Lysippus.[4]   He had imperfect conceptions and was afraid to risk entirely the Schellingian *triple* classification. . . .

---

[1] Evidently Coleridge was giving his audience Schlegel's first lecture. See Schlegel's *Werke,* v. 3–20.   For Coleridge on the classic and romantic cf. i. 174–6, etc.   For his treatment of Gothic chivalry, etc., see *M.C.,* pp. 7–9.

[2] These plays are the trilogy of Aeschylus, not Euripides.   For *Orestes,* read *The Libation-Bearers.*

[3] The subject of this lecture is the same as that of Schlegel's sixth (*Werke,* v. 88–111).   Robinson's brief notes do not allow any discussion of a possible influence.

[4] This comparison is evidently from Schlegel's sixth lecture (*Werke,* v. 89–90).

29. . . . Accompanied Mrs. Becker, Miss Lewis, and a Miss Dowdie to Coleridge's 4th lecture. It was on the nature of comedy, about Aristophanes, etc. The mode of treating the subject very German, and, of course, much too abstract for his audience, which was but thin.—Scarcely any ladies there. . . . Made a call for half an hour on Mr. [P.] He had heard Coleridge's lecture in the morning but thought him infinitely inferior to Campbell, who, it appears, is exceedingly admired. P. thinks C. makes a sad confusion of mythology, metaphysics, etc. etc. This, I have no doubt, is the general opinion, nor is it unfounded.[1] With such powers of original thought and real genius both philosophical and poetical, such as few men in any age have possessed, Coleridge wants certain low and minor qualities which render his great powers almost inefficient and useless, while most subordinate persons obtain all the fame he merits. . . .

[June] Monday 1 . . . (Mem. At Coleridge's last lecture, when there were few people there, C. told [a] me an epigram he once wrote, the point of which lay in this, that he had fallen asleep and that he thought some great people had come to him and made him promises, etc.; and that he awoke and found it was all as much a dream as if the promises had been made him).

5th . . . At Coleridge's last lecture of his first course. He promised to speak of *Othello*, but wasted his time on the *Winter's Tale*. He digressed excessively, so that he hardly allowed himself time to point out the contrast between the jealousy of the husband of that play and that of *Othello*.[2] In the future lectures,[3] money is to be taken at the door. I doubt much whether the experiment will succeed. He announced his lectures ill, as if he felt degraded by allusion to money matters; I felt degraded at hearing a great man refer to such a subject. . . .

Thursday: 13th August. . . . C. praised *Wallenstein* but censured Schiller for a sort of ventriloquism in poetry—by the bye, a happy term to express that common fault of throwing the feelings of the writer into the body, as it were, of other personages—the characters of the poem.[4]. . .

---

[a] *MS. 'told of.'*

[1] P.'s criticism is really directed against the Germans whom Coleridge honoured with his plagiarisms.

[2] Cf. i. 109–13.

[3] Evidently a reference to the lectures which were ultimately given at the Surrey Institution in the winter of this year.

[4] This definition of 'ventriloquism' in poetry is useful elsewhere. (Cf. i. 73; ii. 124.) Cf. *B.L.* ii. 109, and *M.C.*, pp. 54, 90, 394, 411.

Coleridge said he had been reading *Lear* again. And he thinks the Fool in *Lear* unlike all the other fools of Shakespeare, and one of the profoundest and most astonishing of his characters.[1]

[1] Cf. i. 56; ii. 47, 167.

THE LECTURES OF 1812-13

Syllabus.[1]

LECTURE I.

THAT to use each word in a sense peculiarly its own, is an indispensable condition of all just thinking, and at once the surest, easiest, and even most entertaining discipline of the mind.[2] On the words, Beautiful, Sublime, Majestic,[3] Grand,[3] Picturesque, Fancy,[3] Imagination,[3] Taste.

LECTURES II AND III.

THE falsehood of the almost universal opinion, that, in the progress of civilized life, the Invention of Conveniences and Utilities precedes the Arts of Ornament, proved both by facts, and *à priori* (i.e. from the Nature of the Human Being). The *Fine Arts* in the Natural Order of their origination—Dress, Orchesis, (including all the Arts of Bodily Motion, as Mimic Dances, Gymnastic Sports, &c.) Architecture, Eloquence, Music, Poetry, Statuary, Painting, Gardening.[4]

LECTURE IV.

ON Poetry *in genere*, and as common to antient Greece and to Christendom. On the Poetry of the Antients as contradistinguished from that of the Moderns; or, the differences of the *Classical* from the *Romantic* poetry,—exemplified in the Athenian Dramatic Poets.[5]

---

[1] Filed among H. C. Robinson's *Letters*, 1809–17, p. 87. The heading of the syllabus, which is in capitals in the original, runs as follows: Syllabus/of/a Course of Lectures/on the/Belles Lettres/to be Delivered by/S. T. Coleridge, Esq./at the/Surrey Institution/1812.

[2] Cf. i. 221.

[3] These terms are Coleridge's additions to a list drawn from Kant's *Critique of Aesthetic Judgement*.

[4] It seems that Coleridge was drawing on Herder's *Kalligone*. See Robinson's report of the 1808 lectures (cf. ii. 13, note 1).

[5] Evidently Schlegel's first lecture, with illustrations from the succeeding lectures on Greek drama. For additional evidence of Coleridge's use of Schlegel in the lectures at the Surrey Institution cf. ii. 211, note 3.

Lecture V.

ON the Mythology of Antient Greece, its Causes and Effects—and the worse than Ignorance infused by our School Pantheons,—and the mistaken zeal of Religious Controversy. The connection between the Polytheism, Ethics, and Republicanism of Greece: and (as thence deduced) the impossibility, and (were it possible) the uselessness of modelling our Poetry, Architecture, Music, etc. on the remains of the Antients.[1] The *Spirit* of Poetry common to all ages, and to *imitate* the Antients wisely, we should do as they did; that is, embody the Spirit in Forms adapted to all the Circumstances of Time, State of Society, etc.[2]

Lecture VI.

THE *human* causes which the goodness of Providence directed to the Diffusion of Christianity, and its temporal effects, abstracted from all higher and purely theological views. The Deluge of Nations—the Establishment of Christendom—and the formation of mixed languages, in which the decomposed Latin became amalgamated, in different proportions, with the Gothic or Celtic. These, collectively, were called the *Romance*, and in this sense of the *mixed*, as opposed to the *simple* or homogeneous, the word *Romantic* is used,[3]—and not exclusively with reference to what we now call Romances.

Lecture VII.

THE characteristics of the Romantic Poetry, and the true origin of the Romantic Drama in SHAKSPEARE.[4] On the false points of view, from which Shakspeare has been regarded as wild, irregular, &c. and proofs that a profound judgement in the *construction* of his Plays is equally his Characteristic,—as Genius and deep Insight into Human Nature;—or, rather, that they are the same power variously applied.

Lecture VIII.

A PHILOSOPHICAL Analysis of ROMEO and JULIET and of HAMLET.

---

[1] See the preceding note.
[2] Cf. ii. 211, and Schlegel, *Werke*, vi. 158.
[3] Cf. i. 174–6; ii. 216; and Schlegel, *Werke*, v. 9–10.
[4] Cf. Schlegel's first and twenty-fifth lectures for Coleridge's sources.

LECTURE IX.

MACBETH and OTHELLO.

LECTURE X.

HASTY Review of the most important of the other Plays—and the character of SHAKSPEARE as a Poet, and as a *Dramatic* Poet.

LECTURES XI AND XII.

MILTON'S PARADISE LOST.

H. C. Robinson's Reminiscences, 1812.

Nov. 3ᵈ. Coleridge commenced a course of lectures on *belles lettres* at the Surrey Institution, and which were continued down to the 26th of January. As the novelty of these lectures had worn off and I was more familiar with his opinions, they attracted less attention from me; or I was become more lazy, for I have made very few remarks on them. The audience at the Surrey [a] Institution were much more evangelical than at the other lecture rooms and sometimes C. flattered the religious opinions of his hearers, and at other times ran counter to them. . . .

H. C. Robinson's Diary, 1812–13.

[November,] 3 . . . At Coleridge's first lecture on *belles lettres* at the Surrey Institution. It was a repetition of former lectures, and dull. He enlarged on the vagueness of terms and their abuse and in defining taste gave the Kantean theory as to the nature of judgments of taste.[1] He introduced, I had almost said cantingly, some pious parentheses about religion *à la* Wood [2] and did not on the whole gratify me exceedingly. He walked with me to A. Robinson's for Spinoza, which I lent him. . . .

Coleridge informs me his tragedy is accepted at Drury Lane.

---

[a] *MS.* '*Russell*.'

[1] Robinson is rather vague and his reference is sufficient to involve the entire first book ('Analytic of the Beautiful') in Kant's *Critique of Aesthetic Judgement*.

[2] Perhaps this is William Wood (1745–1808), the nonconformist minister, lecturer, and writer.

Whitbread admires it exceedingly, and Arnold, the manager, is confident of its success.   C. now says he has five or six pieces ready for representation ! ! !   At the same time he is about to compose lectures, which are to be the produce of all his talent, and power, on Education.   And each lecture is to be delivered as it may be afterwards sent to the press.   For this purpose he wants Spinoza . . .

10. . . . Took tea with Lamb.   Then heard Coleridge's 2^d lecture at the **Surrey Institution**.   It was very wide of all immediate reference to polite literature.   It was full ^{a} of pious— cant, I fear.   It treated very rhapsodically and obscurely of the primitive and barbarous state of man, etc.[1] . . .

17th, Thursday . . . At Coleridge's lecture, where I slept [2] . . .

24 . . . Evening, heard part of a lecture by Coleridge.   He was in a good vein.

[December,] Tuesday 1. . . .   Evening, at Coleridge's lecture, Surrey Institution.   Three-fourths of the lecture a declamation on atheism.   He meant to introduce by a reference to religion the German antithesis between paganism and Christianity, which was itself to be merely an introduction to the contrast between classic and romantic poetry; but, as usual, he wasted his time on the introduction to the introduction! . . .

8 . . . In the evening I was at a lecture from Coleridge in which was not even a single word on the subject of polite litera- ture in any way.   Tho' he began with an apology for talking too much about atheism last Tuesday, in this lecture he spoke of nothing but Christianity and the circumstances of its early history.[3] . . .

[January, 1813.]   Tuesday 5th . . . In the evening at Cole- ridge's lecture.   Heard but a little. . . .

12 . . . In the evening at Coleridge's lecture. . . .

19th . . . At Coleridge's lecture—Very eloquent and popular on the general character of Shakespeare: he is recovering lost character among the Saints.[4]

26 . . . In the evening heard Coleridge's concluding lecture

---

^{a} MS. '*fully.*'

[1] If one may judge by the syllabus, Robinson was irritated, justly perhaps, by some of Coleridge's plagiarisms from Herder.   (Cf. ii. 13, 199.)

[2] The soporific lecture was again Herder, according to the syllabus above.

[3] Robinson missed Coleridge's seventh lecture (15 December) and the eighth (22 or 29 December).   Otherwise his records give us a complete calendar of the lectures and show that they were delivered on successive Tuesdays.

[4] That is, he is beginning to give his audiences Coleridge instead of Herder and Schlegel.   See the syllabus.

at the Surrey Institution.   He was received with three rounds of applause on entering the lecture room and very loudly applauded at the close.   During the evening he gained great applause by some eloquent *moral* reflections; and he *this* evening, as well as on the three or four preceding nights, redeemed the reputation he lost at the commencement of the course.[1]   That Coleridge should ever become a popular man would once have been thought a very idle speculation.   It depends on himself, and if he would make a sacrifice of some peculiarities of taste (his enemies assert he has made many on essential points of religion and politics) he has talents enough to command success; but he must also add the power of repressing the avowal of his own favorite peculiarities in opinion and feeling, which I doubt he will never be able to obtain.   His general notions on party-topics will suit a large proportion of the public, and, tho' he is not yet a favorite, there is a general opinion in favour of his genius.

[March] 2 . . . In the evening accompanied Aders to see *Coleridge.* . . .   He accused *Schlegel* of *Einseitigkeit* in his exclusive admiration of Shakespeare and in his former work about the Greek poetry [2]—

20. . . .   In the evening a short call on Flaxman and on Coleridge, whom I found in raptures with *Wilhelm Meister.* . . .[3]

---

[1] See the preceding note.   See also his letter to his wife, 'Wednesday afternoon' [27 January], *Letters*, p. 604: 'I concluded my Lectures last night most triumphantly, with loud, long, and enthusiastic applauses at my entrance, and ditto in yet fuller chorus as, and for some minutes after I had retired.   It was lucky that (as I never once thought of the Lecture till I had entered the Lecture Box) the two last were the most impressive and really the best.'   This letter is misdated '[January 20]' instead of 'January 27,' as the reference to Coleridge's last lecture (26 January) and a later reference to the first performance of *Remorse* (23 January), clearly show.   Coleridge's lack of preparation was not due to indolence but to the turmoil attending the last rehearsals and first performances of his successful play

[2] Schlegel's 'former work on Greek poetry' is evidently the part of the *Vorlesungen* which was published in 1809; i.e. the first volume and the first part of the second volume.   Greek drama occupied nearly two-thirds of these lectures, counted by pages.

[3] If this is Coleridge's first reading of *Wilhelm Meister*, as it seems to be, Goethe's analysis of Hamlet's character could have had little or no influence upon him.

THE LECTURES AT BRISTOL, 1813–14

AFTER the lectures of 1812–13 at the Surrey Institution a partial blank occurs in our knowledge of Coleridge's life. He does not seem to have been active in any way until he suggested to his old friends at Bristol that he wished to lecture again in the city where he had first made his acquaintance with the public platform. Cottle tells a charming anecdote of Coleridge's arrival in Bristol several days after the announced date of his first lecture. Coleridge had learned, he says, that a fellow-passenger on the coach was the sister of a particular friend, and had gallantly insisted on accompanying the lady to her destination in North Wales.[1] One wishes to believe this story; but it must be remembered that Cottle was not averse to using his imagination freely in regard to biographical facts. The advertisements in the Bristol weekly newspapers of 1813, of which full files are preserved in the Bristol Library, give no hint of an earlier date for the first lecture than 28 October, when Coleridge actually appeared at the White Lion, Broad Street, and lectured. And an unpublished letter to the Morgans shows that he was in Bristol on 25 October, three days before the first lecture. 'The proposed scheme of lecturing has met with such support that I have resolved on it,'[2] Coleridge writes. This contemporary remark indicated either that Coleridge had misunderstood the definiteness of the announcements which were made before he left London, or—and this is more probable—that Cottle's memory had after twenty odd years become rather too docile before his literary instinct.

No prospectus of the course is known to exist, but we know the subject announced for the first lecture from the report printed in the *Gazette*, 28 October, which says that Coleridge was to lecture on 'The Characteristics of Shakespeare.' The advertisement of the second lecture in the *Mirror*, 30 October, gives us all the information which is necessary in regard to the later lectures of the course. After the first lecture on the characteristics of Shakespeare, the five remaining lectures, which were given on Tuesday and Thursday evenings, were to deal with the following subjects: 2. the construction of the two tragedies, *Hamlet* and *Macbeth*, with an analysis of the characters of Hamlet, of Macbeth, and of Lady Macbeth; 3. *The Winter's Tale* and *Othello*, with an analysis of the characters of Othello, Iago, and of Shakespeare's female characters in general; 4. The historic plays of Shakespeare, with an analysis of *Richard II* and of *Richard III*; 5. the comedies and comic characters of Shakespeare, with an analysis of the character of Falstaff; 6. the New System of Education, as applicable to the higher and middle classes of Society.[3] The price of admission

[1] Cottle's *Reminiscences*, pp. 353–4.
[2] Quoted from a transcript by Ernest Hartley Coleridge.
[3] Omitting dates, etc., and ignoring the erratic capitals and italics of the original, I give the subjects announced in the advertisement *verbatim*.

was five shillings for a single lecture, or six admission tickets at one guinea.

Cottle tells us that 'the lectures gave great satisfaction,' and the report in the *Gazette* of the second lecture says that 'the room over-flowed.' Coleridge carried out his engagements in the subjects announced for each lecture, except that the second lecture, on *Hamlet* and *Macbeth*, required two evenings instead of one. Besides the lecture on education first announced, Coleridge announced [1] and gave a supplementary lecture on 'the practical improvements in the technical education of boys in the higher and middle classes of life, and on female education in general.' These eight lectures were reported briefly in the *Gazette*.[2] The lectures on Shakespeare were discovered by Mr George, the Bristol bookseller, and were first republished by Thomas Ashe in the Bohn edition of Coleridge's *Lectures on Shakspere*, 1883.

Several of these reports were republished in the two London papers with which Coleridge had established friendly associations by his past contributions of prose and verse.[3] The *Morning Post* published the report of Coleridge's second lecture on 20 November, and the *Courier* published the second lecture [4] on 19 November, the first on 17 December, and part [5] of the sixth on 20 December. These reports were simply reprinted from the reports in the *Bristol Gazette*, and it is possible that Coleridge sent clippings to the editors of the *Morning Post* and *Courier*. The use in *Literary Remains* of these Bristol and London reports of Coleridge's lectures presents some curious problems. Revising the text and distributing its parts to different places, H. N. Coleridge used for the notes on *Hamlet* all of his uncle's third lecture at Bristol except its patriotic conclusion; and in the section entitled 'Recapitulation and Summary' he introduced most of the first lecture, on the 'General Characteristics of Shakespeare,' acknowledging his obligations for the greater part of his materials to his brother, Mr Justice Coleridge. All the other materials in this latter section come from manuscripts, and one may presume that Mr Justice Coleridge furnished H. N. Coleridge with the clipping from the London or Bristol newspaper; but there is no acknowledgment of the source of the lecture on *Hamlet*, which appeared, so far as I know, only in the *Bristol Gazette*. The other reports in the *Gazette* were not used at all in *Literary Remains*.

Before this first series of lectures came to an end, Coleridge began another, not in Bristol proper, but in Clifton, the large suburb which is

---

[1] *Mirror*, 20 November 1813.

[2] The dates of the lectures were as follows: I. 28 October; II. 2 November; III. 4 November; IV. 9 November; V. 11 November; VI. 16 November; VII. 18 November; VIII. 23 November. The reports, two to each number of the *Gazette* (a weekly), were published on 4, 11, 18, 25 November. The two lectures on education have no connection with Shakespearean criticism. They are therefore omitted in this text, but may be found in *S.C.* ii. 288–98.

[3] Both the *Morning Post* and the *Courier* were successively owned by Coleridge's friend Stuart, but at this date Stuart had sold the *Morning Post* and had practically turned over the management of the *Courier* to his partner, Street.

[4] Omitting the reporter's introduction and conclusion.

[5] The second paragraph.

continuous with the older city.   The first notice of this is an advertisement in the *Gazette*, 4 November: 'Mr. Coleridge proposes to deliver at Mangeon's Room, at the Hotel, at one o'clock on Monday, Wednesday, and Friday afternoons, a course, of from six to eight lectures, on the following subjects: on the construction, metre, and characteristic beauties of the *Paradise Lost*, with illustrative readings; on Milton in general, as a man, and a poet; on the distinction between the poetry of polytheism, as existing in the republics of ancient Greece, and the poetry of Christendom—the causes, and their results; [1] that a just taste may, and must, be grounded on fixed principles; and the rules deducible therefrom, by which a tenable judgment, both positive and comparative, may be formed concerning poetry, and the works of different poets.   The lectures to commence on Monday next, 8th of November.' [2]

The same advertisement appeared in *Felix Farley's Bristol Journal*, Saturday, 6 November, but set the first lecture for 10 November. Coleridge was apparently urged by others to give these lectures, against his own judgment, for he writes to the Morgans on 'Tuesday, November 10' [9 ?], 'tomorrow at one o'clock I must be at Clifton, tho' with no probability of even more than enough to pay the lecture room and the printing.'   On 17 November he wrote again to the same correspondents: 'It just happened as I had stated to those who had insisted on my attending at Clifton Hotel to-day—some twelve persons present, and among those one only of the score who had over-persuaded me to hazard the negotiations and to incur the expense.'   The next night he repeated this complaint with an interesting addition: 'Well, my dear Loves! I have made a famous lecture to a crowded room, and all the better, because on account of my mortification at the ill-conduct of those who had *forced* me against my own exprest convictions on the Cliftonian lectures, I had not prepared one single word or thought till ten minutes before the lecture commenced.   It was, therefore, quite in my [best vein ?] and pleased more than any.   This was to have been the last.   However, I am to go on Tuesday next—and probably for an indefinite time I might with advantage.' [3]

Evidently the successful extemporaneous lecture [4] was the seventh, on the New System of Education, and the one 'on Tuesday next' was the eighth, the supplementary lecture on education.   It appears from the date of this letter that Coleridge must have reached at least his fourth lecture at Clifton, in spite of the small attendance, but speculation on this subject is unprofitable.

Though the Clifton lectures were a failure, the course in Bristol itself was evidently successful enough to encourage Coleridge in beginning a new series.   In the last lecture, that of 23 November, he

---

[1] Cf. Schlegel's first lecture.

[2] The advertisement is quoted literally, but without regard to typographical details.

[3] These unpublished letters are quoted from the transcripts of E. H. Coleridge.

[4] One must guard against the impression that this extemporaneous lecturing was habitual.   Of the six lectures on Shakespeare, Coleridge had full notes for all except the first and sixth, and at least partial notes for these. (Cf. i. 34–7, 69–72, 109–13, 137–41, 204–7.)

proposed to begin a new course, which was to begin on 8 December. He suggested two lectures 'on the epic and romantic of Shakespeare, not yet spoken of; and four on Milton as a man and a poet.' [1]   This course was advertised in *Felix Farley's Bristol Journal*, 4 December, with some alterations.   The lectures were announced as follows: 'Two on those plays of Shakespeare which were not referred to in the former course and illustrative of the poetic and romantic character of our great dramatist, namely, *The Tempest*, *Midsummer Night's Dream*, *Merchant of Venice*, *As You Like It*, *Twelfth Night*, etc.; and four on the *Paradise Lost* and the character of Milton as a man and a poet; with an examination of Dr. Johnson's Preface to Shakespeare and his life of Milton.'   We hear again of this course in an advertisement in the *Gazette*, 30 December: 'Mr. Coleridge having been surprised and confined by sudden and severe illness at his arrival at Bath, six days before the promised commencement of his second course, 7th December, 1813, respectfully informs his friends that this second course will commence on Tuesday, 4th January, 1814, at the White Lion. . . .'   The advertisement then repeats the announcement of Coleridge's subjects, without specifying individual plays.   The weekly newspapers, the *Gazette*, the *Mirror*, and the *Journal*, take no further notice of this course; but it was probably delivered, for Cottle speaks of a second 'course of six lectures, which was well attended.' [2] If all the plays specified in the first advertisement were actually discussed, our loss in the disappearance of these lectures is great, since only *The Tempest* was among Coleridge's usual subjects.

For several months after this announcement there is a complete gap in Coleridge's life, which is partly explained by what we know of his subjection to opium, described by Cottle only too clearly.   On 2 April 1814, however, another course is announced in the *Journal*: 'Mr. Coleridge informs the former attendants at his lectures, and his friends in general, that being now recovered from his severe and protracted illness, he proposes to give six lectures on the following subjects and in the following order on Tuesday and Thursday evenings . . . : 1st. on the life, character, and prose writings of Milton; 2nd. on the minor poems of Milton; 3rd and 4th. on the plan, metre, characters, and distinguishing beauties of the *Paradise Lost*; [3] 5th on the means of acquiring a just and austere poetic taste and its close connection with religious and moral feelings; and 6th (by particular desire) a philosophic analysis of the *Don Quixote* of Cervantes.   It is intended to give the first lecture on Tuesday next, 5th April, 1814. . . .'

It is certain that the first four lectures announced for this course were delivered; the *Gazette*, 7 April, announced the second and third

---

[1] Cf. note 3, below.

[2] Cottle, *Reminiscences*, p. 354.

[3] The announcement of these lectures on Milton makes one suspect that the second course dealing with the same subject may not have been delivered, in spite of Cottle's vague evidence.

After writing the description of the course on Milton, the editor discovered in the Harvard College Library a prospectus of the course, which is apparently unique.   The prospectus is bound in the back of a copy of Cottle's *Early Recollections* (London, 1837), vol. ii.   The catalogue number is 19477. 260. 2*.   The advertisement quoted above reproduced the prospectus *verbatim*; but see also the postscript quoted in ii. 210, note 1.

lectures; the *Mirror* and the *Journal*, 9 April, announced the third and fourth.   The advertisement of the fourth lecture in the *Gazette*, 14 April, is worth quoting, like many others of Coleridge's advertisements.   'Tomorrow evening, seven o'clock, at the White Lion, Mr. Coleridge will give his fourth lecture; namely, 1st, on the metre of the *Paradise Lost*; 2nd, on the construction of the periods; 3rd, on the characters, principally those of Adam and Eve, and of Satan; and he will conclude with a full analytical character of the late "French Emperor," so entitled by the opprest Continent and—[sic]; but who, thank Heaven! has never been for *Britons*, or by acknowledgement of Great Britain, other than Napoleon Bonaparte, the cowardly Corsican, Usurper, Rebel, and Assassin.'

This blast of red-hot patriotism was echoed *verbatim* in the *Journal*, 16 April, which inserted a complimentary notice of the 'lectures upon Milton [which] have been attended by those numerous and respectable audiences which the splendid talents of this gentleman cannot fail to attract and draw together.'   After the reference to Napoleon, the *Journal* continues as follows: 'We are only performing an act of justice to inform our readers that it was Mr. Coleridge who wrote those essays and leading paragraphs in the *Morning Post* during the treacherous Peace of Amiens, which procured for all the English Newspapers, except the *Morning Chronicle*, the honour of exclusion from France; and which, as Mr. Fox asserted, produced the war with France, that war which has liberated Europe and human nature.[1]   Since that time Mr. Coleridge has not ceased to fight the same good fight; and as he informed us in his Lectures, in consequence, when he was on the Continent, his life was hunted for by the blood-thirsty tyrant, an order for his arrest was sent by express to Rome, and he escaped only by the providential favour of a noble Italian.'

It is to be feared that the *Journal's* account of 'numerous and respectable audiences' was written more in the spirit of compliment than of fact, for Cottle, in his account of Coleridge's third series [2] (of four lectures), says that they were 'but indifferently attended,' and he prints a letter, evidently written at this time, in which Coleridge complains that the receipts have not quite paid for the expenses of the lecture-room and advertisements.[3]   In the same letter Coleridge speaks doubtfully of his plans for three lectures 'on the rise, and progress and conclusion of the French Revolution, with a critique on the proposed constitution,' [4] and of two proposed lectures upon the education of girls.   The three lectures on the French Revolution were advertised in the *Journal*, 23 April, and the dates were set for 26, 29 April, 3 May.   The first of these lectures was delivered on 26 April, but Coleridge was so ill that he was obliged to postpone the second and third lectures,[5] which were probably never delivered, since the newspapers make no reference to them.   The lectures on 'female education' were proposed in a postscript to Coleridge's announcement of

---

[1] Cf. *B.L.* i. 145, for a similar claim.

[2] Cottle, *Reminiscences*, p. 354.

[3] Ibid., p. 357.

[4] 'The present constitution accepted by Louis the Eighteenth.'   Coleridge's advertisement in the *Journal*, 23 April.

[5] *Journal*, 30 April.

his course on Milton, but only tentatively.[1]   Since they were not advertised, it is probable that the requisite number of subscribers was not forthcoming.   Cottle says that Coleridge gave a series of lectures on Homer which 'only a few of his old stanch friends attended,' but the newspapers seem to take no notice of this last attempt, of which we do not even know the date.

It may be worth while to mention here the few remaining references to Coleridge in the newspapers of 1814.   On 28 July the *Gazette* announced that *Remorse* was to be performed in the Bristol theatre on 1 August; in August and September the *Journal* published Coleridge's essays on the fine arts, which were rescued from oblivion by Cottle, and republished in *Early Recollections*; finally, on 1, 15, 29 September, the *Gazette* published a series of letters to the editor from 'Cosmo,' a rather naïve but violent critic of those essays which Coleridge was at that time publishing in the *Journal*; Coleridge responded contemptuously in a letter to the editor of the *Journal* on 10 September, and then ignored his assailant.[2]   Here, apparently, ends the record of the newspapers.[3]   Coleridge remained in Bristol until early in September, under medical treatment; but lectures were no part of his occupations, whatever they may have been.

---

[1] 'P.S. MR. COLERIDGE has been desired by several highly respectable Ladies to carry into effect a plan of giving one or two lectures, in the morning, on the subject of FEMALE EDUCATION, of a nature altogether practical, and explaining the whole machinery of a school organized on rational principles, from the earliest age to the completion of FEMALE EDUCATION, with a list of the books recommended, &c. so as to evolve gradually into utility and domestic happiness the powers and qualities of Womanhood.   Should a sufficient number of Ladies and Gentlemen express their design to patronize this plan, Mr. Coleridge will hold himself ready to realize it, at such time as may be found most convenient to his auditors.'   (*Journal*, 2 April 1814.)

[2] The editor has published a brief account of this controversy in *Modern Language Notes*, xliii. (1928), 375–7.

[3] In this account of Coleridge's advertisements in the newspapers, the editor has ignored duplicates.   Sometimes Coleridge advertised in all three newspapers, sometimes only in one.

[LECTURE I.[1]]

[*General Characteristics of Shakespeare.*]

IN lectures of which amusement form[s] a share, difficulties are common to the first. The architect places his foundation out of sight, the musician tunes his instrument before his appearance, but the lecturer has to try his chords in the hearing of the assembly. This will not tend to increase amusement, but it is necessary to the right understanding of the subject to be developed.[2]

Poetry in essence is as familiar to barbarous as civilized nations. The Laplander and the savage Indian are equally cheered by it, as the inhabitants of Paris or London; its spirit incorporates and takes up surrounding materials, as a plant clothes itself with soil and climate, whilst it bears marks of a vital principle within, independent of all accidental circumstances.[3]

---

[1] The report of the first lecture was introduced as follows:
'MR. COLERIDGE.'
'Were Milton to return among the living, and to select from our poets him, who from profoundness of thought and unworldly abstraction of feeling, joined to the prodigality of fancy in glowing conceptions, the nearest resembled himself, he would probably fix his choice on the author of "The Nightingale" and of "Fears of Solitude"—poems which will continue to stir the heart and elevate the mind, when the *Epics* and *Romaunts* of our time are referred to only by literary antiquaries, as the quaint curiosities of a wonder-gaping and sophisticated age. If it be true that a Poet alone can criticise a Poet, few will dispute the qualifications of Mr. COLERIDGE as a Lecturer on Shakspeare.

'This Gentleman has commenced a Course of Lectures in this city; the following is an imperfect Outline of his first:—OUTLINE/of an INTRODUCTORY LECTURE by Mr./COLERIDGE on the *Characteristics* of SHAKESPEAR, &c., &c./ as delivered in Bristol on Thursday, October 28th, 1813.' (*Bristol Gazette*, 4 November 1813.)

[2] Coleridge found this introduction convenient on more than one occasion. Cf. *B.L.* ii. 227; *The Friend, Works* (Shedd ed.), ii. 25; and i. 158, above.

[3] This paragraph paraphrases passages from Schlegel (*Werke*, v. 5; vi. 158). The influence of Schlegel on this series of lectures lends especial interest to an unpublished letter which Coleridge wrote to the Morgans on 25 October. 'The subscription promises to go on with a steady breeze, but you must be so good as immediately on the receipt of this to hunt out for me the three volumes of Schlegel's *Vorlesungen* . . . and likewise my two *square* thick memorandum books. . . . I am sure you will be able in the title-pages of the books, that are not bound, to distinguish the words "Vorlesungen" on the top and "Schlegel" as the author's name at the end. . . . Besides

To judge with fairness of an author's works, we must observe, firstly, what is essential, and secondly, what arises from circumstances. It is essential, as Milton [1] defines it, that poetry be *simple, sensuous,* and *impassionate* [a]:—simple, that it may appeal to the elements and the primary laws of our nature; *sensuous,* since it is only by sensuous images that we can elicit truth as at a flash; *impassionate,*[a] since images must be vivid, in order to move our passions and awaken our affections.

In judging of different poets, we ought to inquire what authors have brought into fullest play our imagination and our reason, or have created the greatest excitements and produced the completest harmony. Considering only great exquisiteness of language, and sweetness of metre, it is impossible to deny to Pope the title of a delightful writer; whether he be a poet must be determined as we define the word: doubtless if everything that pleases be poetry, Pope's satires and epistles must be poetry. Poetry, as distinguished from general modes of composition, does not rest in metre; it is not poetry if it make no appeal to our imagination, our passions, and our sympathy. One character attaches to all true poets: they write from a principle within, independent of everything without. The work of a true poet, in its form, its shapings and modifications, is distinguished from all other works that assume to belong to the class of poetry, as a natural from an artificial flower; or as the mimic garden of a child, from an enamelled meadow.[2] In the former the flowers are broken from their stems and stuck in the ground; they are beautiful to the eye and fragrant to the sense, but their colours soon fade, and their odour is transient as the smile of the planter; while the meadow may be visited again and again, with renewed delight; its beauty is innate in the soil, and its bloom is of the freshness of nature.

The next ground of judging is how far a poet is influenced by *accidental circumstances.* He writes not for past ages, but for that in which he lives, and that which is to follow. It is natural

---

you will remember that I used to take them to the Surrey Institution.' Quoted from a transcript by E. H. Coleridge. The 'two square thick memorandum books' are notebooks No. 18 and either 25 (not quite square) or 17. (Cf. i. 126, ii. 18, and notes.) Coleridge's use of Schlegel at the Surrey Institution is borne out by the syllabus. (Cf. ii. 199–200.)

For the manuscript notes of the present lecture see i. 204–5.

[a] *Read 'passionate.'*
[1] Cf. i. 148 and note.
[2] This comparison, continuing to the end of the paragraph, is taken from Schlegel (*Werke*, v. 5–6). Coleridge merely paraphrases the passage in Schlegel without essential change.

that he should conform to the circumstances of his day, but a true genius will stand independent of these circumstances: and it is observable of Shakespeare that he leaves little to regret that he was born in such an age. The great aera in modern times was what is called the restoration of literature; the ages which preceded it were called the dark ages; it would be more wise, perhaps, to say, the ages in which we were in the dark. It is usually overlooked that the supposed dark aera was not universal, but partial and successive or alternate; that the dark age of England was not the dark age of Italy; but that one country was in its light and vigour, while another was in its gloom and bondage. The Reformation sounded through Europe like a trumpet; from the king to the peasant there was an enthusiasm for knowledge; the discovery of a MS. was the subject of an embassy. Erasmus read by moonlight, because he could not afford a torch, and begged a penny, not for the love of charity, but for the love of learning. The three great points of attention were morals, religion, and taste, but it becomes necessary to distinguish in this age mere men of learning from men of genius; all, however, were close copyists of the ancients, and this was the only way by which the taste of mankind could be improved, and the understanding informed. Whilst Dante imagined himself a copy of Virgil, and Ariosto of Homer, they were both unconscious of that greater power working within them, which carried them beyond their originals; for their originals were polytheists. All great discoveries bear the stamp of the age in which they were made; hence we perceive the effect of their purer religion, which was visible in their lives; and in reading of their works we should not content ourselves with the narration of events long since passed, but apply their maxims and conduct to our own.[1]

Having intimated that times and manners lend their form and pressure to the genius, it may be useful to draw a slight parallel between the *ancient* and *modern stage*, as it existed in Greece and in England. The Greeks were polytheists, their religion was local, the object of all their knowledge, science, and taste, was their gods; their productions were, therefore (if the expression may be allowed), *statuesque*. The moderns we may designate as *picturesque*; the end, complete harmony.[2] The Greeks reared a structure, which, in its parts and as a whole, filled the mind

[1] At least the three final sentences of this paragraph are based on Schlegel (*Werke*, v. 7–8). (Cf. i. 196, 204.)

[2] Cf. ii. 121–2, the ninth lecture of 1811–12, reported by J. P. Collier. The comparison is from Schlegel (*Werke*, v. 10; vi. 32–3).

with the calm and elevated impression of perfect beauty and symmetrical proportion. The moderns, blending materials, produced one striking whole. This may be illustrated by comparing the Pantheon with York Minster or Westminster Abbey. Upon the same scale we may compare Sophocles with Shakespeare:[1] in the one there is a completeness, a satisfying, an excellence, on which the mind can rest; in the other we see a blended multitude of materials, great and little, magnificent and mean, mingled, if we may so say, with a dissatisfying, or falling short of perfection, yet so promising of our progression, that we would not exchange it for that repose of the mind which dwells on the forms of symmetry in acquiescent admiration of grace. This general characteristic of the ancient and modern poetry might be exemplified in a parallel of their ancient and modern music: the ancient music consisted of melody by the succession of pleasing sounds; the modern embraces harmony, the result of combination and effect of the whole.[2]

Great as was the genius of Shakespeare, his judgment was at least equal. Of this we shall be convinced, if we look round on the age, and compare the nature of the respective dramas of Greece and England, differing from the necessary dissimilitude of circumstances by which they are modified and influenced. The Greek stage had its origin in the ceremonies of a sacrifice, such as the goat to Bacchus. It were erroneous to call him only the jolly god of wine; among the ancients he was venerable; he was the symbol of that power which acts without our consciousness from the vital energies of nature,[3] as Apollo was the symbol of our intellectual consciousness. Their heroes under his influence performed more than human actions; hence tales of their favourite champions soon passed into dialogue. On the Greek stage the chorus was always before the audience—no curtain dropt. *Change of place* was impossible; the absurd idea of its improbability was not indulged. The scene cannot be an exact copy of nature, but only an imitation. If we can believe

---

[1] Schlegel, *Werke*, v. 11.

[2] Ibid., v. 10. These references are merely the most striking borrowings from Schlegel in this paragraph. The whole paragraph is ultimately based on Schlegel (*Werke*, v. 9–17).

[3] Schlegel makes a similar remark (*Werke*, v. 92), but the coincidence is of little importance with such a commonplace. A. C. Dunstan (*Modern Language Review*, xviii. 195) points out a similar passage in the *Vorlesungen* (p. 115) of C. G. Heyne, a professor of Greek art, poetry, and mythology at Göttingen, under whom both Coleridge and Schlegel studied. Moreover, Coleridge made this same point in his lecture of 5 Feb. 1808 (cf. i. 164–5; ii. 6).

ourselves at Thebes in one act, we can believe ourselves at Athens in the next. There seems to be no just boundary but what the feelings prescribe. In Greece, however, great judgment was necessary where the same persons were perpetually before the audience. If a story lasted twenty-four hours or twenty-four years, it was equally improbable. They never attempted to impose on the senses, by bringing places to men, though they could bring men to places.

Unity of time was not necessary, where no offence was taken at its lapse between the acts, or between scene and scene, for where there were no acts or scenes it was impossible rigidly to observe its laws. To overcome these difficulties the judgment and great genius of the ancients supplied music, and with the charms of their poetry filled up the vacuity. In the story of the *Agamemnon* of Aeschylus, the taking of Troy was supposed to be announced by the lighting of beacons on the Asiatic shore: the mind being beguiled by the narrative ode of the chorus, embracing the events of the siege, hours passed as minutes, and no improbability was felt at the return of Agamemnon; and yet examined rigidly he must have passed over from Troy in less than fifteen minutes. Another fact here presented itself, seldom noticed: with the ancients three plays were performed in one day; they were called trilogies. In Shakespeare we may fancy these trilogies connected into one representation. If *Lear* were divided into three, each part would be a play with the ancients. Or take the three plays of Agamemnon, and divide them into acts, they would form one play:

1st Act would be the Usurpation of Ægisthus, and Murder of Agamemnon;

2nd. Revenge of Orestes, and Murder of his Mother;

3rd. The Trial of Orestes before the Gods;

consuming a time of twenty-two years. The three plays being but three acts, the dropping of the curtain was as the conclusion of a play.[1]

Contrast the stage of the ancients with that of the time of Shakespeare, and we shall be struck with his genius: with them, it had the trappings of royal and religious ceremony; with him, it was a naked room, a blanket for a curtain; but with his vivid appeals the imagination figured it out

A field for monarchs.[2]

[1] This paragraph is based upon a similar passage in Schlegel (*Werke*, vi. 26), with omissions and additions.

[2] This line is a faint echo of the Prologue to *Henry V*. (Cf. i. 117; ii. 57.)

After the rupture of the Northern nations, the Latin language, blended with the modern, produced the *Romaunt* tongue, the language of the minstrels: to which term, as distinguishing their songs and fabliaux, we owe the word and the species of *romance*.[1]   The romantic may be considered as opposed to the antique, and from this change of manners, those of Shakespeare take their colouring.   He is not to be tried by ancient and classic rules, but by the standard of his age.   That law of unity which has its foundation, not in factitious necessity of custom, but in nature herself, is instinctively observed by Shakespeare.

A *unity of feeling* pervades the whole of his plays.[2]   In *Romeo and Juliet* all is youth and spring—it is youth with its follies, its virtues, its precipitancies; it is spring with its odours, flowers, and transiency:—the same feeling commences, goes through, and ends the play.   The old men, the Capulets and Montagues, are not common old men; they have an eagerness, a hastiness, a precipitancy—the effect of spring.   With Romeo his precipitate change of passion, his hasty marriage, and his rash death, are all the effects of youth.   With Juliet love has all that is tender and melancholy in the nightingale, all that is voluptuous in the rose, with whatever is sweet in the freshness of spring; but it ends with a long deep sigh, like the breeze of the evening.[3]   This unity of character pervades the whole of his dramas.

Of that species of writing termed *tragi-comedy*, too much has been produced, but it has been doomed to the shelf.   With Shakespeare his comic constantly re-acted on his tragic characters.   Lear, wandering amidst the tempest, had all his feelings of distress increased by the overflowings of the wild wit of the Fool, as vinegar poured upon wounds exacerbate[s] their pain; thus even his comic humour tends to the development of tragic passion.

The next character belonging to Shakespeare as Shakespeare, was the *keeping at all times the high road of life*.   With him there were no innocent adulteries; he never rendered that amiable which religion and reason taught us to detest; he never clothed vice in the garb of virtue, like Beaumont and Fletcher, the

[1] Cf. i. 175 and note.   See also Schlegel, *Werke*, v. 9.

[2] The two preceding sentences are probably based on Schlegel (*Werke*, vi. 20–1).

[3] This lyrical sentence is Schlegel's, not Coleridge's (see *Werke*, vi. 242–3): 'All that is intoxicating in the fragrance of a southern spring, all the yearning in the song of the nightingale and the voluptuousness of the first blooming of the rose,—all breathe forth from this poem. . . .   The echo which the whole leaves behind in the mind, is like that of a single, but endless sigh.'

Kotzebues of his day: his fathers were roused by ingratitude, his husbands were stung by unfaithfulness; the affections were wounded in those points where all may and all must feel. Another evidence of exquisite judgment in Shakespeare was that he seized hold of popular tales. *Lear* and the *Merchant of Venice* were popular tales, but so excellently managed, [that] both were the representation of men in all ages and at all times.

His dramas do not arise absolutely out of some one extraordinary circumstance; the scenes may stand independently of any such one connecting incident, as faithful reflections of men and manners. In his *mode of drawing characters* there were no pompous descriptions of a man by himself; his character was to be drawn as in real life, from the whole course of the play, or out of the mouths of his enemies or friends.[1] This might be exemplified in the character of Polonius, which actors have often misrepresented. Shakespeare never intended to represent him as a buffoon. It was natural that Hamlet, a young man of genius and fire, detesting formality, and disliking Polonius for political reasons, as imagining that he had assisted his uncle in his usurpation, should express himself satirically; but Hamlet's words should not be taken as Shakespeare's conception of him. In Polonius a certain induration of character arose from long habits of business; but take his advice to Laertes, the reverence of his memory by Ophelia, and we shall find that he was a statesman of business, though somewhat past his faculties. One particular feature which belonged to his character was, that his recollections of past life were of wisdom, and shewed a knowledge of human nature, whilst what immediately passed before, and escaped from him, was emblematical of weakness.[2]

Another excellence in Shakespeare, and in which no other writer equalled him, was in the *language of nature*. So correct was it that we could see ourselves in all he wrote; his style and manner had also that felicity, that not a sentence could be read without its being discovered if it were *Shakespearian*. In observations of living character, such as of landlords and postilions, Fielding had great excellence; but in drawing from his own heart, and depicting that species of character which no observation could teach, he failed in comparison with Richardson, who perpetually placed himself, as it were, in a day-dream. But Shakespeare excelled in both; witness an accuracy of

---

[1] Cf. i. 201, 205 and note.
[2] This excellent character of Polonius is taken from Dr Johnson's note on *Hamlet*, II. iv (Cambridge edition, II. ii).

character in the Nurse of Juliet.   On the other hand, [consider] the great characters of Othello, Iago, Hamlet, and Richard III.; as he never could have witnessed anything similar, he appears invariably to have asked himself, How should I act or speak in such circumstances? [1]   His comic characters were also peculiar. A drunken constable was not uncommon; but he could make folly a vehicle for wit, as in Dogberry.[2]   Every thing was as a substratum on which his creative genius might erect a super-structure.

To distinguish what is *legitimate* in Shakespeare from what does not belong to him, we must observe his varied images symbolical of moral truth, thrusting by and seeming to trip up each other, from an impetuosity of thought, producing a metre which is always flowing from one verse into the other, and seldom closing with the tenth syllable of the line—an instance of which may be found in the play of *Pericles*, written a century before, but which Shakespeare altered, and where his alteration may be recognized even to half a line.[3]   This was the case not merely in his later plays, but in his early dramas, such as *Love's Labour['s] Lost*.   The same perfection in the flowing continuity of interchangeable metrical pauses is constantly perceptible.

Lastly, contrast his *morality* with the writers of his own or the succeeding age, or with those of the present day, who boast of their superiority.   He never, as before observed, deserted the high road of life; he never made his lovers openly gross or profane; for common candour must allow that his images were incomparably less so than those of his contemporaries.   Even the letters of females in high life were coarser than his writings.

The writings of Beaumont and Fletcher bear no comparison; the grossest passages of Shakespeare were purity to theirs; and it should be remembered that though he might occasionally disgust a sense of delicacy, he never injured the mind: he caused no excitement of passion which he flattered to degrade, never used what was faulty for a faulty purpose; carried on no warfare against virtue, by which wickedness may be made to appear as not wickedness, and where our sympathy was to be entrapped by the misfortunes of vice; with him vice never walked, as it were, in twilight.   He never inverted the order of nature and pro-priety, like some modern writers, who suppose every magistrate to be a glutton or a drunkard, and every poor man humane and

---

[1] Cf. with all this ii. 101, 85 and note.
[2] Cf. i. 199.
[3] Cf. ii. 165.

temperate; with him we had no benevolent braziers or sentimental ratcatchers.[1]   Nothing was purposely out of place.

If a man speak injuriously of a friend, our vindication of him
is naturally warm.   Shakespeare had been accused of profane-
ness.   He (Mr. C.) from the perusal of him, had acquired a
habit of looking into his own heart, and perceived the goings on
of his nature, and confident he was, Shakespeare was a writer of
all others the most calculated to make his readers better as well
as wiser.[2]

[1] For this phrase cf. *B.L.* ii. 162.   For the whole paragraph cf. Schlegel's
Werke, vi. 195.   'He has . . . never varnished over wild and blood-thirsty
passions with a pleasing exterior, never clothed evil with a false glitter of
magnanimity.'   The reference from *B.L.* is from 'Satyrane's Letters,' first
published in *The Friend*, 1809–10 (No. 16, 7 December 1809), and shows that
Coleridge anticipated Schlegel in this excellent remark; but the coincidence is
worthy of notice.   Cf. the two preceding paragraphs with i. 54; ii. 29–30.

[2] 'Yesterday evening's lecture was tolerably attended.'   Coleridge to the
Morgans, 29 October.   Unpublished letter transcribed by E. H. Coleridge.

Coleridge's old schoolfellow, J. M. Gutch, introduced a much briefer
report of this same lecture in *Felix Farley's Bristol Journal*, of which he
was the editor.   The report reads almost like a short summary of that printed
above.   Gutch did not report any of the later lectures, and in an unpublished
letter to the Morgans (17 November), Coleridge complained that this was due
to his rivalry with Mills, editor of the *Gazette*.

[LECTURE II.]

[*Macbeth.*]

THIS gentleman's [1] lecture of last evening on *Macbeth* was marked, characteristically, with that philosophical *tact* which perceives causes, and traces effects, impalpable to the common apprehension. He seemed to have been admitted into the closet of Shakespeare's mind; to have shared his secret thoughts, and been familiarized with his most hidden motives. Mr. Coleridge began by commenting on the vulgar stage error which transformed the Weird Sisters into witches with broomsticks. They were awful beings, and blended in themselves the Fates and Furies of the ancients with the sorceresses of Gothic and popular superstition.[2] They were mysterious natures: fatherless, motherless, sexless; they come and disappear: they lead evil minds from evil to evil, and have the power of tempting those who have been the tempters of themselves. The exquisite judgment of Shakespeare is shown in nothing more than in the different language of the Witches with each other, and with those whom they address: the former displays a certain fierce familiarity, grotesqueness mingled with terror; the latter is always solemn, dark, and mysterious.[3] Mr. Coleridge proceeded to show how Macbeth became early a tempter to himself; and contrasted the talkative curiosity of the innocent-minded and open-dispositioned Banquo, in the scene with the Witches, with the silent, absent, and brooding melancholy of his partner. A striking instance of this self-temptation was pointed out in the disturbance of Macbeth at the election of the Prince of Cumberland; but the alarm of his conscience appears, even while meditating to remove this bar to his own advancement, as he exclaims, 'Stars! hide your fires!' The ingenuity with which a man evades the promptings of conscience before the commission of a crime, was compared with his total imbecility and helplessness when the crime had been committed, and when conscience can

---

[1] This lecture is under the same heading as the first.
[2] Cf. i. 60, note, and Schlegel (*Werke*, vi. 253).
[3] 'Among themselves, the witches converse like women of the lowest class, for this they are intended to be; with Macbeth, however, their tone is elevated.' (Schlegel, *Werke*, vi. 255.)

be no longer dallied with or eluded. Macbeth in the first instance enumerates the different worldly impediments to his scheme of murder: could he put them by, he would 'jump the life to come.' Yet no sooner is the murder perpetrated, than all the concerns of this mortal life are absorbed and swallowed up in the avenging feeling within him: he hears a voice cry, 'Macbeth has murder'd sleep: and therefore, Glamis shall sleep no more.' [a]

The lecturer alluded to the prejudiced idea of Lady Macbeth as a monster, as a being out of nature and without conscience: on the contrary, her constant effort throughout the play was, if the expression may be forgiven, to *bully* conscience. She was a woman of a visionary and day-dreaming turn of mind; her eye fixed on the shadows of her solitary ambition; and her feelings abstracted, through the deep musings of her absorbing passion, from the common-life sympathies of flesh and blood. But her conscience, so far from being seared, was continually smarting within her; and she endeavours to stifle its voice, and keep down its struggles, by inflated and soaring fancies, and appeals to spiritual agency.

So far is the woman from being dead within her, that her sex occasionally betrays itself in the very moment of dark and bloody imagination. A passage where she alludes to 'plucking her nipple from the boneless gums of her infant,' [b] though usually thought to prove a merciless and unwomanly nature, proves the direct opposite: she brings it as the most solemn enforcement to Macbeth of the solemnity of his promise to undertake the plot against Duncan. Had *she* so sworn, she would have done that which was most horrible to her feelings, rather than break the oath; and as the most horrible act which it was possible for imagination to conceive, as that which was most revolting to her own feelings, she alludes to the destruction of her infant, while in the act of sucking at her breast. Had she regarded this with savage indifference, there would have been no force in the appeal; but her very allusion to it, and her purpose in this allusion, shows that she considered no tie so tender as that which connected her with her babe. Another exquisite trait was the faltering of her resolution, while standing over Duncan in his

---

[a] ' *Glamis hath murder'd sleep, and therefore Cawdor*
   Shall sleep no more; Macbeth shall sleep no more.'
                                                   II. ii. 42–3.

[b] ' *I would, while it was smiling in my face,*
   Have pluck'd my nipple from his boneless gums,
   And dash'd the brains out, had I so sworn as you.'
                                                   I. vii. 56–8.

slumbers: '*Had he not resembled my father as he slept*, I had done it.' [a]

Mr. Coleridge concluded the lecture, of which we have been only able to touch upon a few of the heads, by announcing his intention of undertaking in his next discourse the analysis of the character of Hamlet.   It is much to the credit of the literary feeling of Bristol that the room overflowed.

[a]   '*Had he not resembled*
      My father as he slept, I had done't.'
                                              II. ii. 12–13.

[LECTURE III.]

[*Hamlet.*]

THE [1] seeming inconsistencies in the conduct and character of
Hamlet have long exercised the conjectural ingenuity of critics;
and as we are always loth to suppose that the cause of defective
apprehension is in ourselves, the mystery has been too commonly
explained by the very easy process of supposing that it is, in fact,
inexplicable, and by resolving the difficulty into the capricious
and irregular genius of Shakespeare.

Mr. Coleridge, in his *third* lecture, has effectually exposed the
shallow and stupid arrogance of this vulgar and indolent decision.
He has shewn that the intricacies of Hamlet's character may be
traced to Shakespeare's deep and accurate science in mental
philosophy. That this character must have some common
connection with the laws of our nature, was assumed by the
lecturer from the fact that Hamlet was the darling of every
country where literature was fostered. He thought it essential to
the understanding of Hamlet's character that we should reflect
on the constitution of our own minds. Man was distinguished
from the animal in proportion as thought prevailed over sense;
but in healthy processes of the mind, a balance was maintained
between the impressions of outward objects and the inward
operations of the intellect: if there be an overbalance in the con-
templative faculty, man becomes the creature of meditation, and
loses the power of action. Shakespeare seems to have conceived
a mind in the highest degree of excitement, with this over-
powering activity of intellect, and to have placed him in circumstances where he was obliged to act on the spur of the moment.
Hamlet, though brave and careless of death, had contracted a
morbid sensibility from this overbalance in the mind, producing
the lingering and vacillating delays of procrastination, and
wasting in the energy of resolving the energy of acting. Thus
the play of *Hamlet* offers a direct contrast to that of *Macbeth*:
the one proceeds with the utmost slowness, the other with
breathless and crowded rapidity.[2]

[1] Heading in the *Gazette*: '*Mr. Coleridge's Third Lecture.*'
[2] Cf. i. 49, note, 71, and Schlegel, *Werke*, vi. 257, the origin of this remark.

The effect of this overbalance of imagination is beautifully illustrated in the inward brooding of Hamlet—the effect of a superfluous activity of thought. His mind, unseated from its healthy balance, is for ever occupied with the world within him, and abstracted from external things; his words give a substance to shadows, and he is dissatisfied with commonplace realities. It is the nature of thought to be indefinite, while definiteness belongs to reality. The sense of sublimity arises, not from the sight of an outward object, but from the reflection upon it; not from the impression, but from the idea.[1] Few have seen a celebrated waterfall without feeling something of disappointment: it is only subsequently, by reflection, that the idea of the waterfall comes full into the mind, and brings with it a train of sublime associations. Hamlet felt this: in him we see a mind that keeps itself in a state of abstraction, and beholds external objects as hieroglyphics. His soliloquy, 'Oh that this too, too solid flesh would melt,' arises from a craving after the indefinite: a disposition or temper which most easily besets men of genius; a morbid craving for that which is not. The self-delusion common to this temper of mind was finely exemplified in the character which Hamlet gives of himself: 'It cannot be, but I am pigeon-liver'd, and lack gall, to make oppression bitter.' He mistakes the seeing his chains for the breaking of them; and delays action, till action is of no use; and he becomes the victim of circumstances and accident.

The lecturer, in descending to particulars, took occasion to defend from the common charge of improbable eccentricity, the scene which follows Hamlet's interview with the Ghost. He showed that after the mind has been stretched beyond its usual pitch and tone, it must either sink into exhaustion and inanity, or seek relief by change. Persons conversant with deeds of cruelty contrive to escape from their conscience by connecting something of the ludicrous with them, and by inventing grotesque terms, and a certain technical phraseology, to disguise the horror of their practices.

The terrible, however paradoxical it may appear, will be found to touch on the verge of the ludicrous. Both arise from the perception of something out of the common nature of things,—something out of place: if from this we can abstract danger, the uncommonness alone remains, and the sense of the ridiculous is excited. The close alliance of these opposites appears from

---

[1] Coleridge is here quoting Kant's definition of the sublime (*Critique of Aesthetic Judgement*, ed. Meredith, pp. 94, 104, 114, etc.).

the circumstance that laughter is equally the expression of extreme anguish and horror as of joy: in the same manner that there are tears of joy as well as tears of sorrow, so there is a laugh of terror as well as a laugh of merriment.   These complex causes will naturally have produced in Hamlet the disposition to escape from his own feelings of the overwhelming and supernatural by a wild transition to the ludicrous,—a sort of cunning bravado, bordering on the flights of delirium.

Mr. Coleridge instanced, as a proof of Shakespeare's minute knowledge of human nature, the unimportant conversation which takes place during the expectation of the Ghost's appearance: and he recalled to our notice what all must have observed in common life, that on the brink of some serious enterprise, or event of moment, men naturally elude the pressure of their own thoughts by turning aside to trivial objects and familiar circumstances.   So in *Hamlet*, the dialogue on the platform begins with remarks on the coldness of the air, and inquiries, obliquely connected indeed with the expected hour of the visitation, but thrown out in a seeming vacuity of topics, as to the striking of the clock.   The same desire to escape from the inward thoughts is admirably carried on in Hamlet's moralizing on the Danish custom of wassailing; and a double purpose is here answered, which demonstrates the exquisite judgment of Shakespeare. By thus entangling the attention of the audience in the nice distinctions and parenthetical sentences of Hamlet, he takes them completely by surprize on the appearance of the Ghost, which comes upon them in all the suddenness of its visionary character. No modern writer would have dared, like Shakespeare, to have preceded this last visitation by two distinct appearances, or could have contrived that the third should rise upon the two former in impressiveness and solemnity of interest.

Mr. Coleridge at the commencement of this lecture drew a comparison between the characters of Macbeth and Bonaparte— both tyrants, both indifferent to means, however barbarous, to attain their ends; and he hoped the fate of the latter would be like the former, in failing amidst a host of foes, which his cruelty and injustice had roused against him.   At the conclusion of his lecture, he alluded to the successes of the Allies,[1] and complimented his country on the lead she had taken, and the example she had set to other nations, in resisting an attack upon the middle classes of society; for if the French Emperor had succeeded in

[1] Cf. i. 37, note 4.

his attempts to gain universal dominion, there would have been but two classes suffered to exist—the high and the low. England, justly proud, as she had a right to be, of a Shakespeare, a Milton, a Bacon, and a Newton, could also boast of a Nelson and a Wellington.

[LECTURE IV.]

[*Winter's Tale.   Othello.*]

AT the commencement of the fourth lecture last evening, Mr. Coleridge combated the opinion held by some critics, that the writings of Shakespeare were like a wilderness, in which were desolate places, most beautiful flowers, and weeds; he argued that even the titles of his plays were appropriate and shewed judgment, presenting as it were a bill of fare before the feast. This was peculiarly so in *The Winter's Tale*,—a wild story, calculated to interest a circle round a fireside.[1]   He maintained that Shakespeare ought not to be judged of in detail, but on the whole.   A pedant differed from a master in cramping himself with certain established rules, whereas the master regarded rules as always controllable by and subservient to the end.   The passion to be delineated in *The Winter's Tale* was *jealousy.* Shakespeare's description of this, however, was perfectly philosophical: the mind, in its first harbouring of it, became mean and despicable, and the first sensation was perfect shame, arising from the consideration of having possessed an object unworthily, of degrading a person to a thing.   The mind that once indulges this passion has a predisposition, a vicious weakness, by which it kindles a fire from every spark, and from circumstances the most innocent and indifferent finds fuel to feed the flame.   This he exemplified in an able manner from the conduct and opinion of Leontes, who seized upon occurrences of which he himself was the cause, and when speaking of Hermione, combined his anger with images of the lowest sensuality, and pursued the object with the utmost cruelty.   This character Mr. Coleridge contrasted with that of Othello, whom Shakespeare had portrayed the very opposite to a jealous man: he was noble, generous, open-hearted; unsuspicious and unsuspecting; and who, even after the exhibition of the handkerchief as evidence of his

---

[1] Cf. i. 37, 107, 109, 206.   Schlegel also comments on the appropriateness of this name and also contrasts the jealousy of Leontes and Othello (*Werke*, vi. 237–8).   In both instances he may have given Coleridge his original suggestion; but in the first case the parallel is so insignificant that it may easily be due to coincidence; in the second Coleridge's treatment of the jealousy of Leontes and Othello is entirely different from that of Schlegel, and overwhelmingly superior.

wife's guilt, bursts out in her praise.   Mr. C. ridiculed the idea
of making Othello a negro.   He was a gallant Moor, of royal
blood, combining a high sense of Spanish and Italian feeling,
and whose noble nature was wrought on, not by a fellow with a
countenance predestined for the gallows, as some actors represented Iago, but by an accomplished and artful villain, who was
indefatigable in his exertions to poison the mind of the brave and
swarthy Moor.   It is impossible, with our limits, to follow Mr.
Coleridge through those nice discriminations by which he
elucidated the various characters in this excellent drama.
Speaking of the character of the women of Shakespeare, or
rather, as Pope [1] stated, the absence of character, Mr. Coleridge
said this was the highest compliment that could be paid to them:
the elements were so commixed, so even was the balance of
feeling, that no one protruded in particular,—everything amiable
as sisters, mothers, and wives, was included in the thought.
To form a just estimation and to enjoy the beauties of Shakespeare, Mr. Coleridge's lectures should be *heard* again and again.
Perhaps at some future period we may occasionally fill our
columns with an analysis of his different lectures similar to what
we presented last week of the first; at present we must content
ourselves with generals.[2]

[1] Cf. i. 120, note.
[2] 'The lecture of to-night, which I had expected to have been the best and
to have produced the most lively effect, that on *Othello*, was the worst I ever
delivered and a humiliating contrast to the lectures before.'   Coleridge to the
Morgans: 'Tuesday, November 10' [9 ?], E. H. Coleridge's transcript of an
unpublished letter.   Coleridge's adverse opinion of this lecture does not
seem to be justified.

[LECTURE V.]

[*Historical Plays. Richard II.*]

FULLY to comprehend the nature of the Historic Drama, the difference should be understood between the epic and tragic muse. The latter recognizes and is grounded upon the free-will of man; [1] the former is under the control of destiny, or, among Christians, an overruling Providence. In epic, the prominent character is ever under this influence, and when accidents are introduced, they are the result of causes over which our will has no power. An epic play begins and ends arbitrarily; its only law is, that it possess beginning, middle, and end. Homer ends with the death of Hector; the final fate of Troy is left untouched. Virgil ends with the marriage of Aeneas; the historical events are left imperfect.

In the tragic, the free-will of man is the first cause, [2] and accidents are never introduced; if they are, it is considered a great fault. To cause the death of a hero by accident, such as slipping off a plank into the sea, [3] would be beneath the tragic muse, as it would arise from no mental action.

Shakespeare, in blending the epic with the tragic, has given the impression of the drama to the history of his country. By this means he has bequeathed as a legacy the pure spirit of history. Not that his facts are implicitly to be relied on, or is he to be read, as the Duke of Marlborough read him, as an historian; [4] but as distance is destroyed by a telescope, and by the force of imagination we see in the constellations, brought close to the eye, a multitude of worlds, [5] so by the law of impressiveness, when we read his plays, we seem to live in the era he portrays.

One great object of his historic plays, and particularly of that to be examined (*Richard II.*), was to make his countrymen more

---

[1] Schlegel, *Werke*, v. 73, 75; vi. 17, etc. Schlegel dwells on this point frequently and at length and is probably Coleridge's source.

[2] See preceding note.

[3] The instance is probably taken from Schiller's preface to *Fiesco*, in which he explains that he had been obliged to alter historical fact in regard to the death of Fiesco to avoid so undramatic a conclusion. See A. C. Dunstan, *Modern Language Review*, xvii. 278.

[4] Cf. i. 130, note 2. [5] Cf. i. 126, 138.

patriotic; to make Englishmen proud of being Englishmen.
It was a play not much acted. This was not regretted by the
lecturer; for he never saw any of Shakespeare's plays performed,
but with a degree of pain, disgust, and indignation.[1] He had
seen Mrs. Siddons as Lady, and Kemble as Macbeth:—these
might be the Macbeths of the Kembles, but they were not the
Macbeths of Shakespeare. He was therefore not grieved at the
enormous size and monopoly of the theatres, which naturally
produced many bad and but few good actors; and which drove
Shakespeare from the stage, to find his proper place in the heart
and in the closet, where he sits with Milton, enthroned on a
double-headed Parnassus; and with whom everything that was
admirable, everything praiseworthy, was to be found.

Shakespeare shewed great judgment in his first scenes; they
contained the germ of the ruling passion which was to be
developed hereafter. Thus Richard's hardiness of mind, arising
from kingly power; his weakness and debauchery from continual
and unbounded flattery; and the haughty temper of the barons;
one and the other alternately forming the moral of the play, are
glanced at in the first scenes. An historic play requires more
excitement than a tragic; thus Shakespeare never loses an opportunity of awakening a patriotic feeling. For this purpose Old
Gaunt accuses Richard of having '*farmed* out the island.' What
could be a greater rebuke to a king than to be told that

> 'This realm, this England,
> .   .   .   .   .   .
> Is now leased out . . .
> Like to a tenement, or pelting farm.'

This speech of Gaunt is most beautiful; the propriety of putting
so long a speech into the mouth of an old dying man might easily
be shown. It thence partook of the nature of prophecy:—

> 'Methinks I am a prophet new inspired,
> And thus expiring, do foretell of him.'

The plays of Shakespeare, as before observed of *Romeo and
Juliet*, were characteristic throughout:—whereas *that* was all
youth and spring, *this* was womanish weakness; the characters
were of extreme old age, or partook of the nature of age and
imbecility. The length of the speeches was adapted to a

---

[1] Cf. ii. 57, 68, and Gillman's *Life*, p. 280.

delivery between acting and recitation, which produced in the auditors a docility or frame of mind favorable to the poet, and useful to themselves:—how different from modern plays, where the glare of the scenes, with every wished-for object industriously realized, the mind becomes bewildered in surrounding attractions; whereas Shakespeare, in place of ranting, music, and outward action, addresses us in words that enchain the mind, and carry on the attention from scene to scene.

Critics who argue against the use of a thing from its abuse, have taken offence to the introduction in a tragedy of that play on words which is called *punning*.   But how stands the fact with nature?   Is there not a tendency in the human mind, when suffering under some great affliction, to associate everything around it with the obtrusive feeling, to connect and absorb all into the predominant sensation?   Thus Old Gaunt, discontented with his relation, in the peevishness of age, when Richard asks 'how is it with aged Gaunt,' breaks forth [1]—

> 'O! how that name befits my composition!
> Old Gaunt, indeed; and Gaunt in being old.
>
> .   .   .   .
>
> Gaunt am I for the grave, Gaunt as a grave,' &c.

Shakespeare, as if he anticipated the hollow sneers of critics, makes Richard reply—

> 'Can sick men play so nicely with their names?'

To which the answer of Gaunt presents a confutation of this idle criticism—

> 'No, misery makes sport to mock itself.' [2]

The only nomenclature of criticism should be the classification of the faculties of the mind, how they are placed, how they are subordinate, whether they do or do not appeal to the worthy feelings of our nature.   False criticism is created by ignorance, light removes it; as the croaking of frogs in a ditch is silenced by a candle.

The beautiful *keeping of the character of the play* is conspicuous in the Duke of York.   He, like Gaunt, is old, and full of a religious loyalty struggling with indignation at the king's vices

---

[1] Cf. i. 135, 138; ii. 144.
[2] All of the preceding quotations are from *Richard II*, ii. i. 31–85.

and follies, is an evidence of a man giving up all energy under a feeling of despair. The play throughout is a history of the human mind, when reduced to ease its anguish with words instead of action, and the necessary feeling of weakness which such a state produces. The scene between the Queen, Bushy, and Bagot, is also worthy of notice, from the characters all talking high, but performing nothing; and from Shakespeare's tenderness to those presentiments, which, wise as we will be, will still adhere to our nature.

Shakespeare has contrived to bring the character of Richard, with all his prodigality and hard usage of his friends, still within the compass of our pity; for we find him much beloved by those who knew him best. The Queen is passionately attached to him, and his good Bishop (Carlisle) adheres to the last. He is not one of those whose punishment gives delight; his failings appear to arise from outward objects, and from the poison of flatterers around him; we cannot, therefore, help pitying, and wishing he had been placed in a rank where he would have been less exposed, and where he might have been happy and useful.

The next character which presented itself, was that of Bolingbroke. It was itself a contradiction to the line of Pope—'Shakspere grew immortal in spite of himself.' [1]   One thing was to be observed, that in all his plays he takes the opportunity of sowing germ[s], the full development of which appears at a future time. Thus in *Henry IV*. he prepares us for the character of Henry V.; and the whole of Gloucester's character in *Henry VI*. is so different from any other that we are prepared for Richard III.   In Bolingbroke is defined the struggle of inward determination with outward shew of humility. His first introduction, where he says to the nobles who came to meet him—

> 'Welcome, my lords, I wot your love pursues
> A banished traitor; all my treasury
> Is yet but unfelt thanks,' &c.[2]

could only be compared to Marius, as described by Plutarch, exclaiming, on the presentation of the consular robes, Do these 'befit a banished traitor?' concealing in pretended disgrace the implacable ambition that haunted him.

In this scene old York again appears, and with high feelings of

---

[1] 'And grew immortal in his own despite,' Pope's *Imitation of the First Epistle of the Second Book of Horace*, 72.   (Cf. i. 138, 194.)
[2] II. iii. 59–61.

loyalty and duty reproves Bolingbroke in boldness of words, but with feebleness of action—

> 'Show me thy humble heart, and not thy knee.' [1]

> . . . .

> 'Tut! tut!
> Grace me no grace, nor uncle me no uncle:
> I am no traitor's uncle.' [2]

> . . . .

> 'Why, foolish boy, the king is left behind,
> And in my loyal bosom lies his power.' [3]

Yet after all this vehemence he concludes—

> 'Well, well, I see the issue of these arms;
> I cannot mend it . . .

> . . . .

> But if I could, by Him that gave me life,
> I would attach you all . . .

> . . . .

> . . . . So fare you well,
> Unless you please to enter in the castle,
> And there repose you for this night—' [4]

the whole character transpiring in verbal expression.

The overflowing of Richard's feelings, and which tends to keep him in our esteem, is the scene where he lands—

> 'Dear earth, I do salute thee with my hand,
> Tho' rebels wound thee with their horses' hoofs;' [5]

so beautifully descriptive of the sensations of a man and a king attached to his country as his inheritance and his birthright. His resolution and determination of action are depicted in glowing words, thus—

> 'So when this thief, this traitor Bolingbroke,
> Shall see us rising in our throne,' &c., &c.

> . . . .

> For every man that Bolingbroke hath press'd,
> God for his Richard hath in heavenly pay
> A glorious angel.' [6]

Who, after this, would not have supposed great energy of action?   No! all was spent, and upon the first ill-tidings, nothing

---

[1] II. iii. 83.   [2] II. iii. 86–8.   [3] II. iii. 97–8.
[4] II. iii. 152–61.   [5] III. ii. 6–7.   [6] III. ii. 47–61.

but despondency takes place, with alternatives of unmanly despair and unfounded hopes; great activity of mind, without any strength of moral feeling to rouse to action, presenting an awful lesson in the education of princes.

Here it might be observed, that Shakespeare, following the best tragedies, where moral reflections are introduced in the choruses, &c., puts general reflections in the mouths of unimportant personages. His great men never moralize, except under the influence of violent passion; for it is the nature of passion to generalize. Thus, two fellows in the street, when they quarrel, have recourse to their proverbs, 'It is always the case with such fellows as those,' or some such phrase, making a species their object of aversion. Shakespeare uniformly elicits grand and noble truths from passion,[1] as sparks are forced from heated iron. Richard's parade of resignation is consistent with the other parts of the play—

> . . . . 'Of comfort no man speak;
> Let's talk of graves, of worms, of epitaphs,' &c.,[2]

easing his heart, and consuming all that is manly in words; never anywhere seeking comfort in despair, but mistaking the moment of exhaustion for quiet. This is finely contrasted in Bolingbroke's struggle of haughty feeling with temporary dissimulation, in which the latter says—

> 'Harry Bolingbroke,
> On both his knees doth kiss King Richard's hand,' &c.,[3]

but, with the prudence of his character, after this hypocritical speech, adds—

> 'March on, and mark King Richard how he looks.' [4]

Shakespeare's wonderful judgment appears in his historical plays, in the introduction of some incident or other, though no way connected, yet serving to give an air of historic fact. Thus the scene of the Queen and the Gardener realizes the thing, makes the occurrence no longer a segment, but gives an individuality, a liveliness and presence to the scene.

---

[1] Cf. i. 202, 203; ii. 14.
[2] III. ii. 144–5. Read 'and epitaphs.'
[3] III. iii. 35–6. For 'Harry' read 'Henry
[4] III. iii. 61.

After an observation or two upon Shakespeare's taking advantage of making an impression friendly to the character of his favourite hero Henry V., in the discourse of Bolingbroke respecting his son's absence, Mr. Coleridge said he should reserve his definition of the character of Falstaff until he came to that of Richard III., for in both was an overprizing of the intellectual above the moral character; in the most desperate and the most dissolute the same moral elements were to be found.

Of the assertion of Dr. Johnson, that the writings of Shakespeare were deficient in pathos,[1] and that he only put our senses into complete peacefulness, Mr. Coleridge held this much preferable to that degree of excitement which was the object of the German drama; and concluded a very interesting lecture with reading some observations he penned after being present at the representation of a play in Germany, in which the wife of a colonel who had fallen into disgrace was frantic in the beginning, middle, and end; frantic first for grief, and afterwards for joy.[2] A distortion of feeling was the feature of the modern drama of Kotzebue and his followers; its heroes were generous, liberal, brave, and noble, just so far as they could, without the sacrifice of one Christian virtue; its misanthropes were tender-hearted, and its tender-hearted were misanthropes.

---

[1] Dr Johnson does not by any means deny pathos to Shakespeare, but he does protest vehemently that Shakespeare's pathos is always 'polluted with some unexpected depravations'; i.e. puns. 'His persons, however distressed, *have a conceit left to them in their misery, a miserable conceit.*' (Final note to *Romeo and Juliet*. See also his Preface, to the same effect.) Schlegel (*Werke*, vi. 192) attacks Dr Johnson for these remarks, but Coleridge does not borrow his argument.

[2] This German lady is to be found described in the second of 'Satyrane's Letters,' from which Coleridge was obviously reading. See *B.L.* ii. 157–9. The whole discussion of sentimental drama which there follows is brilliant criticism.

[LECTURE VI.]

[*Richard III.   Falstaff.   Iago.   Shakespeare as a Poet.*]

In our fourth page may be seen an analysis of the fifth lecture of this gentleman.[1]   Last evening [2] he delivered his sixth.   It may be necessary here to remark that Mr. Coleridge in his second lecture stated that from the diffuseness he unavoidably fell into in his introductory discourse, he should be unable to complete the series he had designed without an additional lecture, which those who had regularly attended would be admitted to gratis.[3] This was the one delivered last night; that, therefore, intended on education, would be the seventh instead of the sixth, which is to take place on to-morrow (Thursday).   We must content ourselves with giving to-day a very brief account of the lecture of last night.   Mr. Coleridge commenced by tracing the history of tragedy and comedy among the ancients, with whom both were distinct.   Shakespeare, though he had produced comedy in tragedy, had never produced tragi-comedy.   With him, as with Aristophanes, opposites served to illustrate each other.   The arena common to both was ideal; the comedy of the Greek and the English dramatist was as much above real life as the tragedy. Tragedy was poetry in the deepest earnest, comedy was mirth in the highest zest, exulting in the removal of all bounds; an intellectual wealth squandered in sport; it had nothing to do with morality; [4] its lessons were prudential; it taught to avoid vice;

---

[1] Heading in the *Gazette*: 'Mr. Coleridge.'

[2] This report was published Thursday, 18 November; it was written Wednesday, 17 November; and Coleridge's sixth lecture was delivered Tuesday, 16 November.   See the reference, a few lines below, to 'to-morrow (Thursday).'

[3] The announcement of Coleridge's subjects in the *Mirror*, 30 October, which has already been quoted in the introductory note on these lectures, indicates that the diffuseness for which Coleridge apologized came in the second rather than in the first lecture.   The second lecture required two evenings instead of one, as Coleridge had planned.

[4] At this point Coleridge evidently shifted from the 'old comedy' to the 'new comedy' of Athens but was misunderstood by the reporter.   For this whole discussion of tragedy, 'old comedy,' and 'new comedy,' which is taken from Schlegel, see the fragment of a lecture on 'Greek Drama,' i. 151–5. The present lecture is particularly badly reported, and Coleridge expressed his contempt of the report to the Morgans: 'O mercy! such an account of my last night's (6th) lecture in Mills' paper!   It is so strangely throughout the *direct opposite* of what I said, that I triumph in it.'   Unpublished letter of 17 November, transcribed by E. H. Coleridge.

but if it aimed at admonition, it became a middle thing, neither tragedy nor comedy. Mr. C., in deciphering the character of Falstaff, was naturally led to a comparison of the wit of Shakespeare with that of his contemporaries (Ben Jonson, &c., &c.), and aptly remarked, that whilst Shakespeare gave us wit as salt to our meat, Ben Jonson gave wit as salt instead of meat. After wit, Mr. C. proceeded to define *humour*, and entered into a curious history of the origin of the term, distinguishing the sanguine, the temperate,[1] the melancholy, the phlegmatic. Where one fluid predominated over the other, a man was said to be under the influence of that particular *humour*. Thus a disproportion of *black bile* rendered a man melancholy. But when nothing serious was the consequence of a predominance of one particular fluid, the actions performed were humorous, and a man capable of describing them termed a humorist.

Shakespeare, possessed of wit, humour, fancy, and imagination, built up an outward world from the stores within his mind, as the bee builds a hive from a thousand sweets, gathered from a thousand flowers. He was not only a great poet but a great philosopher. The characters of Richard III., Iago, and Falstaff, were the characters of men who reverse the order of things, who place intellect at the head,[2] whereas it ought to follow like geometry, to prove and to confirm. No man, either hero or saint, ever acted from an unmixed motive; for let him do what he will rightly, still conscience whispers 'it is your duty.' Richard, laughing at conscience, and sneering at religion, felt a confidence in his intellect, which urged him to commit the most horrid crimes, because he felt himself, although inferior in form and shape, superior to those around him; he felt he possessed a power that they had not. Iago, on the same principle, conscious of superior intellect, gave scope to his envy, and hesitated not to ruin a gallant, open, and generous friend in the moment of felicity, because he was not promoted as he expected. Othello was superior in place, but Iago felt him inferior in intellect, and unrestrained by conscience, trampled upon him. Falstaff, not a degraded man of genius, like Burns, but a man of degraded genius, with the same consciousness of superiority to his companions, fastened himself on a young prince, to prove how much his influence on an heir apparent could exceed that of statesmen.

---

[1] Another reportorial error. Read *choleric*.
[2] Cf. i. 206; ii. 26, 141, 165, and *B.L.* ii. 189. Beginning at this point, and continuing to the end of the next sentence, the reporter seems again to have become confused.

With this view he hesitated not to practise the most contemptu-
ous [a] of all characters—an open and professed liar: even his
sensuality was subservient to his intellect, for he appeared to
drink sack that he might have occasion to shew his wit.   One
thing, however, worthy of observation, was the contrast of labour
in Falstaff to produce wit, with the ease [with] which Prince
Henry parried his shaft, and the final contempt which such
a character deserved and received from the young king, when
Falstaff, calling his friends around him, Nym, Bardolph, Pistol,
&c., expected the consummation of that influence which he
flattered himself to have established.

Mr. C. concluded by delivering his opinion of Shakespeare's
general character as a poet, independent of a dramatist.   His
Venus and Adonis, written at an early age, contained evidence of
his qualifications as a poet: great sweetness and melody of sound,
with an exquisite richness of language, were symptoms of that
genius which, further displayed in his *Lucrece*, received its consummation in his dramatic writings.[1]   Our limits prevent us
from following Mr. Coleridge further.   We do not offer an
apology to our readers for having consumed so many of our
columns in a brief outline of his interesting lectures.   To gain an
insight into human nature, to enjoy the writings and genius of
the first dramatic poet of any age, and above all to obtain that
knowledge of ourselves, which the lectures of Mr. Coleridge,
rich in imagery, language, and wisdom, were calculated to
produce, have afforded us so much genuine gratification, that
we could not resist the desire of imparting a share to our readers.[2]

---

[a] *Read 'contemptible.'*

[1] Cf. the section on 'Shakespeare's Poetry' (i. 189–93), the fourth lecture
of 1811–12, and ch. xv. of *B.L.*

[2] At the end of this report a list was given of three *errata* in the first and
second lectures.   These corrections have been incorporated in the text.

THE LECTURES OF 1818

After the lectures at Bristol in 1813–14 Coleridge dropped lecturing entirely for a time and would willingly have abandoned it altogether. He had found his final haven of refuge with the Gillmans in 1816, had begun to wrench himself partly free from the tyranny of opium, had accomplished more in a literary way than he had found possible at any other time after his return from Germany in 1799, and was full of hopes to carry on his philosophical studies to a glorious conclusion. But the need for money drove him back to literary lectures, partly, at least, for the sake of Derwent Coleridge's university education.[1]

He wrote on 18 January 1818 to H. C. Robinson, 'I shall have written every lecture, first as if I h[ad intende [2]]d to [read the [2]]m; but shall deliver them without book, which plan will, I trust, answer all purposes—that of order in the matter, and of animation in the manner.' As Coleridge was at this time extremely busy finishing the 1818 edition of *The Friend*, this promise would be regarded with some suspicion but for the testimony of Gillman [3] that Coleridge lectured from carefully prepared notes. But, Gillman said, his audience was most delighted in the extemporaneous passages.

The prospectus which follows is reprinted from a copy in the British Museum.[4]

PROSPECTUS OF A COURSE OF LECTURES

By S. T. COLERIDGE

There are few families, at present, in the higher and middle classes of English society, in which literary topics and the productions of the Fine Arts, in some one or other of their various forms, do not occasionally take their turn in contributing to the entertainment of the social board, and the amusement of the circle at the fire-side. The acquisitions and attainments of the intellect ought, indeed, to hold a very inferior rank in our estimation, opposed to moral worth, or even to professional and specific

---

[1] Derwent Coleridge, *Poems by Hartley Coleridge, with a Memoir of His Life by his Brother. Memoir*, p. lxiii.
[2] A hole in the MS. I quote from the original letter.
[3] *Life of Coleridge*, p. 335. [4] Pressmark, 1890, e (41).

skill, prudence, and industry. But why should they be *opposed*, when they may be made subservient merely by being *subordinated*? It can rarely happen that a man of social disposition, altogether a stranger to subjects of taste (almost the only ones on which persons of both sexes can converse with a common interest), should pass through the world without at times feeling dissatisfied with himself. The best proof of this is to be found in the marked anxiety which men who have succeeded in life without the aid of these accomplishments shew in securing them to their children. A young man of ingenuous mind will not wilfully deprive himself of any species of respect. He will wish to feel himself on a level with the average of the society in which he lives, though he may be ambitious of *distinguishing* himself only in his own immediate pursuit or occupation.

Under this conviction, the following Course of Lectures was planned. The several titles will best explain the particular subjects and purposes of each; but the main objects proposed, as the result of all, are the two following:—

I. To convey, in a form best fitted to render them impressive at the time and remembered afterwards, rules and principles of sound judgment, with a kind and degree of connected information, such as the hearers, generally speaking, cannot be supposed likely to form, collect, and arrange for themselves, by their own unassisted studies. It might be presumption to say, that any important part of these Lectures could not be derived from books; but none, I trust, in supposing, that the same information could not be so surely or conveniently acquired from such books as are of commonest occurrence, or with that quantity of time and attention which can be reasonably expected, or even wisely desired, of men engaged in business and the active duties of the world.

II. Under a strong persuasion that little of real value is derived by persons in general from a wide and various reading; but still more deeply convinced as to the actual *mischief* of unconnected and promiscuous reading, and that it is sure, in a greater or less degree, to enervate even where it does not likewise inflate; I hope to satisfy many an ingenuous mind, seriously interested in its own development and cultivation, how moderate a number of volumes, if only they be judiciously chosen, will suffice for the attainment of every wise and desirable purpose: that is, *in addition* to those which he studies for specific and professional purposes. It is saying less than the truth to affirm, that an excellent book (and the remark holds almost equally good of a

Raphael as of a Milton) is like a well-chosen and well-tended fruit-tree.   Its fruits are not of one season only.   With the due and natural intervals, we may recur to it year after year, and it will supply the same nourishment and the same gratification, if only we ourselves return with the same healthful appetite.

The subject of the Lectures are indeed very *different*, but not (in the strict sense of the term) *diverse*: they are *various*, rather than *miscellaneous*.   There is this bond of connexion common to them all,—that the mental pleasure which they are calculated to excite is not dependant on accidents of fashion, place, or age, or the events or the customs of the day; but commensurate with the good sense, taste, and feeling, to the cultivation of which they themselves so largely contribute, as being all in *kind*, though not all in the same *degree*, productions of GENIUS.

What it would be arrogant to promise, I may yet be permitted to hope,—that the execution will prove correspondent and adequate to the plan.   Assuredly, my best efforts have not been wanting so to select and prepare the materials, that, at the conclusion of the Lectures, an attentive auditor, who should consent to aid his future recollection by a few notes taken either during each Lecture or soon after, would rarely feel himself, for the time to come, excluded from taking an intelligent interest in any general conversation likely to occur in mixed society.

S. T. COLERIDGE.

SYLLABUS OF THE COURSE

LECTURE I. *Tuesday Evening, January* 27, 1818.—On the Manners, Morals, Literature, Philosophy, Religion, and the State of Society in general, in European Christendom, from the eighth to the fifteenth Century (that is, from A.D. 700 to A.D. 1400), more particularly in reference to England, France, Italy, and Germany: in other words, a portrait of the (so called) Dark Ages of Europe.

LECTURE II. *Friday Evening, January* 30.—On the Tales and Metrical Romances common, for the most part, to England, Germany, and the North of France; and on the English Songs and Ballads; continued to the Reign of Charles the First.—

A few Selections will be made from the Swedish, Danish, and German Languages, translated for the purpose by the Lecturer.

LECTURE III. *Tuesday Evening, February* 3.—Chaucer and Spenser; of Petrarch; of Ariosto, Pulci, and Boiardo.

LECTURES IV. V. and VI. on *Friday Evening, February* 6; on *Tuesday Evening, February* 10; and on *Friday Evening, February* 13.—On the Dramatic Works of SHAKSPEARE. In these Lectures will be comprised the substance of Mr. Coleridge's former Courses on the same subject, enlarged and varied by subsequent study and reflection.

LECTURE VII. *Tuesday Evening, February* 17.—On Ben Jonson, Beaumont and Fletcher, and Massinger; with the probable Causes of the Cessation of Dramatic *Poetry* in England with Shirley and Otway, soon after the Restoration of Charles the Second.

LECTURE VIII. *Friday Evening, February* 20.—Of the Life and *all* the Works of CERVANTES, but chiefly of his Don Quixote. The Ridicule of Knight-Errantry shewn to have been but a secondary Object in the Mind of the Author, and not the principal Cause of the Delight which the Work continues to give in all Nations, and under all the Revolutions of Manners and Opinions.

LECTURE IX. *Tuesday Evening, February* 24.—On Rabelais, Swift, and Sterne: on the Nature and Constituents of genuine Humour, and on the Distinctions of the Humourous from the Witty, the Fanciful, the Droll, the Odd, &c.

LECTURE X. *Friday Evening, February* 27.—Of Donne, Dante, and Milton.

LECTURE XI. *Tuesday Evening, March* 3.—On the Arabian Nights Entertainments, and on the *romantic* Use of the Supernatural in Poetry, and in Works of Fiction not poetical. On the Conditions and Regulations under which such Books may be employed advantageously in the earlier Periods of Education.

LECTURE XII. *Friday Evening, March* 6.—On Tales of Witches, Apparitions, &c. as distinguished from the Magic and Magicians of Asiatic Origin. The probable Sources of the former, and of the Belief in them in certain Ages and Classes of Men. Criteria by which mistaken and exaggerated Facts may be distinguished from absolute Falsehood and Imposture. Lastly, the Causes of the Terror and Interest which Stories of Ghosts and Witches inspire, in early Life at least, whether believed or not.

LECTURE XIII. *Tuesday Evening, March* 10.—On Colour, Sound, and Form, in Nature, as connected with POESY: the word 'Poesy' used as the *generic* or class term, including Poetry, Music, Painting, Statuary, and ideal Architecture, as its Species. The reciprocal Relations of Poetry and Philosophy to each other; and of both to Religion, and the Moral Sense.

LECTURE XIV. *Friday Evening, March* 13.—On the Corruptions of the English Language since the Reign of Queen Anne, in our Style of writing Prose. A few easy Rules for the Attainment of a manly, unaffected, and pure Language, in our genuine Mother-Tongue, whether for the purposes of Writing, Oratory, or Conversation. Concluding Address.

———————

By Permission of the PHILOSOPHICAL SOCIETY of London, the Lectures will be delivered at their Great Room, Fleur-de-Luce Court, Fleet-Street; and will commence on each Evening at a Quarter after Eight precisely.

Single Subscription Tickets for the whole Course, *Two Guineas* each; and Tickets admitting a Gentleman and Lady, *Three Guineas* each; may be procured at Messrs. TAYLOR and HESSEY, 93, Fleet-Street; HOOKHAM and SONS, Old Bond-Street; BOOSEY and SONS, New Broad-Street; and at the Society's Rooms, on the Lecture Nights.

Admission to the Single Lecture, *Five Shillings.*

———————

Jas Adlard and Sons, Printers, 23, Bartholomew-Close.

———————

Gillman tells us that these lectures were Coleridge's most profitable course.[1] The previous courses must have given Coleridge a considerable reputation, and he had recently added to this by a series of important publications.[2] He himself felt that the support of the newspapers contributed materially to his financial success, and expressed his gratitude to Mudford, assistant editor of the *Courier*, in a letter [3] which should be quoted in full.

———————

[1] *Life*, p. 335.
[2] *Christabel, Kubla Khan*, etc. (1816), *The Statesman's Manual* (1816), *A Lay Sermon* (1817), *Biographia Literaria* (1817), *Sibylline Leaves* (1817), *Zapolya* (1817).
[3] *Canterbury Magazine*, September 1834, pp. 125–6.

Woe is me! that at 46 I am under the necessity of appearing as a lecturer, and obliged to regard every hour that I give to the PERMANENT, whether as poet or philosopher, an hour stolen from others' as well as from my own maintenance—so that after a life (for I might be said to have commenced in earliest childhood)— a life of observation, meditation, and almost encyclopedic studies, I am forced to bewail, (as in my poem addressed to Mr. Wordsworth:—)

> Sense of past youth and manhood come in vain,
> And genius given and knowledge won in vain;
> And all which I had cull'd in wood walks wild,
> And all which patient toil had rear'd, and all,
> Commune with Thee had open'd out—but flowers
> Strew'd on my corse, and borne upon my bier
> In the same coffin to the self-same grave.[1]

Woe from without, but well for me, however, from within, that I have been 'more sinned against than sinning.'

My lectures are, though not very numerously, yet very respectably attended—and as respectfully *attended* to. For no small portion of the former I am indebted to the favorable notice taken of them in the ——; and, occasionally, in the *New Times* and *Morning Chronicle*. My next Friday's lecture [2] will, if I do not grossly *flatter-blind* myself, be interesting, and the points of view not only original, but new to the audience. I make this distinction, because, 16 or rather 17 [3] years ago, I delivered 18 lectures on Shakespeare, at the Royal Institution—three-fourths of which appeared at that time startling paradoxes, which have since been adopted even by men who at the time made use of them as proofs of my flighty and paradoxical turn of mind—all tending to prove that Shakspeare's judgment was, if possible, still more wonderful than his genius: or rather, that the contra-distinction itself

---

[1] *Poetical Works* (Oxford), p. 407. Although Coleridge bewails his inability to give time to 'the Permanent, whether as poet or philosopher,' it must be remembered that he had long since consciously bade farewell to poetry. He might have, more properly, described his ambitions at this period as those of 'theologian or philosopher.' Without attempting to appraise his very real influence in theology, or the possible value of the great philosophical system which he hoped to achieve, the student of literature may well disagree with him and mourn his deliberate neglect, at the height of his mature genius, of those superb critical endowments which had just produced *Biographia Literaria*.

[2] The first lecture on Shakespeare was delivered Friday, 6 February. This letter probably belongs to the week immediately preceding that date.

[3] Read '10 or rather 11.' Mudford has misread the numerals. On this point cf. ii. 3.

between judgment and genius, rested on an utterly false theory. This, and its proofs and grounds have been, I should not have said *adopted*, but produced as their own legitimate children— nay, the merit given to a foreign writer [1] whose lectures were not given orally till two years after mine, rather than to their country- man, though I dare appeal to the most adequate judges—as Sir G. Beaumont, the Bishop of Durham, Mr. Sotheby—and after- wards to Mr. Rogers and Lord Byron—whether there is one single principle in Schlegel's work, (which is not an admitted drawback from its merits,) that was not established and applied in detail by me.   Plutarch tells us, that egotism is a venial fault in the unfortunate, and justifiable in the calumniated,—yet, I should not have done this violence to me, but that Mr. Words- worth, for whose fame I had felt and fought with an ardour that amounted to absolute self-oblivion, and to which I owe mainly the rancour of the Edinburgh clan, and (far more injurious to me) the coldness, neglect, and equivocal compliments of the *Quarterly Review*, has affirmed *in print*, that a German critic *first* taught us to think correctly concerning Shakspeare.[2]

The name of the newspaper which Mudford modestly leaves blank is, of course, the *Courier*.   Mudford was probably directly responsible for its kindness in calling attention to Coleridge's lectures.   In the early nineteenth century, when newspapers were limited to four pages, of which two were exclusively devoted to advertisements and only two remained for the leading article and political, diplomatic, military, naval, aristocratic, and criminal news—practically the only interests of the newspapers—any attention to matters of literary interest might be regarded as an act of infinite condescension and personal kindness on the part of the editor.

[1] Schlegel, of course.   On this claim of priority cf. Introduction, vol. i, pp. xxvi–xxviii.

[2] Cf. i. 16 for a similar complaint.   It seems that Coleridge refers to Wordsworth's account of Shakespeare's reputation in the Essay Supple- mentary to the Preface, 1815.   In this extremely inaccurate paragraph, Wordsworth does not mention Schlegel by name and may, perhaps, have referred primarily to Lessing, whom Coleridge himself overpraised in *B.L.* (ii. 182), almost in the terms against which he is here complaining.

Cf. ii. 126 for Coleridge's own tribute to Schlegel: 'The sentiments and opinions are coincident with those to which I gave utterance in my lectures at the Royal Institution.   It is not a little wonderful . . . that it should remain for foreigners first to feel truly, and to appreciate justly, his [Shakespeare's] mighty genius.'

Coleridge was right, however, in feeling that Wordsworth had been ungenerous.   According to Wordsworth, the Germans first recognized that Shakespeare's judgment was equal to his genius, and this view was not yet established in England.   The injustice to Coleridge's predecessors is probably inadvertent, but that to Coleridge himself can scarcely be attributed to inadequate knowledge of the facts.

The *Courier* printed seven announcements (not advertisements) of Coleridge's lectures in February, when help was most needed; the *New Times* (Stoddart's paper) and the *Morning Chronicle* followed the example of the *Courier* four or five times. And Coleridge used two of his poems to give further publicity to his lectures, publishing 'Fancy in Nubibus' in the *Courier*, 30 January, and 'The Solitary Date Tree,'[1] in the *New Times* on 31 January. After receiving this letter, Mudford increased his efforts for Coleridge and published on 9 February a brief report of the lecture of 6 February (cf. ii. 249), following this on 13 February with a little article presenting Coleridge's claims of priority to Schlegel, very much in the words of Coleridge's letter.

In another letter of this period,[2] written on the back of a prospectus to H. F. Cary, 9 February 1818, Coleridge attached marginal notes to the announcement in his syllabus of each lecture: I. 'Tho' I was dreadfully hoarse—it went off famously'; II. 'Not so hoarse, but I failed by attempting too much'; III. 'This was very popular'; IV. 'Went off very well but the general opinion was that it was much more instructive . . . [?] but not so splendid as the third.'

The comment on the second lecture, that on the ballads and metrical romances, is particularly interesting. On 4 February Coleridge published in the *New Times* a letter to the public, apologizing for his failure to cover the whole ground. 'I solicited, and now solicit the attendance of all who had or shall have attended me, to a supernumerary Lecture, at the end of the course, given gratis, and composed wholly of poetic translations, in chronological order, and concluding with an original Poem.'[3] This promise was not entirely forgotten, for on 22 May *The Times* carried an advertisement announcing that the 'Supernumerary Lecture, consisting chiefly of free translations from the poets of the middle age, woven into a poem descriptive of the same, will be given on Tuesday evening, May 26.' This advertisement contains also a tentative announcement of a new course of six lectures on *Richard II*, *Lear*, *Macbeth*, *Antony and Cleopatra*, *Twelfth Night*, and certain doubtful plays.[4] But I have been able to find no further notice of this proposal in the newspapers, and even the supernumerary lecture seems to have been neglected. On 25 November Mrs Clarkson wrote to Robinson as follows: 'You heard perhaps what

---

[1] With variations from the later text. This poem was published as an 'Imitation of one of the Minnesinger of the Thirteenth Century, introduced by Mr. Coleridge in his lecture on the literature of the Middle Ages' [30 January?]. The publication of these poems in the *Courier* and the *New Times* has not hitherto been noted.

[2] Transcript by E. H. Coleridge. The notes mentioned above have not hitherto been published.

[3] For this announcement see also Hammond's report of the second lecture, *M.C.*, p. 15.

[4] Coleridge specifically listed *Henry VI*, *Richard III*, and *Pericles* as plays wholly or partly non-Shakespearean. A manuscript draft of this notice, apparently in Green's hand, specifies the *Two Gentlemen of Verona* 'and a large proportion of the three parts of Henry the 6, and some scenes of Richard the third.' These doubts regarding plays attributed to Shakespeare were to be 'illustrated from Pericles, Titus Andronicus, and some extraordinary scenes of an old Drama.'

an ungracious leave he [Coleridge] took of his auditory last spring—calling them together to hear a gratuitous lecture, causing them to be told that he was too ill to meet them, but as soon as he recovered they should be sure of the Lecture.—Either he never recovered or he forgot his promise.' [1]

This melancholy little story is the only evidence of any failure of Coleridge to live up to his engagements for the course. Robinson attended every lecture loyally until after the tenth, when he was obliged to go on circuit, and his calendar of the lectures shows that Coleridge delivered them all on the date announced, and, so far as Robinson informs us, on the subject announced also. For the last four lectures, the advertisements in the *Morning Chronicle*, etc., show that Coleridge continued to observe his schedule punctually. Some of these notices in the *Morning Chronicle* specify Coleridge's subjects in greater detail than the prospectus and, in default of fuller information, deserve quotation. According to the advertisement of 6 February, Coleridge's fourth lecture (the first on Shakespeare) was to 'comprise the Comedies and romantic Dramas'; the fifth was to deal with 'the Historical Plays'; and the sixth was to take up 'the great Tragedies—Hamlet, Othello, Macbeth, &c.' [2] When reannounced, the fifth lecture was to include 'the characters of Richard III. and Falstaff,' while the sixth lecture was limited to 'the characters of Hamlet and Othello,' [3] Coleridge's favourite themes. The seventh lecture became, not primarily a lecture on Shakespeare's contemporaries, but a lecture on Shakespeare himself, illustrated by comparisons with Jonson, Beaumont and Fletcher, and Massinger. [4] The tenth lecture became a lecture on Dante and Milton alone, and the name of Donne was wisely omitted in the advertisement; [5] and the subject of the final lecture was announced as 'the Correspondence of Language to Good Sense, in Conversation, Writing and Public Speaking.' [6]

The subject matter of this course is interesting in its variety and comparative newness. The three lectures on Shakespeare were, of course, drawn chiefly from the earlier series of lectures. [7] Milton was another old subject, [8] and Spenser and Chaucer had at least appeared in Coleridge's tentative programme of the 1808 lectures.

---

[1] From the manuscript in Robinson's papers.

[2] *Morning Chronicle*, 6 February. The advertisement says that the first lecture on Shakespeare was Coleridge's third, but the prospectus and Robinson's record of the actual lectures correct this error. On 30 January the advertisement of the second lecture announced Coleridge's intention of publishing the first lecture—an intention which was never carried out.

[3] *Morning Chronicle*, 10, 13 February.

[4] Ibid., 17 February.

[5] Ibid., 27 February.

[6] Ibid., 10 March.

[7] Campbell (Introduction, p. civ, note 3) speaks of marginalia 'on a copy of Warburton's Shakespeare,' probably because of Coleridge's references to Warburton in his marginalia. These references to Warburton in *Literary Remains* are almost all from Coleridge's marginalia on Theobald's edition of Shakespeare. Theobald constantly prints notes supplied by Warburton. Since Campbell refers to the marginalia already published, he could not have had a clue to unknown materials.

[8] Lectures of 1808, 1811–12, Bristol courses.

The two lectures on the Middle Ages and medieval literature were partly new, partly old material of Coleridge's own,[1] and partly borrowings from Schlegel.[2]   But more than half of the course was quite new. It included some brilliant criticism of Shakespeare's contemporaries, of Sterne, and of English prose, for which Coleridge's preparation is proved by the manuscripts which he left behind him.   We have less concrete evidence of his success in dealing with foreign literatures, but manuscripts remain at least for the lectures on Dante[3] and on Cervantes,[4] of which the first, at least, is among his best achievements in criticism.   He drew upon his old notebooks and fragmentary memoranda for lectures upon ghosts and the supernatural generally, and he excavated new materials from the German mines, gathering an abstract discussion of wit and humour from Richter's *Vorschule der Aesthetik*[5] and a lecture on the relation of the fine arts to nature from Schelling's lecture on the same subject.[6]   The German importations and the notes on the supernatural were not very desirable additions to the lectures, if we may judge by the manuscripts printed by H. N. Coleridge.[7]   But the rest of the material is valuable; and it is supplemented by excellent lectures on Spenser and Milton, which are probably based on Coleridge's earlier courses.

Besides these new materials, which evidently came from manuscripts, H. N. Coleridge prints a few marginalia on the subjects of the various lectures, as well as brief reports by auditors of no less than seven lectures.[8]   A brief report of the fourth lecture appeared in the *Courier*, 9 February 1818; reports of the ninth and fourteenth lectures were published in the *Tatler*, 23, 24, May 1837; and some notes on the

---

[1] The account of the old play by Hans Sachs. Cf. i. 171–2, ii. 7, and *M.C.*, p. 16.

[2] See Helmholtz, *Indebtedness of Coleridge to Schlegel*, p. 368.

[3] This lecture on Dante contains a long passage borrowed from Schiller's essay 'On Naive and Sentimental Poetry.'   Cf. Introduction, vol. i, p. xxiii, and A. C. Dunstan, 'German Influence upon Coleridge,' *Mod. Lang. Rev.*, vol. xvii. (1922), pp. 274–5.

In this lecture on Dante (see *M.C.*, p. 152, note) Coleridge kindly used his influence in favour of his recent friend H. F. Cary, by a public recommendation of Cary's translation of Dante. Cary's son tells us that the result was the immediate sale of a thousand copies! (*Memoir of H. F. Cary*, ii. 28.) This evidence of Coleridge's great critical influence is all the more valuable because we have so little other information on the subject, and might gather from Coleridge's own statements that he was rather an object of literary persecution.   Cf. ii. 121 for Byron's testimony.

[4] This subject was announced at Bristol, but the lecture was probably not delivered.   (Cf. ii. 208.)

[5] See Brandl's *Coleridge*, p. 360 (Eng. trans. by Lady Eastlake).   Brandl is reliable in citing this influence, although he is not usually so.   Cf. *M.C.*, pp. 111–20, 440–6, with Richter's *Vorschule*, sections 26, 28–9, 32–4, 43–5, 48–50.

[6] See Sara Coleridge's notes to Lecture XIII, Coleridge's *Works*, iv. 482–7, and *M.C.*, pp. 204–13.

[7] The present editor has seen only part of the manuscripts above enumerated, and relies chiefly on *Literary Remains* for the evidences of Coleridge's definite preparation of lecture notes.

[8] Lectures I, II, III, VII, IX, XI, XII.   Most of these reports are extremely brief.

first and fourth by a certain Mr H. H. Carwardine were published in *Notes and Queries*.[1]

Of these reports only those which deal with Shakespeare are here republished.[2]

REPORTS OF THE FOURTH LECTURE

I. *The Courier*,[3] *February* 9, 1818.

ON Friday evening Mr. Coleridge gave his first lecture on Shakespeare to a numerous and genteel audience. He stated the permanent objects Shakespeare had in view in drawing his characters, and how obviously he disregarded those that were of a transitory nature. The character of Caliban, as an original and caricature of Jacobinism, so fully illustrated at Paris during the French Revolution,[4] he described in a vigorous and lively manner, exciting repeated bursts of applause. He commenced an inquiry into the order of succession in which Shakespeare wrote his plays, and decided that *Love's Labour['s] Lost* must have been the first, as there are so many allusions in it such as a youth would make, few or none resulting from an experience of the world. That play and *The Tempest* were the chief objects of his discourse, into which, however, he introduced a great variety of new and striking remarks, not confined to any particular play. As, for instance, he said, wherever Shakespeare had drawn a character addicted to sneering, and contempt for the merits of others, that character was sure to be a villain. Vanity, envy, and malice, were its certain accompaniments: too prudent to praise itself, it fed its concentrated egotism by sarcasm and lowering others.[5] This is but a poor description of the very glowing language, ample detail, and profound thought Mr. Coleridge displayed on this topic, which produced a thunder of applause.

---

[1] 1870.   Series IV, vol. v, pp. 335–6.

[2] The other reports are republished in my edition of Coleridge's *Miscellaneous Criticism*.

[3] Heading, 'Lectures on Shakespeare.'

[4] This remark fell under the avenging eye of Hazlitt, who consequently made the *Courier*'s brief report an occasion for an exasperated but amusing review of Coleridge's politics, etc.   See *Works* (Waller-Glover), vol. xi, pp. 416–20.   Except in Hazlitt's quotation, this report has not before been reprinted.

[5] Cf. i. 112, note 1, 121, etc.

II. *Carwardine Report.*[1]

'Coleridge, 6 Feb. "On Shakespear." His predecessors, the poets of Italy, France, and England, &c., drew their aliment from the soil; there was a nationality; they were of a country, of a genus, grafted with the chivalrous spirit and sentiment of the North, and with the wild magic imported from the East. He bore no direct witness of the soil from whence he grew; compare him with the mountain pine.

'Self-sustained, deriving his genius immediately from heaven, independent of all earthly or national influence. That such a mind involved itself in a human form is a problem indeed which my feeble powers may witness with admiration, but cannot explain. My words are indeed feeble when I speak of that myriad-minded man, whom all artists feel above all praise. Least of all poets, antient or modern, does Shakespear appear to be coloured or affected by the age in which he lived—he was of all times and countries.

'He drew from the eternal of our nature.

'When misers were most common in his age, yet he has drawn no such character; and why? because it was mere transitory character. Shylock no miser, not the great feature of his character.

'In an age of political and religious heat, yet there is no sectarian character of politics or religion.

'In an age of superstition, when witchcraft was the passion of the monarch, yet he has never introduced such characters. For the weird sisters are as different as possible.

'Judgment and genius are as much one as the fount and the stream that flows from it; and I must dwell on the judgment of Shakespear.

'When astrological predictions had possession of the mind, he has no such character. It was a transient folly merely of the time, and therefore it did not belong to Shakespear; and in company with Homer and Milton and whatever is great on earth, he invented the Drama.

'The Greek tragedy was tragic opera differing only in this, that in Greek the scenery and music were subservient to the poetry. In modern opera the poetry is subservient to the music and decoration.

[1] The manuscript for the first page of this report is probably that printed on i. 214–17.

'A *mere* copy never delights us in anything. Why do we go to a tragedy to witness the representation of the woe which we may daily witness? The antient tragedians confined their subjects to gods and heroes, and traditional people. Shakespear—a more difficult task—in drawing not only from nature, but from the times as well as things before him, and so true to nature that you never can conceive his characters could speak otherwise than they do in the situation in which they are placed.

'—— common expression—"How natural Shakespear is"—and yet so peculiar that if you read but a few detached lines you immediately say, "this must be Shakespear."

'Such peculiar propriety and excellence, and truth to nature, that there is nothing in any man at all like him—a research for that felicity of language current in the courts of Elizabeth and James, but so was Massinger, B. Jonson, Beaumont & Fletcher, &c., but yet they are not like Shakespear's language. Divide his works into three great classes; no division can be made that applies to tragedy and comedy, for nature acknowledges none of these distinct sharp lines, and Shakespear is the Poet of Nature, pourtraying things as they exist. He has, as it were, prophesied what each man in his different passions would have produced.

'1. His Comedies and Romantic Dramas.

'2. His Historical Plays.

'3. His Great Tragedies.

'There is a character of observation, a happiness of noticing whatever is external, and arranging them like a gallery of pictures, representing passions, which no man appropriates to himself, and yet acknowledges his share.

'Character of his mind, depth, and energy of thought. No man was ever a great poet without being a great philosopher. In his earliest poems the poet and philosopher are perpetually struggling with each other till they found a field where they were blended, and flowed in sweetest harmony and strength.

'*Love's Labour Lost*, I affirm, must have been the first of his plays—firstly, it has the least observation, and the characters are merely such as a young man of genius might have made out himself. But it has other marks; it is all intellect. There is little to interest as a dramatic representation, yet affording infinite matter of beautiful quotation. King and Biron, "Light seeking light blinds us,"[1] no instance in which the same thought so happily expressed. In the character of Biron he has the germ of

---

[1] 'Light seeking light, doth light of light beguile,' *L.L.L.* I. i. 77.

Benedict and Mercutio; it was the first rough draft, which he afterwards finished with Ben. and Mer.

'In Holofernes is contained the sketch of Polonius. He never on any occasion spares pedantry—

> "remunerative.
> *Nathaniel.* I praise God for your sin," &c.[1]

'Much of this wordiness (here ridiculed) shown in modern poetry; words nicely balanced till you come to seek the meaning, when you are surprised to find none.

'His blank verse has nothing equal to it but that of Milton. Such fulness of thought gives an involution of metre so natural to the expression of passions, which fills and elevates the mind, and gives general truths in full, free, and poetic language.

'*Lear, Macbeth*, &c.

'Shakespear, the only one who has made passion the vehicle of general truth, as in his comedy he has made even folly itself the vehicle of philosophy. Each speech is what every man feels to be latent in his nature; what he would have said in that situation if he had had the ability and readiness to do it, and these are multiplied and individualized with the most extraordinary minuteness and truth.

'Of the exquisite judgment of the . . . must conceive a stage without scenery—acting a poor recitation. He frequently speaks to his audience. If, says he, you will listen to me with your minds and not with your eyes to . . . and assist me with your imaginations, I will do so and so.

'Characteristic of his comedy and romantic drama.

'1st. His characters never introduced for the sake of his plot, but his plot arises out of his characters, nor are all these involved in them. You meet people who meet and speak to you as in real life, interesting you differently, having some distinctive peculiarity which interests you, and thus the story is introduced which you appear casually made acquainted with, yet still you feel that it excites an interest—that there is something that is applicable to certain situations, &c.

'Again, his characters have something more than a mere amusing property.

'For example, in *The Tempest*, the delight of Trinculo at

---

[1] The quotation is clearly wrong. For 'remunerative' read 'remuneration.' See the play on this word in *L.L.L.* III. i. The verse following in the text has no connection with this illustration. It seems to be a perversion of 'I praise the Lord for you,' *L.L.L.* IV. ii. 70.

finding something more sottish than himself and that honours him—the characteristic of base and vulgar minds which Shakespear is fond of lashing and placing in a ridiculous light [reads scene between Trinculo and Caliban]; but Shakespear can make even rude vulgarity the vehicle of profound truths and thoughts. Prospero, the mighty wizard, whose potent art could not only call up all the spirits of the deep, but the characters as they were and are and will be, seems a portrait of the bard himself. No magician or magic, in the proper sense of the word—a being to excite either fear or wonder—nothing in common with such characters as were brought from the East.

'If there be any imitation in Shakespear, of what is it imitation? What so earthly as Caliban, so aerial as Ariel, so fanciful, so exquisitely light, yet some striving of thought of an undeveloped power.

'I know no character in Shakespear to which he has given a propensity to sneer, or scoff, or express contempt, but he has made that man a villain.'

Reports from Robinson's Diary, 1818.

Tuesday, [January] 27 . . . I called at Collier's and taking Mrs. C. with me I went to a lecture by Coleridge in Fleur de Luce Court, Fleet Street. I was gratified unexpectedly by finding a large and respectable audience—generally of very superior looking persons, in physiognomy rather than dress.

But the lecture was heavy. C. treated of the origin of poetry and of oriental works, but he was little animated and an exceedingly bad cold rendered his voice scarcely audible.

I met Hundleby there, whom I had sent to in the course of the day, and he seemed quite pleased with the lecture, and will subscribe for the whole course, which he had not at first intended. . . .

Friday 30. . . . I then went to Coleridge's second lecture. It was much more brilliant than the first and seemed to give general satisfaction . . .

[February] 3 . . . I accompanied Mrs. Collier to Coleridge's lecture. C. lectured on Dante, Ariosto, etc. More entertainment than instruction—splendid irregularities, throughout . . .

Friday 6 . . . After eight I accompanied Mrs. John Collier to Coleridge's lecture, which was like his other lectures in most particulars, but rather less interesting.—He treated of Shakespeare, and dwelt on mere accidents which served to bring out some of his favorite ideas, which after a certain number of repetitions become tiresome . . .

10 . . . I dined with Walter . . . I was obliged to leave the party to attend Coleridge's lecture. On Shakespeare and as usual; but he was apparently ill . . .

12 . . . I called late on Lamb, who does not attend Coleridge's lectures. C. had not sent him a ticket, which I cannot account for.

13 . . . Coleridge's lecture, to which I accompanied Mrs. Flaxman . . . The lecture was as usual interesting . . .

Tuesday 17 . . . I then went alone to Coleridge's lecture. He spoke of Ben Jonson, Beaumont and Fletcher, etc. Spoke of their impurity, etc., as he had done before, and further convinced me that his circle of favorite ideas he is confined within as much as any man, and that his speculations have ceased to be living thoughts, in which he is making progress. They are closed, I believe, and he has not the faculty of giving them consistency and effect.

20 . . . We found the lecture room fuller than I had ever seen it and were forced to take back seats, but it was a pleasure to Mrs. P[attison] to sit behind Sir James Mackintosh. He was with Serjt. Bosanquet and Rolland and some genteel woman. The party was, however, in a satirical mood and made sneering remarks, as it seemed, throughout the lecture.

Indeed, Coleridge was not in one of his happiest moods to-night. His subject was Cervantes, but he was more than usually prosing and his tone peculiarly drawling. His digressions on the nature of insanity were carried too far, and his remarks on the book but old and by him often repeated . . .

Tuesday, 24 . . . The lecture was on Wit and Humour and the great writers of Wit and Humour. There was much obscurity and metaphysics in the long introduction and not a little cant and commonplace in the short criticisms.[1] I fear that Coleridge will not on the whole add to his reputation by these lectures . . .

27 . . . I took tea with Gurney and invited Mrs. G. to accompany me to Coleridge's lecture. It was on Dante and Milton—one of his very best. He digressed less than usually and really gave information and ideas about the poets he professed to criticise [2]. . . .

---

[1] This was from Richter's *Vorschule der Aesthetik*. (Cf. ii. 248, note 5.)
[2] After this lecture Robinson went on circuit.

THE LECTURES OF 1818-19

Until the publication of James Dykes Campbell's life of Coleridge, as an introduction to his edition of *Coleridge's Poetical Works*, the lectures of 1818 had been generally considered Coleridge's last course. Campbell saw the references to a later course in Allsop's *Letters, Conversations, and Recollections of S. T. Coleridge*, and described the course from the prospectus in the possession of E. H. Coleridge. The prospectus announces two courses of lectures which were to be given at the 'Crown and Anchor' Tavern, in the Strand—a course of fourteen lectures on the history of philosophy, beginning 7 December, and continuing on successive Mondays; and an alternate course of literary lectures, to be delivered on successive Thursdays, beginning on 10 December.[1] The prospectus bears a correction of these two dates to 14 December and 17 December. Besides the prospectus there was published a 'Historical and Chronological Guide' to the lectures on philosophy. John Hookham Frere paid a shorthand reporter to take down the philosophical lectures, and his reports are still extant.[2] Most of the prospectus to the philosophical lectures has been printed by Allsop,[3] and I shall here reprint only the prospectus of the literary lectures.[4]

Alternate Course of Lectures.

On the Thursday Evenings, in the same room, Mr. COLERIDGE will give a course of Six Lectures, each having for its subject some one play of Shakespear's, scene by scene, for the purpose of illustrating the conduct of the plot, and the peculiar force, beauty, and propriety, of the language, in the particular passages, as well as the intention of the great Philosophic Poet in the prominent characters of each play, and the unity of interest in the whole and in the apparent contrast of the component parts.

Thursday, December 10, 1818.—THE TEMPEST, as a specimen of the Romantic or Poetical Drama of Shakespear.—17, RICHARD the SECOND, of his Dramatic Histories.—Thursday, January 7, 1819, HAMLET.—14, MACBETH.—21, OTHELLO.—28, LEAR.

Double Ticket, admitting a Lady and Gentleman, *Two*

---

[1] Campbell, Introduction, p. cv.
[2] Coleridge's *Philosophical Lectures* (ed. Kathleen Coburn), 1949.
[3] *Letters, Conversations, and Recollections of S. T. Coleridge* (1858), pp. 240–2. See also pp. 187–90 for Coleridge's 'Historical and Chronological Guide' (incomplete).
[4] From the third page of the prospectus for the first course.

Guineas. Single Ticket, *One Pound Five Shillings.* Admission to each Lecture, *Five Shillings.* Tickets and Prospectuses to be had, as above.

The Courses are postponed to the 14*th and* 17*th.*[1]

It has not been previously noticed that at the end of the literary lectures, Coleridge announced a new course on Shakespeare and other literary subjects to continue concurrently with the philosophical lectures on Mondays.[2] These new lectures, seven in number, were to begin on 4 February and continue on successive Thursdays, three on Shakespeare and the remaining four on ' Milton—Dante—Petrarch, Spencer and Ariosto—and Don Quixote; with the Life, Character and Genius of Cervantes.' A note which followed informed the public that ' By particular request, Mr Coleridge will begin the course with a Second Lecture on Hamlet, in which after a brief recapitulation of the substance of the former, the Criticisms will be continued scene by scene, through the third, fourth, and last Acts.'

On 1 February the *Morning Chronicle* carried a second advertisement of this new course, announcing that the philosophical lectures would be intermitted for a week and that the new course would begin on 11 February, instead of 4 February.[3] After the lecture on *Hamlet,* the second lecture was advertised as dealing with 'the Tragedy of *Romeo and Juliet,* with the characters of Antony and Cleopatra; or Shakespeare's double portrait of Love, as it displays itself in Youth and in Manhood.' [4] The same advertisement announced that the subject of the third and last lecture on Shakespeare would be 'the ascent of his Genius from its Rise to its Zenith.' On 4 March the *Morning Chronicle* announced the fourth lecture on 'Paradise Lost, and the Character of Milton'; and on 11 March the subject of the fifth lecture was given briefly as Dante, omitting the name of Petrarch. On 18 March we learn from the same source that Coleridge's sixth lecture would deal with 'the Fairy Queen of Spenser, the Italian School of Poetry, and the Nature of Allegory'; and on 25 March the subject of the seventh and last lecture was announced, with no alteration, as *Don Quixote* and Cervantes.

The subjects of each lecture, with the various slight alterations, are given in detail because they are the only records of this course which have appeared. The subjects announced indicate little or no attempt to find new materials to attract new audiences, and this course, as well

[1] Manuscript note. The philosophical lectures were to begin on 7 December, the literary on 10 December.

[2] *Morning Chronicle,* 28 January 1819.

[3] A slight alteration in the subjects announced may be noted. After the three lectures on Shakespeare, the remaining lectures were to deal with the following subjects: 1. Milton, 2. Dante and Petrarch, 3. Spenser compared with Chaucer and Ariosto. 4. Don Quixote.

[4] *Morning Chronicle,* 18 February. I do not preserve typographical details. This is the lecture on *Romeo and Juliet* mentioned in Coleridge's letter to Mudford of the next paragraph. Campbell's conjecture that *Romeo and Juliet* was substituted for one of the plays to be discussed in the first course is not needed to fit the facts.

as that immediately preceding, seems to have been a distinct failure. Several brief undated notes to Mudford, which were published in the *Canterbury Magazine*, September 1834,[1] evidently belong to this period, though Mudford himself informed the public that they referred to the lectures of 1818. 'I was very sorry to miss you last night, because my lecture gave, and I believe, would have given even *you*, more than ordinary satisfaction. But alas! the audience (including free tickets) were scarcely enough to pay the rooms. Perhaps the Christmas parties are inauspicious.'. . . The next note may be dated,[2] 5 January 1819. 'You saw and I doubt not regretted, for my sake, how scanty an audience I had yester-evening.' This reference is to one of the lectures on philosophy, which one would scarcely expect to attract large audiences; and perhaps most of the notes speak of this course. But one refers definitely to the literary lectures: 'I hope you will come, and give the farewell shake by the hand to *my* Shakespeare. The *Romeo and Juliet* pleased even beyond my anticipation; but alas! scanty are my audiences!' The references to the second and third lectures on Shakespeare date this note between 19 February and 24 February. Another note in which Coleridge complains that 'that week's break was indeed unfortunate' probably is written soon after the intermission between the first and second courses at the beginning of February.[3] Still another note, which gives no hint as to its date, is worth quoting. 'When I tell you, that yester-evening's receipts were somewhat better than many of the preceding; and that these did not *equal* one half of the costs of the room, and of the stage and hackney coach, (the advertisements in the *Times* and *Morning Chronicle*, and the printer's prospectus bill not included), you will find no difficulty in understanding the warmth with which I express my sense of your kindness.'. . .[4]

Though the philosophical lectures were fully reported, no records of the literary lectures are known to the present editor, except those discovered by Campbell,[5] which are here reprinted from the *Champion*, 20 December 1818 and 10 January 1819.

[*Report of the First Lecture.*[6]]

Mr. Coleridge commenced his lecture on the *Tempest*, as a specimen of the romantic or poetical drama of Shakespeare, on

---

[1] pp. 127–8.

[2] From the record of the sale of the manuscript at Sotheby's, 2 December 1896, No. 349.

[3] Mudford says that this break was due to 'temporary indisposition.'

[4] Notices in the *Courier*, calling attention to the lectures. (Cf. ii. 245–6.) I have omitted one of this series of notes.

[5] Published in the *Athenaeum*, 26 December 1891, and 2 January 1892, with interesting comments.

[6] *Champion*, 20 December 1818. I have omitted the long critical introduction on Coleridge's character. The editor of the *Champion* was the radical, John Thelwall, one of the friends of Coleridge's young manhood. His criticism of Coleridge is a weak imitation of Hazlitt's and is scarcely capable of interesting even the most earnest student of Coleridge's life.

Thursday, by investigating the true nature and foundation of poetic probability.   To give a *rule*, it is necessary first to investigate the end to which it is to be subservient.   The end of dramatic poetry is not to present a *copy*, but an *imitation* of real life.   Copy is imperfect if the resemblance be not, in every circumstance, exact; but an imitation essentially implies some difference.   The mind of the spectator, or the reader, therefore, is not to be deceived into any idea of reality, as the French critics absurdly suppose; neither, on the other hand, is it to retain a perfect consciousness of the falsehood of the presentation.   There is a state of mind between the two, which may be properly called illusion,[a] in which the comparative powers of the mind are completely suspended; as in a dream, the judgment is neither beguiled, nor conscious of the fraud, but remains passive. Whatever disturbs this repose of the judgment by its harshness, abruptness, and improbability, offends against dramatic propriety.

Observing this distinction, Mr. C. proceeded to show that many natural improbabilities were innocent in the groundwork or outset of the play, which would break the illusion afterwards; and the contrary.   The temper of mind in the spectator must be considered; a strong improbability in the story, founded on some known tradition, does not offend in the outset of a play; but the interest and plot must not depend upon that improbability. Again, violent emotions must not be excited at the very commencement; for if the mind is not prepared, the judgment is awakened and the illusion vanishes at once.

Mr. C. proceeded to apply those principles to the *Tempest*, a romantic drama, in which the interest depends on the imagination rather than the feelings.   The plot has little intricacy, and its interest ceases in the 3rd act, in which the conclusion becomes evident.

It would be endless to refer to all the beautiful illustrations of his theory which Mr. C. drew from the successive scenes of this play; the truth, the harmony which he made apparent, and the softening touches that he produced, to show how this great master tempered every thing (the wonderful and the terrible) to the feelings of his audience.   This was illustrated in the circumstances of the shipwreck, and in the character of the magician Prospero.   Criticism of this kind cannot be abridged; but it would be doing injustice to Mr. C. to pass over the beautiful manner in which he commented on the scene of the intended

[a] *Champion*, '*allusion*.'

murder.   Contempt, he remarked, is never attributed in Shakespeare, but to characters deep in villainy, as Edmund, Iago,
Antonio and Sebastian in the play before us—the sophistry of
guilt diminishing the crime in its own eyes, by contempt for the
object of its purpose, and by veiling in metaphor and mild language the horrors from which the mind would revolt; all which
was admirably exposed in comments upon this scene.

Mr. C. concluded with some beautiful observation[s] on the
versification of Shakespeare, which he compared to the sinuous
and ever-varied [a] lapses of a serpent, writhing in every direction,
but still progressive, and in every posture [b] beautiful.

The connection between the character of the versification and
of the language, and between the metre and the sense, one
elucidating and assisting the other, were demonstrated with a
truth and beauty which he only can arrive at who writes profound
philosophy with exquisite taste and depth of poetic feeling.

                                                                  A. S.

[*Report of the Third Lecture*.[1]]

Coleridge's Lecture on Thursday [2] was, as we expected, a
splendid and ingenious display of metaphysical criticism and
poetic enthusiasm.   Many of his ideas were as just as they were
beautiful; but we wish that he had given some portion of the
time consumed by the almost unintelligibly ambiguous apologies
for belief in ghosts and goblins, to the elucidation of the yet
obscure traits of the character of Hamlet.   In many particulars
Mr. C. at least accords with, if he has not availed himself of, the
opinions of Hazlitt, and of another lecturer, whose disquisition
on the character of Hamlet, during the last season, excited very
popular attention.[3]   But still we are of opinion that he has not
gone into the entire depths of this extraordinary delineation of
physical, moral, and intellectual peculiarity of human character.

---

[a] *Champion*, '*over-varied*.'   [b] Ibid., '*postsure*.'
[1] *Champion*, 10 January 1819.   The number of 3 January contained a report of one of the philosophical lectures.
[2] 9 January.
[3] Thelwall, the editor, modestly refers to his own lectures in 1818.   We
need not comment on the impudence of this suggestion.   The suggestion
of an influence from Hazlitt is, of course, equally baseless.

A LETTER TO J. BRITTON ON
PROPOSED LECTURES OF 1819

No evidence has ever appeared to indicate that Coleridge gave any courses of lectures [1] besides those which have here been discussed; but it is by no means certain that other courses may not yet come to light. The most important clue is a letter of February 1819, evidently written in answer to a request that Coleridge repeat at the Russell Institution those lectures previously given at the Surrey Institution in 1812–13.[2] I have made some search of the newspapers for announcements of this course, but without success. In any case, the letter is so important a discussion of Coleridge's lectures that it is worth reprinting for its own sake.[3]

28th Feb. 1819, Highgate.

DEAR SIR,—First permit me to remove a very natural, indeed almost inevitable mistake, relative to my lectures; namely,[a] that I *have* them, or that the lectures of one place or season are in any way repeated in another. So far from it, that on any point that I had ever studied (and on no other should I dare discourse—I mean, that I would not lecture on any subject for which I had to *acquire* the main knowledge, even though a month's or three months' previous time were allowed me; on no subject that had not employed my thoughts for a large portion of my life since earliest manhood, free of all outward and particular purpose)—on any point within my habit of thought, I should greatly prefer a

---

[a] *Gazette*, '*not.*'

[1] He gave at least one or two individual lectures. Gillman speaks of an extemporaneous lecture on 'The Growth of the Individual Mind,' delivered at the London Philosophical Society, on some date which Gillman does not specify (*Life of Coleridge*, pp. 354–7). E. H. Coleridge is inclined to identify this lecture with that given in December 1817. (Coleridge's *Letters*, p. 680, note.) But Coleridge refers to this lecture as in part identical with his essay 'On Method' in the *Encyclopaedia Metropolitana* (*Letters*, p. 681), and in an unpublished letter to Mr Williams, 12 December 1817, he outlines it as a lecture on the nature and limitations of metaphysics. (This letter is in the Manuscript Room of the British Museum, Additional MS. 36, 532, ff. 3–4.) It seems, therefore, that the lecture is not that to which Gillman refers.

[2] Not 1814, as Coleridge implies below.

[3] From the *Literary Gazette*, 1834, pp. 628–9. Part of the letter was republished by H. N. Coleridge in *L.R.* ii. 2–5; the part unpublished by H. N. Coleridge was republished by Campbell in the *Athenaeum*, 2 January 1892. p. 18.

subject I had never lectured on, to one which I had repeatedly given; and those who have attended me for any two seasons successively will bear witness that the lecture given at the London Philosophical Society, on the *Romeo and Juliet* for instance, was as different from that given at the Crown and Anchor as if they had been given by two individuals who, without any communication with each other, had only mastered the same *principles* of philosophic criticism. This was most strikingly evidenced in the coincidence between my lectures and those of Schlegel; such, and so close, that it was fortunate for my moral reputation that I had not only from five to seven hundred ear-witnesses that the passages had been given by me at the Royal Institution two years before Schlegel commenced his lectures at Vienna, but that notes had been taken of these by several men and ladies of high rank. The fact is this: during a course of lectures, I faithfully employ *all* the intervening days in collecting and digesting the materials, whether I have or have not lectured on the same subject before, making no difference. The day of the lecture, till the hour of commencement, I devote to the consideration, what of the mass before me is best fitted to answer the purposes of a lecture—*i.e.* to keep the audience awake and interested during the delivery, and to leave a *sting* behind—*i.e.* a disposition to study the subject anew, under the light of a new principle. Several times, however, partly from apprehension respecting my health and animal spirits, partly from the wish to possess copies that might afterwards be marketable among the publishers, I have previously written the lecture; but before I had proceeded twenty minutes, I have been obliged to push the MSS. away, and give the subject a new turn. Nay, this was so notorious, that many of my auditors used to threaten me, when they saw any number of written papers on my desk, to steal them away; declaring they never felt so secure of a good lecture as when they perceived that I had not a single scrap of writing before me.[1] I take far, far more pains than would go to the set composition of a lecture, both by varied reading and by meditation; but for the words, illustrations, &c., I know almost as little as any one of my audience (*i.e.* those of any thing like the same education with myself) what they will be five minutes before the lecture begins. Such is *my way*, for such is *my nature*; and in attempting any other, I should only torment myself in order to disappoint my auditors—torment myself during the delivery, I mean; for in all

---

[1] Cf. ii. 82.

other respects it would be a much shorter and easier task to deliver them from writing. I am anxious to preclude any semblance of *affectation*; and have therefore troubled you with this lengthy preface before I have the hardihood to assure you that you might as well ask me what my dreams were in the year 1814, as what my course of lectures was at the Surrey Institution. *Fuimus Troës*. I regret that I cannot say the same of all my intellectual life. At least, were it in my power, my works should be confined to the second volume of my 'Literary Life,' [1] the Essays of the third volume of the 'Friend,' from page 67 to page 265,[2] with about fifty or sixty pages from the two former volumes, and some half-dozen of my poems.

If, therefore, I *should* be able to employ the time required for a course of six or eight lectures at the Russell Institution, that is, comparatively with other employment for the bread and beef of the day—God knows how laboriously, and yet scarcely earned!—I should greatly prefer your committee's making their own choice of the subjects from English, Italian, or German literature; and even of the Fine Arts, as far as the *philosophy* of the same is alone concerned. I have learnt, what I might easily have anticipated, that the *Lear* of Shakespeare is not a good subject for a whole lecture, in *my* style; with that exception, any of the plays of Shakespeare, the *Twelfth Night*, or the *Tempest*, the *Henry IVth's*, *Richard II.* with the character of *Richard III.*, *Romeo and Juliet*, *Antony and Cleopatra*, *Macbeth*, *Hamlet*, *Othello*,[3] &c. &c.; the *Paradise Lost*, with the character of Milton, (which I appear to remember was the favourite lecture of those given at the Surrey Institution); Spencer, Dante, old English ballads and metrical romances; on the uses of poetry in the process of the mind's education, especially on the supernatural; the comparison of English poetry from Chaucer to Milton, with the period from Dryden (inclusive) to the Wartons;—of all these, and of any other congenerous subjects, the committee might take their

---

[1] *Biographia Literaria*, chs. xiv–xxiv. Coleridge is here disparaging his theory of the imagination in favour of his magnificent criticism of Wordsworth. Professor Irving Babbitt has pointed out, in various unpublished lectures on this subject, that in chs. i.–xiii. of *Biographia Literaria* Coleridge is a follower of Schelling, while in the remainder of the book, he is an enlightened Aristotelian, criticizing Wordsworth's theory and practice by reference to the universality demanded of art, and to the doctrines of decorum and probability.

[2] Section II of *The Friend*, ending at the 'Third Landing-Place.' This is the Essay on Method.

[3] Coleridge's list of preferred plays is very significant. From the evidence of his marginalia the modern reader will be startled at his exclusion of *Lear* and somewhat surprised by the inclusion of *Twelfth Night* and *Henry IV*.

choice; and it would be much more agreeable to me (who am so utterly unfit to arrange any pecuniary matters, and have in consequence suffered so much in *mind*, to leave all else unnoticed, that I have vowed and promised never to attempt it again, but to leave it to some friend) if the committee would state the sum they are disposed to offer, and I would instantly decide.—Oh! how much more genial would my feelings be, could I but address so respectable an audience with unhired eloquence. Even as it is, and bleak as my vineyard (potatoe-ground would be a metaphor more *germain* to the occasion) lies on the north aspect of Parnassus, yet the accounts I have received, from the best authority, of the character of the audience at the Russell Institution, have *alone* induced me to return an hesitating answer to the inquiry which, at all events, I must have acknowledged as a high compliment to, dear sir, yours with unfeigned respect,

S. T. COLERIDGE.

To J. Britton, Esq.

INDEX

INDEX